305-235 GID

KT-451-877

1832823

UNIVERSITY OF WALES, NEWPORT
LIBRARY
AND
INFORMATION
SERVICES
CAERLEON

YOUTH FUTURES

YOUTH FUTURES

Comparative Research and Transformative Visions

Edited by

Jennifer Gidley and Sohail Inayatullah

UNIVERSITY OF WALES COLLEGE NEWPORT
LIBRARY
AND
INFORMATION
SERVICES
ALLT-YR-YN

UNIVERSITY OF WALES COLLEGE NEWPORT
LIBRARY
AND
INFORMATION
SERVICES
ALLT-YR-YN

PRAEGER

Westport, Connecticut
London

Library of Congress Cataloging-in-Publication Data

Youth futures: comparative research and transformative visions /edited by Jennifer Gidley and Sohail Inayatullah.
    p. cm.
  Includes bibliographical references and index.
  ISBN 0–275–97414–6 (alk. paper)
    1. Youth—Attitudes. 2. Forecasting—Study and teaching. 3. Youth—Education. I.
  Gidley, Jennifer. II. Inayatullah, Sohail, 1958–
HQ796.Y5928 2002
305.235—dc21   2001036704

British Library Cataloguing in Publication Data is available.

Copyright © 2002 by Jennifer Gidley and Sohail Inayatullah

All rights reserved. No portion of this book may be reproduced, by any process or technique, without the express written consent of the publisher.

Library of Congress Catalog Card Number: 2001036704
ISBN: 0–275–97414–6

First published in 2002

Praeger Publishers, 88 Post Road West, Westport, CT 06881
An imprint of Greenwood Publishing Group, Inc.
www.praeger.com

Printed in the United States of America

The paper used in this book complies with the
Permanent Paper Standard issued by the National
Information Standards Organization (Z39.48–1984).

10 9 8 7 6 5 4 3 2 1

Contents

Preface

Youth Futures: The Terrain

Jennifer Gidley and Sohail Inayatullah

Youth around the globe are struggling to make sense of a world that has lost its meaning for them (both in postmodern Western societies and mixed—traditional, modern, and postmodern—Asian and African societies).

Growing into a time of the most rapid change known to history—as evidenced by trends such as globalization, genomics, global governance, virtualization, and terrorism—the line between adapting and falling off is a very fine one. We hear so much about the rise in youth suicide and youth violence, yet many young people have positive—indeed transformational—ideas about the future that go unheard. Furthermore, too little attention is given in contemporary policy-making, education, and community development to the hopes, dreams, fears, and anticipations of young people. As a global society, we are failing to actively listen to what young people are saying about the future. Instead we stereotype and disenfranchise them. This lack of dialogue on crucial questions of building less violent, more equitable, and more environmentally sustainable futures indicates insufficient foresight and empathy as well as structural problems in the world economy (in terms of who gets what) and imperialism associated with cultural hegemony (in terms of who defines reality—what is truth, reality, and beauty).

DEFINING THE AREA

Youth futures can be defined initially as how young people think about and envision the future (probable, possible, and preferred). Youth itself is defined demographically as those humans between the ages of fifteen and twenty-five. In Chapter 1, Gidley includes critical analysis of how youth are defined, categorized, and conceptualized.

If we are to go beyond the platitudes of political leaders that youth are the future, we need to explore in a layered manner how it is that we socially construct youth. Thus, while most discourses on youth futures (outside of official press releases) focus on issues concerning youth—unemployment and the environment, for example—we can attribute these discourses to globalization, to the impact on neo-liberal policies on the most vulnerable. At a deeper level, we can explore the context of globalization, of explaining issues such as unemployment and environment as part of a grander breakdown of industrial civilization, for example, as part of the cyclical nature of the crisis of the West. This layered analysis will be explored in more detail by Inayatullah in Chapter 2.

At an even more foundational level, there is a paradox, whereby the "problematique of youth" is also part of the possible solution to the future, in that they, as other disadvantaged, marginal groups, do not share the ethos of the global system. In any attempt to transform global civilizational systems, the ideas and visions of youth must be seen as part of creating a new story, a new myth and metaphor to ground any transformed planetary civilization. Bussey is further develops this approach in Chapter 6.

This, of course, is not the conventional frame. Generally, youth are considered by the population as too materialistic, taking society for granted, unconcerned about the future, and unlikely to lead any nation to economic prosperity. They are the problem—in need of discipline, training. They are the problem—current and future criminals.

Indeed, philosopher Duane Elgin, in his work on the evolution of humanity, reports that when he asks focus groups the likely age of humanity, they respond: adolescent. By this they mean immature, overly concerned about the present (not responsible for the future), cliquish (strong in-group, out-group cultures), impressionistic (latest fad or style), dangerous (destructive of self and others). Clearly, *young* is not a highly respected term. And yet, current world culture is essentially focused fighting aging, through genetics and cosmetics. It is about being young again. Thus the contradiction: youth do not represent the future, yet they are the future; "youth" is not respected, yet it is what the older generation aspires to.

MAPPING YOUTH FUTURES

In mapping youth futures, we have found the following discourses to be dominant:

1. Youth as the future—Communities need to work together to ensure a better future for young people.
2. Youth as commodities—Youth as a market to sell identity to, from Nike to Sega.

3. Youth as the problem—As the age cohort most likely to engage in criminal activities, drugs.
4. Youth as part of transformation—Because youth are not tied into the current culture, they can innovate and produce new futures—in such areas as music—as well as social and political revolution.
5. Youth futures research—Empirical research on how young people view the future (addressed in more detail in Part II).
6. Youth futures as educational curriculum—Can negative views of the future be broadened and changed using futures methods and tools (addressed in more detail in Part III).
7. Youth and education—How can education transform to meet the needs of young people and future generations?

As a balance, this book speaks to all these points by bringing together some of the latest cross- and trans-disciplinary research on youth's anticipations of the future from around the world. It combines diverse theoretical perspectives and up-to-date research, with exemplars of practical initiatives that address young people's hopes, fears, and preferred futures.

DIVERSE PERSPECTIVES ON YOUTH AND THEIR FUTURES

Although most of the contributors to this book do not fall into the youth category, they attempt to break down the barriers to understanding young people's views, fears, hopes, and visions of their futures. This is done first by exploring diverse perspectives on the conceptualization of youth, across disciplines and cultures.

The chapters in Part I are primarily theoretically oriented and span psychosocial, politico-cultural, macro-historical, educational, health, and spiritual perspectives. They also speak to the first four points above, addressing the impact of issues such as globalization, mass media culture, mental health, fragmentation and secularization, and environmental degradation, and their impact on the views and visions of youth globally. The authors of this section are educationists and futures researchers primarily from Australia and the United States. The remaining two sections of the book are linked to the key areas of youth futures research.

Part II of this book (relating to point five above) includes recent research particularly over the last ten to fifteen years on young people's views and visions of the future in a number of countries, including England, Australia, Finland, Japan, Norway, Singapore and Hungary. The contrasts are as sharp between the Hungarian (Chapter 10) and Norwegian (Chapter 12) perspectives as they are between the more controlled scenarios of Singapore (Chapter 9) and the "free-market–influenced" Japanese youth (Chapter 7), while the Australian study (Chapter 13) reflects youth visions borne out of an unconventional educational approach.

Part III reports case studies that involved teaching an actual futures studies curriculum to young people attending schools and universities (and relates to point six above). The chapters in this section include an historical overview of this field by Richard Slaughter (Chapter 14) as well as case studies from Australia, the United States, Germany, and Taiwan. A third area, relating to point seven above, emerges from the other two: critical speculations by educational futurists about how education might respond to some of the disturbing findings of the other key areas of youth futures research. Although this really needs to be the subject of another book, some reference is made to alternative educational models and approaches in Chapters 4 and 13.

Finally, at the end of each section of the book is a short essay from a young person expressing views, visions, and hopes for the future. While it is admittedly a small selection, it does represent less dominant cultures, such as Australia, Pakistan, and the Philippines.

Ultimately, youth futures, like futures studies generally, is about empowering individuals to critically reflect on the futures being created for them so that they can actively create their preferred futures. While not denying the tremendous structural obstacles for many youth (highlighted poignantly by Bilal Aslam in his essay), futures studies processes can provide a point of leverage. We hope that this book will demonstrate this and empower youth and those involved with youth to this end.

Part I

Mapping Youth Futures

Chapter 1

Global Youth Culture:
A Transdisciplinary Perspective

Jennifer Gidley

YOUTH OF THE TWENTY-FIRST CENTURY: CHILDREN OF THE MONOCULTURE

Any attempt to classify "youth" as a group belies the inherent diversity and heterogeneity, as well as the burgeoning individuality, of contemporary youth. Yet, increasingly, as an outcome of globalization over the past ten to fifteen years, the recognition of youth, globally, as a category of human existence requiring acknowledgment, has gained the attention and focus of such organizations as the United Nations (UN), especially UNESCO, the World Bank, and the World Health Organization (WHO).

An "official" definition of youth, created by the United Nations General Assembly in 1999 for the International Youth Year, and refers to youth as "all persons falling between the ages of fifteen and twenty-four inclusive."[1] The limitations of this "definition" will be discussed later in this chapter in light of some psycho-social perspectives, including alternative images of youth since the Middle Ages. The ensuing chapters will present critical analysis of the construct of youth including multiple diverse constructions across a range of cultures. However, this UN definition has given rise to a global picture of the demographic composition of the "group of youth" worldwide.

The "Global Village" of Youth

If the 1 billion-plus youth who currently live in the world (approximately 18 percent of the global population) consisted of a village of one hundred people:

- there would be fifty-one young men and forty-nine young women;
- forty-nine would live in the village center and fifty-one in the rural outskirts;

- there would be sixty young Asians, fifteen Africans, nine Latin Americans and Caribbeans, and only sixteen young people from the industrialized countries of the world;
- fifteen of the villagers would be "illiterate," nine of them young women (this refers to literacy narrowly defined and will be contested elsewhere);
- sixty-four would be living on an average of less than US$1,000 per year, while only eleven would be earning an average income of more than US$10,000 per year;
- by the end of the year, one person would have contracted the HIV virus.[2]

With the available technology, it is also possible to provide statistics on the health and mental health characteristics of the global youth population (as well as figures for unemployment, drug abuse, juvenile delinquency, juvenile pregnancy, and many others).[3] Ironically, this capacity of the "global bureaucracy" to monitor the health and well-being of particular populations globally may contain the seeds of globalization's demise, as it points to the growing psychological "ill-health" of advanced Western societies. While the concern (of global nongovernmental organizations) on the well-being of youth globally has primarily emphasized health and education issues in the "developing" world, the emerging figures for growing mental health issues for young people in the "overdeveloped" world (discussed in a later section) confirm that "development" as part of the modernity project is not the panacea it was once thought to be. Yet globalization (called "Americanization" by some) has amplified the modernity project manyfold, supported by mass education and communication technologies, particularly the Internet and the mass media.

The Impact of Globalization

Globalization is a series of powerful processes that provide both opportunities and threats. While much has been written in the last few years about the impact of globalization, particularly on the less "developed" countries and peoples, the discourse on globalization and youth has remained oddly silent. In its first definitive statement of the impact of globalization on youth, the UN's Youth Information Network took a rather cautious view and conceded that more analysis is needed on the impact of:

Intensified evidence of poverty, unemployment and social exclusion. . . . Furthermore, the trade imbalances between developed and developing economies, favoring the more developed economies, place development at risk in many countries. . . . Hundreds of millions of people are negatively affected by these factors. Young people are particularly affected, because it means that their transition to adulthood is made more difficult. . . . [On the other hand] . . . [t]here are constructive trends. Many countries are experiencing a deepening of democracy. . . . This opens up opportunities for participation by all people. Young people will gain from this move towards democracy.[4]

This cool and balanced weighing of pros and cons masks a deeper, farther-reaching, and profound cultural transgression that is emerging in the literature on the impact of globalization. Globalization is increasingly perceived by many non-Western academics and researchers as "a form of Western ethnocentrism and patronizing cultural imperialism, which invades local cultures and lifestyles, deepens the insecurities of indigenous identities and contributes to the erosion of national cultures and historical traditions."[5]

The tensions thus created have been referred to by Benjamin Barber as "'McWorld,' the moving force of a borderless market towards global homogeneity, and . . . 'Jihad,' the rivaling process of localization, which originates in cultural, ethnic, and linguistic boundaries."[6]

The Industrial Model and Youth

With the onset of the industrial revolution, young people, and even children, became fodder for the industrial machine—cheap labor, used mercilessly by industry to keep the factories churning. These Dickensian images of children in sweatshops are no longer valid for the West; the global sweep of industrial geography has shifted these images into backyards of the newly "developing" nations. As gentrification emerges and child labor becomes unfashionable in one place, the multinational global agenda simply shifts to another locus—from Japan to Korea, from Malaysia to Taiwan, from China to Fiji—as the race for ever-cheaper products meets the craving to buy what the high-tech world offers. Who will be next? Ethiopia? Mongolia?

In addition to these overtly oppressive macro-economic forces, globalization also has an impact on non-Western youth resulting from at least two other major processes: mass education (based on the factory model) and the media. In a critique of the model of education put forward by the World Bank a decade ago at the Education for All (EFA) meeting in Jomtein, Thailand, a number of educationists and social activists cite this model as a further attempt to assert the values and culture of the Western materialist worldview. The Education for All agenda argued that education is essential for economic survival, but Sangeeta Kamat contests this yoking of education with economics. She argues that it is a flawed model for education because it is based on the human capital theory, named after the World Bank's proposals relating to "building human capital for increasing national productivity, as in production and consumption of (economically valued) goods and services." Furthermore, while the rhetoric of the Education for All strategy was to promote "flexibility and adaptability to local culture," according to Anita Dighe, in India at least, the reality of the World Bank–funded District Primary Education Project is homogeneity and "uniformity."[7] In addition, Catherine Hoppers strongly critiques the EFA agenda on literacy: "Instead of looking at literacy as a continuum in different modes of communication, from the oral to the written, we (the EFA) equated being ignorant of the Western alphabet with total ignorance."[8]

As a result of this process of mass education of children of the third world over the last decade has prompted increasing enculturation of the world's youth into the Western worldview. Pawan Gupta describes this view: "The modern education system has used modern science (and vice versa) to successfully perpetuate many modern myths which both advertise the superiority of the modern development paradigm and devalue rural communities and their knowledge systems, values and wisdom." He adds, in a description of what might be called "virtual colonialism," "the West has succeeded in refining the instruments of control to such a high degree that the physical presence of the oppressor is no longer required at the site of exploitation."[9]

The Media as "Global Culture" Amplifier

The mass media (such as television, music), and in particular the new media (such as the Internet) are important tools for spreading the global culture to young people around the world; conversely, it can be used as a platform for networking resistance. Researchers from Denmark, France, and Israel found that as a result of the media-induced processes of globalization, young people in those countries have a preference for transnational fiction and movie material (particularly American "soapies") as well as a new sense of transnational social space provided by the Internet.[10] One of the paradoxes of the media's Western cultural influence is the tension between the homogenizing effect of a dominant culture on diverse cultures, and the inherent individualism at the center of the Western cultural model. This creates a push-and-pull effect of "look-alike" teenage role models masking the ongoing struggle for individuality and identity that is at the heart of adolescence. However, when the individualism being promoted in tandem with the global media images of Western lifestyles is blended with aggressive market-driven consumerism, it can be a rather toxic brew for youth living in poverty unable to attain the image. Sonia Livingstone describes this process in which modern marketing directs popular culture, transforming the global citizen (or viewer) into the consumer. She adds, "Whether conceived optimistically or pessimistically, the processes of globalization of media and culture are seen by many as the means par excellence by which such social changes are effected."[11]

Yet ironically, in the one place where the wealth seems to grow into infinity, the youth of the United States have activated their ethical con-

science. For the first time since the anti-Vietnam War marches of the six-
ties, students in large numbers are demonstrating in American universities.
Paradoxically, the targets of their resistance are the multinationals who continue to abuse young people confined to work in the sweatshops of the
third world manufacturing the very label-brands these students like to buy
and wear. One of the processes used by these students, culture jamming,
co-opts the powerful advertising images of the corporate giants and mod-
ifies them to show their shadow side.[12] This student resistance (United
Students Against Sweatshops) is hailed as the beginning of a new anti-cor-
poratist movement[13] and is just one of the many paradoxes that surround
the complexities of being young and human on earth at the beginning of
the twenty-first century.

In this example, students are using their very commodification as their
point of leverage. As long as globalization continues to be fueled by consumerism, the young (as "market-share") hold some trump cards—their
buying power and their peer influence—the Achilles' heels of the multinationals.

Monoculture (or Toxiculture)

The particular variety of culture underpinned by Western scientific
thought, and in recent decades amplified by information technologies and
the economic rationalist paradigm of commodification, has claimed cultural superiority since the Enlightenment. With this self-imposed authority
(at first European, now American), it has sought to "develop" the "underdeveloped world" using the development paradigms of "deficit" and "dis-
advantage" rather than "diversity" as its justification.[14] This is not to
diminish or underestimate the great gains made by the spread of the
modernity project: the introduction of electricity; technology; and certain
medical and other improvements. Yet, like all great civilizations of the past
that reached their zenith before they begin to decay, the "over-develop-
ment" of the Western culture, with its foundations rooted in a materialist
worldview, has for decades showed signs of decay. The litany of symptoms exhibited by many young people of the "most-developed" nations
exemplify this with great poignancy. As research presented later in this
chapter and book will show, many youth of the West have increasingly
high rates of depression and other forms of mental illness, are committing
suicide and other violent crimes at an alarming rate, and are expressing a
general malaise, loss of meaning, and hopelessness about the future.
Western culture has recently been described by film director Peter Weir as
a "toxic culture," after a spate of violent school shootings by and of fellow
students in the United States.

The next section of this chapter considers what has gone wrong in the
enculturation of youth in Western (and increasingly global) culture.

TRENDS AND CHALLENGES OF CULTURAL BREAKDOWN AND RENEWAL

Before exploring some of the manifestations of this cultural breakdown, it is essential to go to the heart of what is missing from the Western materialist cultural model. Because it is based on a view of human nature that lacks a spiritual dimension (divorcing psychology from theology, science from ethics), all further fragmentations stem from this inherent tendency to segregate rather than integrate. Four forces of change that have emanated from this materialist worldview over recent decades, accelerating the breakdown of society "as it was" particularly in regard to the enculturation of young people:

- individualism versus community;
- the colonization of imagination;
- the secularization of culture;
- environmental degradation.

Individualism versus Community

The current age of the "I," which celebrates self-centered egoism, began in the 1960s and 1970s with the recognition of (and rebellion against) the injustices involved in the long-term cultural dominance of the "wealthy white male." The various movements for "liberation" and human rights (feminism, gay, black, and indigenous rights movements) set in motion a process where rights began to dominate responsibilities. While not wanting to undermine the gains made in equity and human rights, in the process, the needs of family and community have often been compromised. While the development of the individual ego is an important stage in the evolution of human nature, linked to our destiny to discover freedom, it is also evident that the human ego is a double-edged sword. The striving of individual human beings throughout the twentieth century for self-identity and equal rights has culminated in what David Elkind called the "me decade," the 1990s.[15] In the nineteenth century, Soren Kierkegaard (1813–1855) was aware of the dangers of the "free human ego" unless it had some spiritual grounding:

> The most tremendous thing that has been granted to man is: the choice, freedom. And if you desire to save it and preserve it there is only one way: in the very same second unconditionally and in complete resignation to give it back to God, and yourself with it.[16]

It might be added, "to use it in the service of the common good."

From the demise of the tribe (with the breakdown of the chief's authority in indigenous cultures) in the face of globalization, to the breakdown of families and other social structures (linked also to the shift in male–female power relationships), we are seeing an unprecedented fragmentation of the social glue, without which young people are rudderless in their social orientation.

Is it just coincidence that the symptoms observed today among Western young people, such as homelessness, alienation, and depression, have increased during the same few decades? By contrast, this individualism inherent in the West strikes a strong chord with youth as they strive for their own identities. This provides a balance for some of the homogenizing cultural forces.

The Colonization of Imagination

Over roughly the same period, the education of the imaginations of children and youth has changed from the nourishment of oral folk and fairy tales to the poisoning of interactive electronic nightmares. Since the advent of television, and video game parlors, followed by the use of computer games (originally designed to train and desensitize soldiers before sending them off to the killing fields), Western children and youth have been consistently and exponentially exposed to violent images.[17] Toys once made by mothers or fathers from simple materials lying around have given way in this "wealthy consumer age" to what are very often grotesque monsterlike toys given ready-made to young children. These are not food for the souls of children, but the food for nightmares. The imagination, like the intellect, needs appropriate content to develop in a healthy manner. It will be shown in my later chapter that powerful, positive images in education can help young people envision strong, positive futures—which they feel empowered to create.

Is it surprising, then, that over the past decade in particular, symptoms have appeared among young people (particularly in the United States but also other "developed" countries) of ever-increasing violence and suicide. The American Medical Association and American Academy of Pediatrics have recently made a joint statement that "the prolonged viewing of media violence can lead to emotional desensitization towards violence in real life."[18] Most of the research on suicide and suicidal ideation shows strong links with depression and also hopelessness about the future.[19] By contrast, young people educated with an eye to the development of a healthy, positive imagination are not disempowered by their concerns about the future.[20]

The Secularization of Culture

Secularization of society is the third major change that has accelerated over the past few decades. This triumph of secular science over spiritual science, coinciding with the widespread crisis of values reflected in post-modernism as a "belief system" has resulted in a dominant world culture, which, although ostensibly Christian, is in practice amoral. The egoism that brings greed in its wake, the economic rationalism that denudes politics of the principals of social justice, the secularization of education (leading to a loss of the values dimension), the death of churches as inspiring community organizations, and ultimately the cultural fascism (and religious fundamentalism) that leads to ethnic cleansing are all symptoms of societies that have lost connections with moral, ethical, and spiritual values.

The resultant symptoms in young people are a cynical "don't care" attitude, loss of purpose and meaning, and a "dropping out" of mainstream society, assisted of course by the high levels of youth unemployment. On the other hand, the counterpoint is that many young people are beginning to recognize this void and are seeking meaning through a search for spiritual values.

Environmental Degradation

Finally, the culture that has dominated the global environmental agenda, and valued private and corporate profit over community or planet, has been responsible for the systematic and pervasive pollution of our earth, air, and water. What message, we might wonder, has this given our youth? In addition, while the scientific/medical solution of chemical approaches to mental as well as physical illnesses provides "newer and better drugs" for depression, hyperactivity, and anxiety, the numbers of depressed adolescents and children diagnosed as having attention-deficit hyperactivity disorder (ADHD) continue to climb.[21] Meanwhile, genetic engineers push forward to develop improved strains of everything, bringing us closer daily to the age of the "designer baby."

Is it any wonder that in this unnatural world so many youth are turning to drug abuse to escape, or to alcohol binges to drown their sorrows? Conversely, the environmental awareness of youth is high, with "green futures" almost universally present in their preferred futures scenarios.

Cultural Renewal

If we're not allowed to dream, we turn to things that will destroy us, drugs, etc.
    —Jesse Martin, Australian who sailed solo around the world at age 16

In the face of all these cultural stressors and related symptoms, especially among young people, that signal the breakdown of our cultural system, the formal approaches of most government, professional, and academic systems is "business as usual," or try to return to "the way it was." Many right-wing conservative governments have been returned to power as a fear response to all the rapid changes, with the hope that they will take life back to how it was. Such governments also slash spending on education, health, and welfare as part of the "free market" ideology. As a counter-response to renewed conservatism, "alternative" approaches abound (to medicine, education, agriculture). However, most of the responses, even the alternative ones, are responses to symptoms or effects of the cultural malaise of our times. Yet unless this malaise is addressed at its systemic roots and in a transdisciplinary and holistic manner, new symptoms will continue to replace the old ones.

How does one transform a culture, especially one that has become a colonizing monoculture, homogenizing diversity in its path?

There are many ways to attempt to transform a culture, and all are fraught with contention:

1. directly by structural change such as reform and/or cultural revolution;
2. directly by taking charge of the enculturation processes of the young people, as Singapore has tried to do (see Chapter 9);
3. directly by transforming the education system, as some alternative approaches attempt (Steiner, Montessori, Ananda Marga Gurukul);
4. indirectly by making subtle, gradual inroads via literature and the arts;
5. indirectly by telling ourselves and our young people different stories about the future and encouraging them to create and enact their own personal futures stories.

The successes and failures of the first four are well known. The fifth utilizes the processes of futures studies to facilitate for and with young people a cultural renewal, inspired by the hopes and dreams of these young people. This book is about the diverse futures that young people would like to create, a world that would go beyond symptom treatment into a place of hope, renewal, potential, and creativity, a place where a society might reflect the health, not the symptoms, of its members, and where the young people draw physical, emotional, and spiritual sustenance.

Before considering these issues further, some perspectives on how youth have been and are conceptualized are presented.

IMAGES OF YOUTH AND CONTEMPORARY CHALLENGES

A Genealogy of Western Youth since the Middle Ages

All theories about human nature (and therefore youth) are embedded in the broader sociocultural (and more recently politico-economic) milieu in which they are conceived. This is highlighted by the recent shift to the term "youth" (a broader politico-economically defined category than "adolescence"), which raises the age level of the passage to adulthood for expedient purposes. The most frequently used conception of adolescence this century is that of George Stanley Hall, who initiated the seminal psychological study of the period between puberty and adulthood (at around twenty-one) and coined the phrase "storm and stress."[22] Earlier usages of the term youth are synonymous with this period of life.

Prior to the psychological conceptions of this century, we must refer to literature for a historical understanding. In a study by Violato and Wiley (1990), Chaucer's fourteenth-century squire was "frivolous" and demonstrated "adventurousness . . . (and) . . . turbulent sensuality," while Thomas More's sixteenth-century utopian youth experienced a smooth transition, based on an emphasis on moral training as well as academic learning. Shakespeare's youth were sympathetically characterized by "excess, passion and sensuality," while Lewis Bayly, also writing in the seventeenth century, foreshadowed a Freudian view of youth as "untamed beast." By contrast, John Milton, also a Puritan, saw youth as "carefree and joyful" as well as a time for intellectual development. By the eighteenth century, the Romantic era, which began the critique of the materialist worldview with its "narrow rationalism and . . . its mechanized universe," is well represented by William Wordsworth. Influenced by what is called "primitivism" that the earliest conditions of humanity were glorious and that children reflect this—Wordsworth saw youth as a unique stage of cognitive development, in transition from the more spiritual world of childhood, and toward adulthood, which is fully separated from God and Nature. "The Youth, who daily farther from the east/Must travel, still is Nature's Priest" (Ode, II, 72–73). In the nineteenth-century environment of industrialization, child labor, urbanization, and mass education, writers such as Charles Dickens initiated the "sentimental" view depicting the visionary image of the "saintlike young person, battling against the immense forces of evil."[23]

The contemporary Western images of youth seem to be a mixture of those explained above, all of which are inscribed in the collective "cultural memory," depending on one's philosophical standpoint. Further variations can also be taken from different professionalized standpoints, such as the social deviance model, youth as victim, or the youth rights model.[24]

For a cross-cultural perspective, a cultural anthropology study using a world sample of 186 pre-industrial societies recognizes a distinct stage of social adolescence as almost a cultural universal.[25] However, the inevitability of adolescence as a period of "storm and stress" in traditional cultures is strongly contested. Diverse cultural conditions relating to traditional family roles, community embeddedness, and, most importantly, initiation ceremonies appear to reduce and/or ameliorate the stressors of Western adolescence in many non-Western cultures, such as China, Indonesian Java and, Micronesia, to name a few.[26]

How long this will remain so in the face of global cultural change is impossible to say.

Contemporary Psychosocial Perspectives on Adolescence

In the present era, not much has changed in the psycho-social domain since Hall's turn-of-the-century conception, except that the earlier (pre-Hall) images contained a sense of lightheartedness and joyfulness, where today in the West the "storm and stress" for many is increasingly tinged with sadness and even despair. This may be seen as sentimental and even disempowering, but from the "chalkface of school counseling," it is a reality that needs to be addressed. In spite of reports that as many as one in five young people in "developed countries" experiences some form of mental illness (particularly depression),[27] contemporary psychology and pedagogy are surprisingly unable to arrive at any clear understanding of what adolescence is. According to Collins (1991), "The study of adolescence is the Cinderella, the neglected person, of developmental psychology. It is the Forgotten Era, having been the focus of less than 2 percent of research articles on human behavior for many years.[28]

Much contemporary education and social policy, operating in the absence of coherent psychosocial theories of adolescence, takes a "waiting room" approach to the vital years between puberty and adulthood. The economic rationalism underpinning this policy considers secondary, and now post secondary, education to be training for future employment, in spite of the fact that most of this employment no longer exists. The youth labor force in the "developed world" reduced from 106 million to 88 million between 1980 and 1995. A comprehensive study of the psychosocial effects of unemployment on young people found that the transition from school to work is a significant phase in their maturation as "it represents their initiation into the adult world."[29]

It is becoming increasingly evident that with the sleight of hand that is politics, the psychology and sociology of adolescence have been appropriated by expedient politico-economic policy. While psychologists are edged to the sidelines to "manage" the resultant behavioral and emotional chaos that ensues, sociologists are left to argue about how best to situate the crises of today's youth within the polemic of Marxist or Foucaultian approaches to "youth subculture" theory. Further, most of what psychologists and sociologists have written about youth is from the position of outsiders looking at youth as the "other," where the youth themselves are primarily silent. This book attempts to demonstrate the plurality and diversity of voices of many youth from around the world, on their own terms.

A Plurality of Voices from a Monotone of Silence

In spite of the pressure toward homogeneity, of the globalizing influence of Western values, youth everywhere refuse to be suppressed. One of the great challenges and excitements of working with young people is their irrepressible spirit of rebellion. Sociologists and ethnographers (and, more recently, market researchers) have devoted numerous dissertations to the various characteristics and types of "youth subculture" and new-age "tribes" such as "punks," "Goths," "homeys," "surfies," "ferals" and "skinheads" to name a few.[30] One theory suggests that each main youth subculture has been superceded by another, each generation attaching themselves to a drug of choice—the hippies favored LSD, the punks were partial to speed, while the latest metamorphosis, rave culture, prefers designer drugs such as MDMA or Ecstasy.[31]

If we look to the extremes of the Western youth profile, on one end of the spectrum we have recently been hearing of some areas where the young can make it in society—where they can rise to heights of success in certain predefined areas. These would include the Olympic heroes and heroines, popstars, and, of course, the new breed known as "the dot-com boys"—the young twenty-somethings who have made their first million from floating a successful dot-com company.

At the other end of the spectrum are the marginalized and disenfranchised—the "street kids" who spurn society because it has rejected them. In Australia and the United States, growing numbers of young people have become disenchanted with schooling, lack of work prospects, and the general malaise of materialism. It seems the more that policy-makers try to codify and rectify their curricula, to nationalize their agendas, and to increase their retention rates, the more young people will slip through the cracks. They live a life on the streets of cities and rural towns—hanging out with friends to make up for the sense of belonging and meaning that once came from working and community life. Many are children of the long-term unemployed, who don't look to employment as the norm, but others are from diverse backgrounds, who choose the school of life rather than the life of school.[32] Although the "street-frequenting" youth of the "developed" world are living in relative poverty, they are still wealthy compared to the "street kids" in Brazil or the Philippines, who do not have the safety net of Social Security.

In this context, the extent to which Western culture is adequately initiating its youth into the stage of adult maturity needs to be seriously considered.

The Puberty Transition: Initiation into What?

Traditional cultures have always offered rites of passage to their youth around the time of puberty. These diverse forms of culture, being gradually extinguished, formed the basis of the knowledge, the mores, and indeed the wisdom that was the curriculum for the education and enculturation of their children. Each unique culture had also developed, over centuries and even millennia, appropriate initiation ceremonies for marking the stages of acquisition of this knowledge. These initiation ceremonies require disciplined preparation and are a symbolic recognition of an important stage—sexual maturity, and increased consciousness, requiring orientation to and knowledge of the world at a level beyond that of childhood. The teaching of responsibility is an integral part and generally physical challenge especially for males. The spiritual values of the culture are also introduced in a new way, as are life-survival skills.

The importance of honoring the esoteric nature of the crucial changes involved in puberty transition has been ignored by our postmodern Western culture at its peril. It has been suggested that if a society, or the responsible adults, do not provide some adequate initiation or orientation for adolescents, one of two things may happen:

- They may seek to initiate themselves through drugs, and other customs referred to as part of "youth subculture"—dress, body mutilation, "street living," and even risk-taking behaviors.
- They may become disorientated and lose their sense of meaning or hope about the future, or at worst attempt to take their own lives.[33]

Sohail Inayatullah suggests in the next chapter that consumer-oriented processes, such as shopping and buying one's own car, are the contemporary alternatives for youth with spending power.

Animal or Angel? A Transformed View of Youth

Regrettably, the puberty transition issue was discarded as "stage theories" of child development went out of vogue. While stage theory has been unpopular with psychologists and educationists for a number of decades, there is renewed recognition of the importance of learning readiness and of the dangers of intellectually accelerating children beyond their biological maturity.[34] One of the few educational approaches that is still underpinned by an understanding of developmental stages of childhood and adolescence is the Rudolf Steiner (or Waldorf) approach.[35] Steiner's theories, while not entirely inconsistent with the approaches of Piaget, Erickson, and Kohlberg, take developmental stage theory into a comprehensive, coherent pedagogy. There also seems to be a resurgence of interest in Erickson's seminal work on adolescence, which no contemporary theory has really replaced.[36] Perhaps it is also an indication that the moral and spiritual aspects of development are being called for today. One of the great stage theorists, Kohlberg also made important links between the uniqueness and vulnerability of adolescence and the importance of being able to retain idealism and hope and a positive relationship to the future.[37]

Notwithstanding the contentiousness of developmental stage theory, the fact that puberty marks a stage of dramatic changes cannot reasonably be denied. Taking this perspective, I would argue that adolescence is a stage when powerful, opposing forces are emerging that require harmonizing over time. The changes of puberty bring with them, simultaneously, new experiences of two forces:

- the coolness of newfound intellectual reason (with ensuing idealism tempered by opinionated argument, a sense of fragmentation, and critical judgment);
- the heat of passions, romantic emotions, and the generative energy of hormonally charged, emerging sexual capacities (with impulsive, demanding urges).

A culture that polarizes and fragments reality can make the harmonizing of these forces difficult for many and impossible for some. The swings between the polarities are common fare for most. What is required of a culture and an enculturation system to support the adolescent stage of development and maximize the potential of this transition is not what is currently offered. What is needed is enculturation processes that integrate and synthesize and include social, cultural, and educational processes that encourage wisdom, healthy imagination, and creative and ethical activity through:

- an integrated knowledge system, underpinned by wisdom;
- exposure to and involvement with the aesthetics of the arts, music, theater;
- appropriate opportunities for engagement in worthwhile action through employment and/or useful occupation.

Such transformed enculturation processes could provide a powerful balance, harmonizing the conflicting inner forces experienced by contemporary adolescents. Who knows, this may even allow the angel to appear.

NOTES

1. Division for Social Policy and Development, United Nations, *The Definition of Youth*. 1999. www.un.org/esa/socdev/unyin/g-and-a/define.htm.

2. Division for Social Policy and Development, United Nations, "The Global Village," 1999. www.un.org/esa/socdev/unyin/g-and-a/village.htm.

3. United Nations, *The World Program of Action for Youth to the Year 2000 and Beyond*. 1998. www.un.org/events/youth98/backinfo/yreport.htm.

4. Youth Information Network, United Nations, *Global Profiles on the Situation of Youth: 2000–2025*. www.un.org/esa/socdev/unyin/wywatch/glob-1.htm.

5. Dafna Lemish et al., "Global Culture in Practice: A Look at Adolescents in Denmark, France and Israel," *European Journal of Communication* 13, 4 (1998): 540.

6. Ibid., 540.

7. Manish Jain, ed., *Unfolding Learning Societies: Challenges and Opportunities*. (Udaipur, Shikshantar: People's Institute for Rethinking Education and Development, 2000).

8. Catherine Odora Hoppers, "Turning the Monster on Its Head: Lifelong Learning Societies for All," in *Unfolding Learning Societies,* ed. Manish Jain, 18.

9. Pawan Gupta, "Liberating Education from the Chains of Imperialism," in *Unfolding Learning Societies,* ed. Manish Jain, 12–13.

10. Dafna Lemish et al., "Global Culture."

11. Sonia Livingstone, "Mediated Childhoods: A Comparative Approach to Young People's Changing Media Environment in Europe," *European Journal of Communication* 13, (1998): 443.

12. Naomi Klein, *No Logo: Taking Aim at the Brand Bullies* (London: Flamingo, 2000).

13. Lisa Featherstone, "The New Radicals," in *The Sydney Morning Herald.* (16th September 2000): 19–23.

14. Anita Dighe, "Diversity in Education in an Era of Globalization," in *Unfolding Learning Societies,* ed. Manish Jain.

15. David Elkind, *The Hurried Child* (Reading, Mass.: Addison Wesley, 1981).

16. Joseph Campbell, *The Masks of God: Creative Mythology* (New York: Penguin Arkana, 1968): 197–198.

17. Dave Grossman, Gloria Degaetano, and David Grossman, *Stop Teaching Our Kids to Kill: A Call to Action Against TV, Movie and Video Violence* (New York: Random House, 1999).

18. Greg Callahan and Nick Cubbin, "Scream Tests," in *The Australian Magazine* (November 11th–12th, 2000): 21.

19. Aaron Beck et al., "Hopelessness and Eventual Suicide: A 10-Year Prospective Study of Patients Hospitalized with Suicidal Ideation," *American Journal of Psychiatry* 142, 5 (1985): 559–563; Lyn Abramson, Gerald Metalsky, and Lauren Alloy, "Hopelessness Depression: A Theory-Based Subtype of Depression," *Psychological Review* 96, 2 (1989): 358–372; David Cole, "Psychopathology of Adolescent Suicide: Hopelessness, Coping Beliefs and Depression," *Journal of Abnormal Psychology* 98, 3 (1989): 248–255.

20. Jennifer Gidley, "Imagination and Will in Youth Visions of their Futures: Prospectivity and Empowerment in Steiner Educated Adolescents," in *Education, Work and Training* (Southern Cross University: Lismore, 1997).

21. Martin Seligman, *The Optimistic Child: A Revolutionary Approach to Raising Resilient Children* (Sydney: Random House, 1995).

22. George Stanley Hall, *Adolescence,* vols. 1 and 2 (New York: Appleton, 1904).

23. Claudio Violato and Arthur Wiley, "Images of Adolescence in English Literature: The Middle Ages to the Modern Period," *Adolescence* 25, 98 (1990).

24. Nancy Lesko, "Past, Present and Future Conceptions of Adolescence," *Educational Theory* 46, 4 (1996): 453–472.

25. David Levinson and Melvin Ember, eds., *Encyclopedia of Cultural Anthropology* (New York: Henry Holt and Co., 1996).

26. Gwen Broude, ed., "Growing Up: A Cross-Cultural Encyclopedia," *Encyclopedias of the Human Experience,* ed. David Levinson (Santa Barbara: ABC-CLIO., 1995).

27. Marie Bashir and David Bennett, eds., "Deeper Dimensions: Culture, Youth and Mental Health," *Culture and Mental Health: Current Issues in Transcultural Mental Health* (Parramatta: Transcultural Mental Health Center, 2000).

28. J. K. Collins, "Research into Adolescence: A Forgotten Era," *Australian Psychologist* 26, 1 (1991): 1–9.

29. A. H. Winefield, et al., *Growing Up with Unemployment: A Longitudinal Study of its Psychological Impact* (London: Routledge, 1993): 2.

30. Caroline Lees, "Youth Tribes," in *The Bulletin* (June 14, 1988): 42–48; Alison Cotes, "Feral Arts—Culture in the Wild," *Social Alternatives* 10, 3 (1991): 33–35; Mike Harskin, "Czechoslovakia: Skinheads Who Cry," in *New Statesman and Society* (June 19, 1992): 15.

31. Andrew James Smith, "The Third Generation," in *New Statesman and Society* (September 11, 1992): 31–32.

32. Jennifer Gidley and Paul Wildman, "What Are We Missing? A Review of the Educational and Vocational Interests of Marginalized Rural Youth," *Education in Rural Australia Journal* 6, 2 (1996): 9–19.

33. Robert Bly, ed., *The Kabir Book* (Boston: Beacon Press, 1971); David Tacey, "The Rites and Wrongs of Passage: Drugs, Gangs, Suicides, Gurus," *Psychotherapy in Australia* 1, 4 (1995): 5–12.

34. D. Elkind, *The Hurried Child.*

35. Rudolf Steiner, *The Renewal of Education Through the Science of the Spirit* (Lectures, 1920) (Sussex: Kolisko Archive, 1981); Rudolf Steiner, *The Younger Generation: Education and Spiritual Impulses in the 20th Century* (Lectures, 1922) (New York: Anthroposophic Press, 1967).

36. Bruce Singh, "Book Reconsidered," *Australian and New Zealand Journal of Psychiatry* 34, 3 (2000): 701–4.

37. Lawrence Kohlberg and Carol Gilligan, "The Adolescent as a Philosopher: The Discovery of the Self in a Postconventional World," *Daedelus* (1971): 1051–1085.

Chapter 2

Youth Dissent: Multiple Perspectives on Youth Futures

Sohail Inayatullah

Youth is about renewal, fresh ideas challenging old traditions and yearning for the untried. Youth finds change inebriating, not intimidating. Youth is also impetuous, unpredictable: with the promise of a better future comes a veiled threat to tear down the past. . . . Youth breaks all the rules. Youth is colorful, irreverent, entertaining, sometimes shocking, almost always rebellious. Youth is on the vanguard of fashion, music, literature and popular culture. But the young are also the first to hurl stones, to lob bombs, to rush to the barricades. Youth is, in a word, energy.[1]

IDEALISM

In the 1999 movie *Dick,* about the life of Richard Nixon as seen through the eyes of two fifteen-year-olds, Nixon uses the famous line, "Young people are the voice of the future" to end the war in Vietnam. In the scene, Henry Kissinger walks into a meeting between the president and two young girls (who had stumbled on to accounts of the Watergate affair). He asks the president what to do about the war. One of the girls says, "War is not healthy to children and all living beings." While Kissinger and others debate who started the war, Nixon says that we should listen to the girls, since they represent the "voice of the future of America."

Through a series of amusing circumstances, we discover that the two girls are in fact "Deep Throat," the person who brought down the Nixon administration. The movie, while hilarious, shows the power and idealism of youth *and* utterly mocks them. They are in love with Nixon until they find out that he mistreats his dog, Checkers. All other issues escape them—corruption, bribery—but mistreatment of the dog transforms their perspective of the

president. The movie ends with Nixon resigning and flying home by heli-
copter, only to see the girls unfurling a banner from their rooftop that reads,
"You suck, Dick."

In the recently released German movie *Sonnenallee,*[2] about life in East
Berlin during the communist era, we see a similar approach to how young
people construct politics.

First, it is essentially about fun and self-destruction—endless alcohol,
drugs, and sex. However, these are not shown to us in neutral terms but
in politicized language, that is, these practices are used as resistance against
an evil regime. To win the heart of a lovely neighbor girl, the main actor
invents a diary. In the diary he writes lengthy entries of his desire to rebel
against East Germany's tyranny. He makes sure to mention that from an
early age he was not a socialist. Rebellion against the State means music
and drugs. Near the end of the movie, border guards shot a fifteen-year-
old boy, thinking that he is attempting to scale the wall. Fortunately for
him, the Rolling Stones album he has just purchased—*Exile on Main
Street*—saves his life. But he can only lament the album's (a double one)
destruction by the bullet. Freedom—meaning purchasing goods that revile
the staleness of communism—means more than life.

The movie concludes with the young people leading a neighborhood
party by the Wall. Soon, older East Germans join in. The police do nothing
but watch the testament to a different future the youth wish for.

It is this different future that has been the heart of the failed revolution
in Afghanistan. The Taliban, young men between the ages of fifteen and
twenty, were schooled in *madrasses*, religious schools in Pakistan, to
destroy the triple evils of communism, secularism, and tribal feudalism that
had claimed Afghanistan. Unfortunately, they forgot the even greater evil
of patriarchy. It remains remarkable that a group of young people (trained
and armed by the Pakistani Army and the American CIA) can defeat a
much stronger military force. Their unity and determination, as well as
desire for a moral polity, has seen them to victory. The costs of that victory—their intolerance for all other perspectives—have been overwhelming and unforgivable. Still, they have shown what youth can do by
exhibiting creative transformative and chaotic destructive power.

Equally powerful have been youth revolutions in Serbia. When
President Slobodan Milosevic annulled local elections in 1997 and gave city
power to opposition leaders, the students turned out in mass to protest. It
was the final straw. Milosevic was mocked as 500,000 took to the streets.
Eventually, after three months of nonviolent protest, the students were vic-
torious. Most recently, it was the students (with the miners and professionals) who brought down Milosevic himself. As they marched the streets,
many feared for the lives. They knew the tanks would be among them, in
any second, butchering every last protester (as Milosevic's wife and other

associates had requested the ruler to do in the 1997 revolution). But the army did not intervene and history was made that day in Belgrade.

Earlier it was the action of the Otpor (Resistance) movement that had struck fear into the hearts of government officials. Concerned not with debating Milosevic but with tearing down his system—using disobedience in every possible way, from Web anarchy to pouring sugar into the government-owned vehicles—the students had made a clear statement: We want change and we will risk everything for it. They have also made it clear to the new government that unless the last vestiges of Milosevic's regime are cleansed, they will renew their resistance.

We have seen similar student protests against the inequities of globalization, against particular dictators such as Marcos (and now the corrupt Estrada), or the cruel Mahathir, or "wanna-be" tyrants such as Hanson of Australia, or against the destruction of nature, or against permanent refugee status as in Israel/Palestine. The images of young *Intifada* Palestinian youth throwing stones against the heavily armed Israeli forces tell us in no uncertain terms that youth are more than shopping mall consumers. At the same time, even as David versus Goliath is the operating metaphor, the futility and their resultant destruction shows the paradox youth find themselves in. The Israeli army attacks them and the Palestinian political authority uses them for symbolic media purposes. Youth have agency to create a different future and, simultaneously, their vigor is used by others.

Still, this idealism is at the heart of young people's visions of the future. It is essentially the desire to create a world that works for everyone—all humans, plants, and animals. Idealism means the unwillingness to accept adult reasons for why the world cannot change or should not change—the deep structures of history. Idealism, like utopianism, expresses "impulses and aspirations which have been blocked by the existing society."[3]

However, while "the enemy" is easy to see when the forces of oppression are direct, and thus action and inspiration are far more available and accessible, transformation is far more problematic when the problems are associated with the worldview of postindustrialism (advanced and hypercapitalism)—the deeper patterns of thought, of epistemes that organize what constitutes the real.

This becomes the great source of malaise. What to do when the entire system is a lie, when the foundations of civilization, of adult civilization, claim universalism but in fact are the victories of particular politics?[4] How should youth react? How do they react? They show anger when governments express concern for human rights but continue supporting killing animals for food. They are angry when states and corporations express concern for the environment and peace but make no investment in public transport or continue to be part of the global military machine. They express anger at traditional religions when religious leaders profess a love for god but tolerate pedophilia.

When they are unable to find ways to express their bright visions of the future in positive, life-enhancing ways, the same expression comes out as destruction against others (after all, it is youth who do most of the killing)[5] and against themselves through suicide and long-term suicidal behavior (for example, drug and alcohol abuse).

POSTINDUSTRIAL FATIGUE

Based on the massive ten-nation study of how individuals envisioned the year 2000, Johan Galtung writes that the most pessimistic respondents came from the richest nations.[6] Young people expressed a development fatigue. They had seen the limits of technology, and understood that social transformation, inner transformation was required. But instead they received more technologies.[7]

As a result, the young experience cognitive dissonance when they hear talk of fairness but see actions that discriminate against the poor, the indigenous. This brings a range of responses. At one extreme is the rush to join the MBA set, to globalize, to work hard to ensure that one's own future is bright. The second is the global backlash of the right—to resist multiculturalism and the "other" through a return to extreme forms of one's identity. This is the Islamic right wing or the Christian right wing and localist/nationalistic movements throughout the world. In more respectable forms, this is scientism, wherein science (like god) is seen outside of history, the truth for all who convert to the open inquiry of the scientific method.[8] As famed physicist Michio Kaku said in reference to the new world being created by the technologies of genetic engineering, nanotechnology and space research: get on the train or forever be left behind.[9]

A third alternative is common in nations belonging to the Organization for Economic Cooperation and Development (OECD), that of suicide, especially suicide among males. They end their physical life partly because they see no future, they are missing moral male role models and the only rituals left are those of consumption—the shopping mall as the great savior. The fourth alternative is violence against others.

At heart then is a crisis in worldview. Much of the earlier youth futures research presented data as to whether young people are optimistic or pessimistic about the future. Causes of suicide were blamed on unemployment and other social and economic problems.[10] But these causes, to be sensible, must be nested in the limits of the industrial and postindustrial worldview, wherein reality is segmented into work (profit-making) followed by years of retirement. An analysis of worldview must as well speak to an even deeper sense of myth and metaphor. At this level of analysis, the issue is, what stories do young people tell themselves and others? For young people, the foundational problem is a story of the universe in which they are expected to behave in certain ways (become a worker, rational human being) and a reality that denies this possibility (unemployment) and is utterly divorced from their world (the limits of the European enlightenment with respect to accessing other ways of knowing). There is thus a contrast between the world of globalization and secularization and the realities of emotions and identity creation.

Nor is postmodernism the solution for young people. It gives them endless choices—virtuality—but with no foundation. Without this foundation, the result is a reality with too many selves—the swift Teflon vision of the future, in which identity is about speed and the collection of a multitude of experiences, not about understanding the "other." Moreover, the terms remain within the confines of the Western limitless worldview of accumulation. This is at a time in their lives where at least two forces are operating: hormonal expression of the body and idealism of the mind. Virtuality merely creates the illusion of endless choice but not the fulfillment of having met and responded to a challenge. Nature, conditions of inequity, and authentic alternatives to the postmodern are lost in this discourse.

However, as Galtung argues, it is too simplistic to say that the *problematique* is of the Western worldview, of the crises of the West because the West is ubiquitous and even closed societies exhibit similar problems. In Libya, the problems of heroin, atheism, drugs, and hallucinogens prompted Qaddafi to say: "We have lost our youth."[11] And, third, it is a conceptual mistake to argue that the West is in crisis because this is a tautological statement.[12] The West by definition exists in this way (indeed, as do youth, that is, being young is about a crisis in life, the transformation from a child to an adult). That has been the West's success in expanding the last 500 years. The West is not just linear in its evolution, it is also dramatic, apocalyptic. The West by definition searches for the latest breakthrough, the victory, the challenge that can propel it onwards. But the other side of the West is its alter ego focused not on expansion but on human rights, not on the businessman but on the shaman, not on the mature adult ready to live and retire from the company (or kingdom or church) but on the youth that contests reality. Not on domination-focused masculine principles but on partnership-focused feminine principles.

The challenge to official reality comes also from the outside, the periphery, such as the Bedouins not vested in the normative and coercive power of the state, as Ibn Khaldun argues.[13] Indeed, youth are the periphery. Even as many are part of the ego of the West (I shop, therefore I am), many are of the alter-ego (I love, therefore I am and I protest, therefore I am). This ability of the West to appropriate counter movements and to use youth and other cultures to transform itself from within; is how the

West has made itself universal. In this sense, the youth crisis in the West
(the youth movements of the last thirty years) is not new, it is merely the
alter-ego expressing the alternative West.

This is easier when the oppressor is clearer—whether it is in the form
of a tyrant or a multinational such as General Motors (or more recently
Microsoft) or a world organization such as the World Bank. It is more difficult when it is the worldview that must be challenged and transformed.

The challenge to worldview thus comes across in a multitude of movements, each touching some dimension of the critique of what has come to
be called globalization. These are expressed through spiritual movements,
vegetarian movements, cults, green movements, grunge, rap, rock and roll
as well as through the south Asian diaspora, *bhangra* rap. All these movements are supported by youth as cadres, even if managed by aging hippies.

The hypothesis then is that the crisis of youth is part of the West's own
renewal and clearly part of the fatigue of development. This fatigue has
been delayed quite a bit the Internet revolution. Screenagers, as Douglas
Rushkoff accurately calls them, have found a different way to express individuality.[14] It is quick time, quick communication, and a chance to immediately lead instead of follow. This will likely be delayed even more by
revolutions in genetics and nanotechnology. While at one level delayed, at
another level, the dot-com revolution is a youth explosion. Many small
start-ups are multicultural and gender partnership-based, and they challenge traditional notions of working nine-to-five and wearing black suits.
They also offer a network vision of work and organizational structure. In
this sense, they renew even as they delay more basic (needed) changes to
globalization.

SCENARIOS OF THE FUTURE

This ego and alter-ego come across in foundational scenarios of the
future. These can be seen in popular and academic images of the future
and have certainly come across in visioning workshops with young people
(explored in Chapter 19 on case studies).[15] The first is the *globalized* artificial future and the second is the *communicative-inclusive* future.[16]

The globalized scenario is high technology and economy-driven.
Features include the right to plastic surgery and an airplane for each
person. Generally, the vision is of endless travel and shopping, and of a
global society that meets all our desires, where we all have fun. The underlying ethos is that technology can solve every problem and lead to genuine
human progress.

In contrast is the communicative-inclusive society, which is values-
driven. Consumption in this scenario is far less important than communication. It is learning from another that is crucial. While technology is

important, the morality of those inventing and using it is far more important. Instead of solving the world's food problem through the genetic engineering of food, the reorganization of society and softer, more nature-oriented alternatives such as organic foods are far more important. The goal is not to create a world that leads to the fulfillment of desire but one wherein desire is reduced (the Gandhian sentiment) or channeled to spiritual and cultural pursuits.

The underlying perspective is that of a global ethics with a deep commitment to the belief that communication and consciousness transformation can solve all our problems.

MACROHISTORY AND DEPTH

The argument made so far is that there are generally two foundational futures. Of course, the specter of total collapse remains, because of either the exploitation of nature or overconcentration of power and wealth. But this image is used more as a call to action, to either join the technology revolution or the consciousness revolution. The scenario of muddling through is also important but generally rejected by youth.

The basic perspective of the globalization/technologization scenario is that things rise—more progress, more technology, more development, more wealth, more individuality. This is generally the view of older age cohorts and those in the center of power. The underlying perspective of the communicative-inclusive scenario is that of transformation, whether because of green or spiritual values or because of the wise and moral use of technology. This tends to be more the vision of youth. It is idealistic and not beholden to the values of the market. In contrast to the exponential curve of the first scenario, this scenario has a spiral curve (a return to traditional values but in far more inclusive terms).

This pattern oscillates in the West. The West needs the latter, its alterego, to refresh itself. Collapse remains the fear (technology gone wrong or overpopulation from the South) that spurs the West to constantly create new futures.

We have also argued that the West is by definition in crisis, and that is how it refreshes itself. Without these two pillars it would have fallen to the wayside, and other civilizations would have reigned.

Youth and the idealistic futures they imagine are central to this oscillation. Macrohistorian Pitirim Sorokin writes of this in terms of sensate (materialistic) civilization and ideational (mental) civilization.[17] He argues that we are in a phase shift. Eisler writes of this in terms of dominator and partnership society.[18] The first is based on rank ordering a hierarchy system with the goal of moving up. The second is based on different values, on sharing futures, on not winning. This transformation is based on stages of crisis, catharsis, charisma, and then transformation. Youth are foundationally engaged in the first two—in noticing the crisis. As among the most vulnerable, they can see the negative implications of globalization far before elders. Also, as they are less vested in the economic basis and power politics, they are free to protest and to work to create alternatives. However, many youth do not succeed. Others imagine a time with no change when they were not the most vulnerable—when borders protected them against others. This latter is the plea of every sovereignty movement: youth would have jobs if the others (illegal immigrants and large corporations) did not enter the nation and take away employment and other opportunities.

Youth futures (defined as how young people envision possible, probable, preferred, and transformational futures, and how these futures are empirically studied, interpreted, and critically understood) must thus be understood in the context of the code and cosmology of civilization and the patterns of macrohistory.

They must also be understood in the context of layers of reality. At the most superficial (litany level), youth futures are defined by the problematique of unemployment, crime, and family breakdown.[19] At the deeper level of worldview, youth futures express the transition of industrial to postindustrial/postmodern (end of full employment, loss of meaning, breakdown of the nation-state). At the deepest level of metaphor, the crisis of identity is central: do youth have one self, multicultural, many selves, or virtual fragmented selves? In this sense, whether youths are optimistic or pessimistic matters less than their vision of the future, the idealism embedded in it, and whether they believe they have the capacity to realize that vision.

Thus at one level, the discussion of youth futures is an exercise in banality. "The future is the youth" and similar statements are generally symbolic politics used to create an appearance that something for the future is being done—that vitality and innovation are just around the corner. It is code for deep oppressive structures that mitigate against change.

OPPRESSION AND CHANGE

The future of no change, or muddling through, is, however, the reality for most in the world. In the West, this is the scenario of liberal government, of increasing wealth, of all problems solved through the democratic scenario, of not rocking the boat lest the entire project capsize.

In the non-West, "muddling through" is dealing with colonialism and neocolonialism. It means the continued centralization of power in the military and feudal lords. Shifts in power are merely shifts rulers, not transformations of culture and society.

This is especially so in traditional societies, such as Pakistan. Youth futures there are focused on a fatigue not with development but with feudalism and state corruption.[20] While initially the ways out of this oppression were marches against the government or the university vice-chancellor, eventually military dictatorships and violent suppression by rightwing parties engendered a deep fatigue. The result of this deep fatigue has been a desire to escape to high-income areas, either Middle Eastern countries or OECD. Youth who could not escape have generally had to make the best of it. Of course, the "best of it" tends to mean high heroin addiction.[21]

An emerging new factor is the Internet. This has allowed the hundreds of thousands of youths who cannot emigrate to the United States to connect with youth all over the world, and for some, to find ways to earn income (or create viruses). They are dramatically changing the economic and political landscape of regions, especially south Asia and China.

However, while global, these young people are not postmodern in the Western sense, as are Douglas Rushkoff's postmodern youth (who can quickly and swiftly adapt). This is because Pakistan and other third-world nations do not exist in advanced knowledge economies. The day-to-day realities of power surges, blackouts, coup d'états do not allow the victory of life as mediated through the modem. Third-world youth live in conditions of pre-agricultural, agricultural, industrial, modern, and postmodern. It is this authentic diversity of worldviews and commitments to these perspectives that makes Rushkoff's hypothesis problematic. Far more resonating are the images of community/green/sustainability, as well as images of national success, wherein economic development is realized and poverty is escaped. Another image and alternative, mentioned earlier, has been joining the *madrasses* and recognizing Islam as the vehicle to create a purer world. India and other third-world nations are undergoing similar processes. While some take strict anti-West or anti-"other" definitions of their religious sensitivities (and are captured by movements of the right), others, following Ashis Nandy's vision of a Gaia of civilizations, understand that no culture is complete in itself—all cultures exist in fields that make up humanity.[22] When constructive alternatives are not possible, then the result is violence, either against the self, or, as in Pakistan in the last generation, against the other sect of Islam (for example, Sunnis attack Shia and visa versa, and all attack Ahmedis).

YOUTH FUTURES AROUND THE WORLD

What then can we say about youth futures around the world? First, there are clear differences among the futures youth practice around the world. This is partly because of the structures of history. The future is created by three factors. The first is the push of the future—technology (the net, genomics) and demographics (the aging population living in the West and the global teenager living in the third world), for example. The second is deep structures that are difficult, nearly impossible, to change—

feudalism in Pakistan, tribalism in Africa, Confucianism in East Asia, imperialism and colonialism in the OECD, and patriarchy in various forms throughout the world. Third is the image of the future. This is the pull of the future, the vision that transforms. It transforms either because it creates a new pattern of ideas that aids in human social evolution (Sarkar's Microvita,[23] Sheldrake's morphogenetic fields) or it is a point of coherence for practical actions.

In the non-West third world, traditions are stronger: Islam and Confucianism (which cohere) as well as feudalism and patriarchy (which create strong hierarchies). In OECD nations, the problems are associated with a loss of meaning, a loss of a clear vision of the future—except in the banal forms of consumption—the problem of hyper-wealth for a few, a middle class for most (with a strong underclass of others including youth), and the ecological problematique. We see this in the underlying imperialistic nature of the West, for example, in its lack of institutional capacity to apologize to Aboriginals in Australia.

The trends affecting youth are also different. Technological transformations are far more prevalent in the West, as is the aging of society. In the third world, the trend is for huge numbers of teenagers moving to the city to escape the tyranny of community and poverty in the village (while in the West, there is movement away from the tyranny of individuality in the city and a desperate search for community).

The differences are also explained by different expectations. In the third-world context, the expectation is to continue the family tradition, to earn income to support the family. In the West, independence and carving out a life autonomously are far more important.

In both cases, youth are pressured to either conform to structures not of their making or rebel against them. This must be placed in the context of changing hormonal patterns and an idealism to create a better world.

Thus, generally the manner in which youth express their concerns is based on the social and cultural conditions they find themselves in. Australian youth rebel through the green movement and the "dope and dole" culture (drugs and government handouts). Malaysian youth rebel via rock and roll (Western music and clothes) and a return to Islam (challenging state secularism and Westernization). Chinese youth rebel through the symbols of Western democracy, spiritual practices, and the Internet. German youth rebel via the green anti-nuke movement and as well through the neo-nazi movement.

This leads back to the movie, *Dick*. Youth, of course, are the future, more so in the West as they become a scarce demographic commodity (with an aging population, there will be less of them).

Youth revolutions and rebellions have an instrumental in challenging strong state structures, most recently in Belgrade and in Israel/Palestine with the *intifada*. Now, throughout the world they challenge globalization and the more extreme forms of corporate capitalism.

These movements emerged in the 1960s and have evolved in various forms (green movement, nongovernmental movements, spiritual movements, ethical business movements).[24] They continue to hold an important antisystemic view of transforming the capitalism system. This is not a surprise, as they are part of the West's alter-ego.

The non-West is, of course, mirroring the West. While the official discourse is religion, the unofficial is escape from religion and the chase for all things Western (T-shirts, cigarettes, and rock music). However, if the wealthier East Asian nations are a sign of the future, then a shift to a communicative-inclusive or partnership future is a possibility, since these nation's youth are already tiring of endless development.

Youth are one element of the creation of a different future. What role they will play in either solidifying global capitalism (muddling through) and creating the Artificial Society or in helping transform the world to a communicative-inclusive future is not clear. Certainly they are playing dramatic roles in all these scenarios, from street protests against globalization to the dot-com revolution to working with environmental and spiritual social movements. Through their actions and their visions they are creating a different future. Whether they do it through dance or music, student rebellion, or the latest Web site, they should not be ignored. The periphery, after all, was once the center. And if this generation of youth age, normalize, and naturalize themselves in the prevailing paradigm—muddling through—there is always the next generation to come.

NOTES

1. Terry McCarthy, "Lost Generation," *Time* (October 23, 2000): 35.
2. Directed by Leander Haussmann, released 1999.
3. Vincent Geoghegan, *Utopianism and Marxism* (New York: Methuen, 1987): 106.
4. The UNDP annual report tells us that in 1999 the combined wealth of the world's 200 richest individuals hit 1 trillion US$ while the combined incomes of the 582 million people living in the forty-three least developed countries was 146 billion US$; Jeff Gates, *Democracy at Risk: Rescuing Main Street from Wall Street—A Populist Vision for the 21st Century* (Boulder, CO: Perseus Books, 2000). He writes that in the United States, the financial wealth of the top 1 percent of households exceeds the combined wealth of the bottom 95 percent.
5. In the United States, the second leading cause of death among fifteen- to nineteen-year-olds is murdered by a gun. Michelle Slatalla, "Teens: A Primer," *Time* (November 6, 2000): 82.
6. Johan Galtung, "The Future: A Forgotten Dimension," in *Images of the World in the Year 2000,* eds. H. Ornauer, H. Wiberg, A. Sicinki, and J. Galtung (Atlantic Highlands, N.J.: Humanities Press, 1976).
7. Johan Galtung, "Who Got the Year 2000 Right—The People or the Experts," *WFSF Futures Bulletin* 25, 4, (2000): 6.

8. Ziauddin Sardar, *Thomas Khun and the Science Wars* (Cambridge Books: Icon, 2000).

9. Speech at Humanity 3000 Symposium, Seattle, Washington. September 23–26. See for details on this: Sohail Inayatullah, "Science, Civilization and Global Ethics: Can We Understand the Next 1000 Years?," *Journal of Futures Studies* (November 2000).

10. The unemployment figures for youth are generally hovering around the forty to fifty percent mark throughout the world, worse in poorer nations. In most areas, minority groups are hit the hardest. See: www.jobsletter.org.nz.

11. Andrew Cockburn, "Libya: An End to Isolation," *National Geographic* (November 2000): 22.

12. Johan Galtung, "On the Last 2,500 Years in Western History, and some remarks on the Coming 500," in *The New Cambridge Modern History, Companion Volume,* ed. Peter Burke (Cambridge: Cambridge University Press, 1979).

13. Ibn Khaldun, *The Muqaddimah (An Introduction to History),* trans. N.J. Dawood (Princeton: Princeton University Press, 1981).

14. Doug Rushkoff, *Children of Chaos* (New York: Harper Collins, 1996).

15. These include visioning workshops in Thailand, Malaysia, New Zealand, Australia, Germany, Austria, Taiwan, Pakistan, Yugoslavia and the United States. Workshop reports available from <s.inayatullah@qut.edu.au> See, for example, Samar Ihsan, Sohail Inayatullah, and Levi Obijiofor, "The Futures of Communication," *Futures* 27, 8 (October 1995): 897–904.

16. Sohail Inayatullah, "Possibilities for the Future," *Development* 43, 4 (December 2000): 17–21.

17. Johan Galtung and Sohail Inayatullah, eds., *Macrohistory and Macrohistorians* (Westport, Conn: Praeger, 1997). Also see, Pitirim Sorokin, *Social and Cultural Dynamics* (Boston: Porter Sargent, 1970).

18. Riane Eisler, *Sacred Pleasure* (San Francisco: HarperCollins, 1996).

19. For the methodology behind this, see "Layered Methodology," Sohail Inayatullah, ed., *Futures* special issue (2002).

20. In Pakistan, for example, children up to fifteen years old form nearly half of the country's population of 144 million, and every third child lives below the poverty line forcing them into begging and labor. Qurat-ul-Ain Sadozai, "Facts of Child Poverty," *The News* (July 3, 2000): 6.

21. Pakistan has 1.5 million heroin addicts of a population of 150 million. Karachi alone has 600,000 addicts. http://www.unfoundation.org/unwire/archives/ UNWIRE000421.cfm#17

22. Ashis Nandy and Giri Deshingkar, "The Futures of Cultures: An Asian Perspective," in *The Futures of Asian Cultures,* eds. Eleonora Masini and Yoges Atal (Bangkok: UNESCO, 1993).

23. Sohail Inayatullah and Jennifer Fitzgerald, eds., *Transcending Boundaries* (Maleny, Australia: Gurukul, 1999); Rupert Sheldrake, *A New Science of Life* (Los Angeles: Jeremy Tarcher, 1981).

24. Immanuel Wallerstein, *The Politics of the World Economy: The States, the Movements and the Civilizations* (Cambridge: Cambridge University Press, 1984).

Chapter 3

Future Visions, Social Realities, and Private Lives: Young People and Their Personal Well-Being

Richard Eckersley

The relationship between global futures and personal well-being is mediated through the quality of hope. Hope is linked to other qualities crucial to well-being, especially meaning and purpose in life. Frank writes: "A unique feature of human consciousness is its inclusion of the future. Expectations strongly affect all aspects of human functioning. . . . Hope inspires a feeling of well-being and is a spur to action. Hopelessness, the inability to imagine a tolerable future, is a powerful motive for suicide."[1] Nunn describes hope as "a pervasive and significant correlate of health and disorder."[2] In a study of the psychosocial impact of the earthquake that struck Newcastle, Australia, in 1989, he and his colleagues found that hopelessness was as important in explaining post-earthquake illness as exposure to disruption and threat.

In his famous account of life in concentration camps during World War II, *Man's Search for Meaning,* Frankl says the prisoner who had lost faith in the future was doomed.[3] As he lost his belief, he also lost his spiritual hold and went into a physical and mental decline. "It is a peculiarity of man that he can only live by looking to the future." Frankl quotes Nietzsche: "He who has a why to live for can bear with almost any how."

The future and the hope discussed here are personal. They do not concern expectations of the future of the world or humanity. The relationship between this broad vision of the future and personal well-being is a trickier issue. The bleakness of many young people's views on the future of the planet and the fate of humanity first aroused my interest in their well-being, including issues such as suicide, drug abuse, and crime. I came across the research on youth futures while writing a report for the Australian Commission for the Future on Australians' attitudes toward science, technology, and the future.[4] As the father of three young children, I was deeply impressed by the sense of hopelessness that pervades the imagery of many children, teenagers, and young adults. So for my next project, I explored whether these visions might help explain the rising rates of psychosocial problems in young people in much of the Western world, as well as some of the broader traits and attitudes of this generation.[5]

The connection between global threats and personal well-being has been speculated on, but, as far as I am aware, remains to be established. Researchers have warned that the pessimism of many young people could produce cynicism, mistrust, anger, apathy, and an approach to life based on instant gratification rather than long-term goals or lasting commitment.[6] Macy has suggested that people's response to concerns of global catastrophes "is not to cry out or ring alarms. . . . It is to go silent , go numb." She suggests this "numbing of the psyche" takes a heavy toll, including an impoverishment of emotional and sensory life. Energy expended in suppressing despair "is diverted from more creative uses, depleting resilience and imagination needed for fresh visions and strategies."[7] Newcomb found a significant association between anxiety about nuclear threats and less purpose in life, less life satisfaction, more powerlessness, more depression, and more drug use.[8] He concludes that the threat of nuclear war and accidents is significantly related to psychological distress and may disturb normal maturational development. Nevertheless, his study only established statistically significant correlations, not a causal relationship. Elkins and Sanson found in their research on young people's views of the future that nuclear war was seen to impinge on their own personal futures, as well as being feared for its catastrophic effects on the planet.[9] Other global threats, such as environmental destruction, did not have this personal impact. They suggest that the nuclear threat may be more likely to detrimentally affect the psychological development of youth than other concerns.

There is little doubt that many qualities that future fears might intuitively be expected to influence—hope, purpose and meaning in life, coherence, efficacy, or agency—are important to well-being. However, we may never be able to do more than suggest this because of the difficulty disentangling concerns about the fate of the earth from the many other factors that influence these qualities, and hence well-being. There are several dimensions to this entanglement. They relate to both the nature of people's expectations of the world's future and to the nature of human well-being. I argue that there is a dynamic and complex relationship between personal welfare, contemporary social realities, and future visions, with each domain interacting with and influencing the other two.

Some aspects of this relationship are self-evident. For example, current social conditions clearly have an impact on personal well-being and shape how we see the future. But other aspects are not so obvious. There are different ways of thinking about the future, future visions may be as much reflections of the present as expectations of the future; and they may affect personal states of mind less than be affected by them. Given these interactions, each domain provides a point of intervention to change the others.

This chapter emphasizes the need to take a broad, integrated, and holistic view of the future and its social and personal significance. I will examine each of the three domains in turn, beginning with future visions, to explore some of the inter-relationships between them.

FUTURE VISIONS

The complexities of young people's worldview and expectations of the future are evident from the research. Some surveys and commentaries suggest most are optimistic, others that they are pessimistic. Some indicate they are adapted to the postmodern world of rapid change and uncertainty, others that they are anxious and apprehensive. Some of these differences can be readily explained; others require more thorough analysis. I have suggested that we can distinguish between three different images of modern youth, each of which reflects different aspects, or depths, of their lives and relationship to the future.[10]

The *postmodern portrait* represents young people as the first global generation, attuned and adapted to the postmodern world: equipped for its abundant opportunities, exciting choices, and limitless freedoms—and its hazards and risks. They are confident, optimistic, well-informed and educated, technologically sophisticated, self-reliant (even self-contained), street-wise, enterprising and creative, fast on their feet, keeping their options open. This portrait tends to be promoted by a technology- and media-driven consumer culture that the image helps to sustain.

The *modern portrait* suggests most young people successfully negotiate the transitions of adolescence to become well-adjusted adults. Most cherish their families, enjoy life, and are confident they personally will get what they want out of life—a good job, travel, a partner, and eventually a family of their own. This portrait focuses on the more personal, and often more immediate, aspects of young people's lives.

The *problematic portrait* (which I have elsewhere called "transformational" because of the social transformation it suggests is required) reveals young people as understandably cynical, alienated, pessimistic, disillusioned, and disengaged. Many are confused and angry, uncertain of what the future holds and what society expects of them. While they may continue to work within "the system," they no longer believe in it or are willing to serve it. This portrait reflects broader social and deeper psychological perspectives.

Another way to look at young people's views of the future is to distinguish between expected, promised, and preferred futures. Here the social and psychological significance lies in part in the level of tension, or degree of coherence, between these three futures. Of particular importance is that young people do not see the *promised* future of unlimited economic growth and technological development as delivering a *preferred* future, or as addressing the problems characterizing the *expected* future.

These tensions were clearly apparent in a 1995 study by the Australian Science, Technology and Engineering Council (ASTEC).[11] The study sought to better understand what young Australians' expect and want of Australia in 2010, and, from these perspectives, to draw out, the key factors shaping the nation's future, including the role of science and technology. It had two components: a series of eight scenario-development workshops involving a total of 150 young people, most aged between fifteen and twenty-four and from a variety of backgrounds; and a national opinion poll of 800 Australians in this age group. The ASTEC study shows the future most young Australians want is neither the future they expect, nor the future they are promised under current national policy priorities. Most do not expect life in Australia to be better in 2010. They see a society driven by greed; they want one motivated by generosity. Their dreams for Australia are of a society that places less emphasis on the individual, material wealth, and competition, and more on community and family, the environment, and cooperation.

The poll reveals a contrast between expected and promised futures at a global level. One question asked which of two statements more closely reflected the respondent's view of the world in the twenty-first century. More than half (55%) chose: "More people, environmental destruction, new diseases and ethnic and regional conflict mean the world is heading for a bad time of crisis and trouble." Four in ten (41%) chose: "By continuing on its current path of economic and technological development, humanity will overcome the obstacles it faces and enter a new age of peace and prosperity." Pessimism increased with age.

The gulf between expected and preferred futures at a national level emerged in the responses to another question, which asked young people to decide which of two positive scenarios for Australia for 2010 came closer to the type of society they both expected and preferred. Almost two thirds (63%) said they expected "a fast-paced, internationally competitive society, with the emphasis on the individual, wealth generation, and enjoying the good life." However, eight in ten (81%) said they would prefer " a greener, more stable society, where the emphasis is on cooperation, community and family, more equal distribution of wealth, and greater economic self-sufficiency."

The contradictions between young people's views of the future reveal a tension between the real and ideal in the hearts of today's youth. Surveys suggest they appear to be adopting attitudes and values they believe are demanded by the world they live in and the future they expect—mistrust, cynicism, self-reliance, detachment, materialism, impatience, and so on— not those needed to achieve the world they want. We can draw an example from homeless youth. At one level, street kids can be described as savvy, self-reliant, resourceful, adapted to their world. Yet it is a world character- ized by high levels of drug abuse, crime and violence, sexual exploitation, mental illness, and suicide. What street kids want most of all are caring families and trusting relationships. No one would suggest theirs is an acceptable or happy situation.

This response to social realities and future prospects demonstrates how the three domains interact. Young people's growing political disengagement can be seen as an adaptive response to harsher circumstances in which people feel less control over the forces shaping society, they so are determined to focus more on their own welfare. Yet this same response raises the prospects of the expectations becoming self-fulfilling as it, in turn, influences social outcomes and directions.

SOCIAL REALITIES

Visions of the future do not have an external "reality" independent of contemporary social conditions and cultural images. While many people's concerns about future war and conflict, social upheaval, and environmental degradation are plausible future realities, they also obviously reflect perceptions of what is happening today.

The ASTEC study suggests most young people see the future mainly a continuation or worsening of today's global and national problems and difficulties, although they also expect some improvements, even in problem areas.[12] Major concerns included pollution and environmental destruction, including the impact of growing populations; the gulf between rich and poor; high unemployment, including the effect of automation and immigration; conflict, crime, and alienation; family problems and breakdown; discrimination and prejudice; and economic difficulties. In areas such as health and education, opinions were more equally divided between improvement and deterioration. In the preferred future, the problems have been overcome. There are a clean environment, global peace, social harmony and equity, jobs for all, happy families (although not necessarily traditional families), and better education and health.

Thus, apart from reflecting legitimate concerns about the future, young people's fears for the future may also express their anxieties about the present. These anxieties may be ill-defined—especially when, according to conventional measures of progress, most of us are better off than ever before—but are nonetheless personal and deeply felt. By projecting these concerns into the future, they can be described in fictional, and more concrete, terms.

A vague uneasiness about the direction the world is going in and people's impotence to change that course becomes, for many, visions of a world in which a growing gap between rich and poor has produced deeply divided and hostile communities; the arms race has resulted in nuclear warfare (still a concern despite the end of the Cold War); ever-expanding industrialization and populations have plundered the environment; or the development of technologies with powers beyond our comprehension have ended in human obsolescence. This translation is most obvious in the future visions of children, who often relate very personally to global threats and problems and depict them in apocalyptic terms.

Popular culture helps this process. But while science fiction fantasies such as *Blade Runner* and *Terminator* influence the images young people use to describe the future, their fears are not distant and detached. They are related to their perceptions of life today, and they are particularly related to perceptions about the values that dominate our way of life today. My own work in Australia shows that most people do not believe quality of life is improving. In a recent survey we found only 24 percent of Australians think life is getting better, while 36 percent think it is getting worse.[13] Studies in Australia and the United States indicate a widespread concern that greed, selfishness, materialism, and excess characterize modern (Western) life, with family and community life paying the price.[14]

In his acclaimed BBC television series, *Civilization,* historian Kenneth Clark observes that civilization, however complex and solid it seems, is really quite fragile.[15] In the concluding episode, after reviewing thousands of years of the rise and fall of civilizations, he warns that "it's lack of confidence, more than anything else, that kills a civilization. We can destroy ourselves by cynicism and disillusion just as effectively as by bombs." The pessimism of young people's expected futures is one measure of this erosion of confidence, this loss of hope. Conversely, their preferred futures can provide a framework for action to address contemporary social concerns, and therefore prevent the expectations from becoming a reality.

PERSONAL WELL-BEING

The coincidence of a sense of futurelessness among young people with the existence of a constellation of traits and attitudes that researchers have seen as its likely consequences suggests a compelling causal link. Young people are at a stage of development and socialization—deciding who they are, what they believe, and where they belong—that makes them vulnerable to the consequences of a lack of a clear and appealing social vision. Rates of psychological and social problems among young people have risen in almost all "developed nations" over the past fifty years.[16] Highly publicized problems, such as youth suicide and drug-overdose deaths, are only the tip of an iceberg of suffering among the young, with recent studies showing that a fifth to a third of young people today experience significant psychological distress or disturbance. The evidence suggests that while tragedies such as suicide arise from intensely personal circumstances, they also represent one end of a spectrum of responses by many young people to modern life, one end of a gradient of distress. This gradient extends through degrees of suicidal attempt and ideation, depression, drug abuse, and delinquency to a pervasive sense of alienation, disillusionment, and demoralization (traits more likely to be expressed passively than through anger or antisocial behavior).

Many recent surveys of youth attitudes have reinforced the view that many young people are not comfortable with the broader changes taking place in society, even if most are, most of the time, happy and optimistic about their own personal circumstances. Nor are they inspired by the visions of the future that society holds up to them. As already noted, the surveys suggest many are mistrustful, cynical, and fatalistic; wary of commitment; outwardly confident but inwardly insecure; and alienated and disengaged from society. They believe that life should be fast and fun, options should be kept open, governments are incapable of solving our problems, they themselves are powerless to change things they are on their own.

THE GLOBAL PESSIMISM–WELL-BEING NEXUS: SOME QUALIFIERS

There are, however, three important qualifications to the belief that global pessimism is eroding young people's well-being. First, the direction of any causal relationship between future pessimism and diminished well-being can also run in reverse. For example, depression affects people's view of the world, and their place in it: the depressed typically look at themselves, the world and the future with bleakness.[17] The association uncovered by Newcomb, for example, might mean that people's psychological state influenced the degree of nuclear anxiety. This doesn't make their perceptions somehow wrong. However, this link between people's psychological state and their worldview does draw attention to the subjective influences on perceptions of objective realities. If depression levels are increasing, as the evidence suggests, then future visions would become more pessimistic.

The second important qualification concerns the nature of well-being. Research shows subjective well-being is most influenced by the more personal domains of life, such as family, work, school, friends, and leisure.[18] Furthermore, we have the ability to adapt to our circumstances and maintain a high degree of life satisfaction. The great majority of people say they are happy, satisfied with their lives, and optimistic about their futures.[19] This finding is remarkably consistent across countries and over time. My own analysis of future views and well-being found that a psychological safety mechanism seemed to operate: "There is plenty of evidence that people tend to make sharp distinction between their personal future and the future of society or the world: a happy belief that the misfortunes that they believe are increasingly likely to befall others, won't affect them."[20] This psychological barrier is not, however, totally impermeable. It does not mean that what happens in the social, economic, and political spheres is unimportant at a personal level, but that the relationship between the objective and subjective worlds is not linear—that is, a change in the former does not produce a corresponding and equal change in the latter. While people show remarkable resilience in adversity, and while the personal affects well-being more than the global, perceptions of the future of the world and humanity may, nevertheless, have a significant impact on well-being. Research has shown that the abilities to adapt, set goals and progress towards them have goals that do not conflict, and view the world as essentially benevolent and controllable are all associated with well-being.[21] Future visions would certainly affect (and reflect) the latter and may well bear on the other qualities as well. In an unpublished 1988 Australian Commission for the Future study, 53 percent of those surveyed who said they were pessimistic or concerned about the future of humanity were asked if their concerns "in general diminish or reduce your enjoyment of life." Two percent said "very much," and 13 percent "quite a lot," while 48 percent said "not much," and 35 percent "not at all" (meaning 63 percent of this group were personally affected to some degree). Those aged fourteen to nineteen were less likely to say "not at all"—25 percent, compared to 43 percent for those over sixty and 33 to 37 percent for other age groups.

The third important aspect of the personal impact of global pessimism is that, to the extent that it cause psychosocial distress and disturbance, it is acting together, and perhaps synergistically, with other features of modern societies. These include, but go beyond, structural social realities. Pessimism is only one of several cultural traits of modern Western societies that are inimical to well-being. Others include:

- **Consumerism:** This reverses traditional societal values that emphasize social obligations and self-restraint, making traditional vices such as greed, envy, and self-centeredness into virtues, and traditional virtues such as moderation and prudence into vices.
- **Economism:** The more that economics, which is amoral, dictates our choices, individually and as a society (which is what I mean by economism), the more marginalized moral considerations become.
- **Postmodernism:** This is characterized by relativism, pluralism, ambivalence, ambiguity, transience, fragmentation, and contingency—an "anything goes" morality in which values cease to require any external validation or to have any authority or reference beyond the individual and the moment.
- **Individualism:** This is expressed as self-centeredness, the gratification of personal wants, a pre-occupation with entitlements, an abrogation of responsibilities, and a withering of collective effort.

These five cultural traits (including pessimism) each have, or can have, positive dimensions. The inalienable right to "life, liberty, and the pursuit of happiness" is at the core of modern democracy. The loosening of social constraints and obligations can enhance personal freedom and creativity and bring a greater social vitality, diversity, and tolerance. Consumerism has made our lives more comfortable. Pessimism, if it does not destroy hope, can be an incentive for change. But the question is, do the trends increase or decrease well-being and humanity in the broadest, fullest sense?

Taken together, however, and taken too far, they have high costs. The effects are subtle and include a tendency for each of us to make ourselves the center of our moral universe, to assess everything—from personal relationships to taxes—in terms of "what's in it for me." The price of this self-centeredness is a weakening of the personal, social and spiritual attachments conducive to well-being.

Psychological well-being is closely related to meaning in life, with positive life meaning related to strong religious beliefs, self-transcendent values, membership in groups, dedication to a cause, and clear life goals.[22] In their book *Understanding Happiness,* Headey and Wearing note that "a sense of meaning and purpose is the single attitude most strongly associated with life satisfaction."[23] Seligman argues that one necessary condition for meaning is the attachment to something larger than the self. The larger that entity, the more meaning people can derive "the self, to put it another way, is a very poor site for meaning."[24]

FUTURE VISIONS NURTURING MEANING

I have argued that our visions of humanity's future involve complex and subtle relationships between expected future conditions, contemporary social realities, and personal states of mind. Future visions can both reflect and reinforce social conditions and personal attributes. They can act on personal well-being directly and indirectly through their social impacts.

What most delighted and encouraged those involved in the ASTEC youth futures study was the energy and enthusiasm of most young people who participated and the idealism and altruism that shone through when they discussed their preferred futures. Many of the students enjoyed the experience; they clearly would like more of their schooling to be like this. They also valued the opportunity to think about the future in more than just personal terms. Thinking about preferred futures had made them more aware of positive changes that could be made and their personal responsibility to contribute to these changes.

So while the future is an outcome of past and present choices and events, it is also an entry point for nurturing meaning and purpose and other qualities essential to healthy societies and healthy people. Visions of a better world can guide social action and provide personal inspiration and hope. They can help to ensure that the relationships between the three domains constitute a virtuous circle, not a vicious one.

NOTES

1.   Jerome Frank, "The Role of Hope in Psychotherapy," *International Journal of Psychiatry* 5, 5 (1968): 383–395.

2.   Kenneth Nunn, "Personal Hopefulness: A Conceptual Review of the Relevance of the Perceived Future to Psychiatry," *British Journal of Medical Psychology* 69 (1996): 227–245.

3.   Viktor Frankl, *Man's Search for Meaning* (New York: Washington Square Press, Pocket Books, 1985) (first published 1946; this translation first published by Beacon Press, 1959): 94–97.

4.   Richard Eckersley, *Australian Attitudes to Science and Technology and the Future,* (Melbourne: Australian Commission for the Future, August 1987).

5.   Richard Eckersley, *Casualties of Change: The Predicament of Youth in Australia* (Melbourne: Australian Commission for the Future, July 1988).

6.   Michael Newcomb, "Nuclear Attitudes and Reactions: Associations with Depression, Drug Use, and Quality of Life," *Journal of Personality and Social Psychology* 50, 5 (1986): 906–920; Kathryn Elkins and Ann Sanson, "Children's Views of the Future: Concerns Expressed in Letters and Questionnaires in the Post Cold War Period," in *Research on Children and Peace: International Perspectives,* eds. S. Hagglund, I. Hakvoort, and L. Oppenheimer (Department of Education and Educational Research, Goteborg University, 1996).

7.   Joanna Macy, *Despair and Personal Power in the Nuclear Age* (Philadelphia: New Society Publishers, 1983).

8.   Michael Newcomb, "Nuclear Attitudes and Reactions . . . ."

9.   Kathryn Elkins and Ann Sanson, "Children's Views of the Future . . . ."

10.   Richard Eckersley, "Portraits of Youth: Understanding Young People's Relationship with the Future," *Futures* 29, 3 (1997): 243–249.

11.   Richard Eckersley, "Dreams and Expectations: Young People's Expected and Preferred Futures and their Significance for Education," *Futures* 31 (1999): 73–90.

12.   Ibid.

13.   Richard Eckersley, *Quality of Life in Australia: An Analysis of Public Perceptions,* discussion paper no. 23 (Canberra: Australia Institute, September 1999); Richard Eckersley, "The State and Fate of Nations: Implications of Subjective Measures of Personal and Social Quality of Life," *Social Indicators Research* (in press).

14.   Richard Eckersley, "The State and Fate of Nations . . . ."

15.   Kenneth Clark, *Civilization,* four-volume video series (BBC Enterprises Ltd., 1993).

16.   Richard Eckersley, "Psychosocial Disorders in Young People: On the Agenda but Not on the Mend," *The Medical Journal of Australia* 166 (1997): 423–424. Richard Eckersley, "Redefining Progress: Shaping the Future to Human Needs," *Family Matters,* 51 (1998): 6–12.

17. Heinz Katschnig and Matthias C. Angermeyer, "Quality of Life in Depression," in *Quality of Life in Mental Disorders,* eds. H. Katschnig, H. Freeman, and N. Sartorius (Chichester: John Wiley & Sons, 1997).

18. Alex Wearing and Bruce Headey, "Who Enjoys Life and Why: Measuring Subjective Well-Being," in *Measuring Progress: Is Life Getting Better?*, ed., R. Eckersley (Collingwood, Victoria: CSIRO Publishing, 1998); Richard Eckersley, *Casualties of Change* . . . .

19. David Myers and Ed Diener, "The Pursuit of Happiness," *Scientific American* 274, 5 (1996): 54–56; Richard Eckersley, *Quality of Life in Australia* . . .; Richard Eckersley, "The State and Fate of Nations . . . ."

20. Richard Eckersley, Casualties of Change . . . .

21. David Myers and Ed Diener, "Who Is Happy?," *Psychological Science* 6, 1 (1995): 10–19.

22. Sheryl Zika and Kerry Chamberlain, "On the Relation Between Meaning in Life and Psychological Well-Being," *British Journal of Psychology* 83 (1992): 133–145.

23. Bruce Headey and Alex Wearing, *Understanding Happiness: A Theory of Subjective Well-Being* (Melbourne: Longman Cheshire, 1992): 191.

24. Martin Seligman, "Why Is There so Much Depression Today? The Waxing of the Individual and the Waning of the Commons," in *Contemporary Psychological Approaches to Depression—Theory, Research and Treatment*, ed. R. E. Ingram (New York: Plenum Press, 1990).

Chapter 4

Partnership Education for the Twenty-First Century

Riane Eisler

Young people often feel powerless to change the course of their lives, much less the course of the world around them. Many become immersed in the "me-firstism" and "overmaterialism" that permeate mass culture, futilely seeking meaning and belonging in the latest fad or commercial offering. Some bury their pain and anger in drugs, gangs, and other destructive activities, seemingly oblivious of the effect their actions have on themselves and others. Some become violent under the thrall of hate-mongering or religious fanaticism, or simply because video games, television, ads, and movies make violence seem normal and fun.

Many factors contribute to this. But one factor can play a major role in providing young people with the understandings and skills to both live good lives and create a more sustainable, less violent, more equitable future: education.

For over two centuries, educational reformers such as Johann Pestalozzi, Maria Montessori, John Dewey, and Paolo Freire have called for an education that prepares young people for democracy rather than authoritarianism, and fosters ethical and caring relations.[1] Building on the work of these and other germinal educational thinkers and on my research and teaching experiences over three decades, I have proposed an expanded approach to educational reform. I call this approach "partnership education." It is designed not only to help young people better navigate through our difficult times but also to help them create a future oriented more to what, in my study of 30,000 years of cultural evolution, I have identified as a partnership rather than dominator model.

Although we may not use these terms, we are all familiar with these two models. We know the pain, fear, and tension of relations based on domination and submission, on coercion and accommodation, of jockeying for control, of trying to manipulate and cajole when we are unable to express our real feelings and needs, of the miserable, awkward tug of war for that illusory moment of power rather than powerlessness, of our unfulfilled yearning for caring and mutuality, of all the misery, suffering, and lost lives and potentials that come from these kinds of relations. Most of us also have, at least intermittently, experienced another way of being, one where we feel safe and seen for who we truly are, where our essential humanity and that of others shines through, perhaps only for a little while, lifting our hearts and spirits, enfolding us in a sense that the world can after all be right, that we are valued and valuable.

But the partnership and dominator models describe not only individual relationships. They describe systems of belief and social structures that either nurture and support—or inhibit and undermine—equitable, democratic, nonviolent, and caring relations. Once we understand the partnership and dominator cultural, social, and personal configurations, we can more effectively develop the educational methods, materials, and institutions that foster a less violent, more equitable, democratic, and sustainable future. We can also more effectively sort out what in existing educational approaches we want to retain and strengthen or leave behind.

HUMAN POSSIBILITIES

Young people are given a false picture of what it means to be human. We tell them to be good and kind, nonviolent and giving. But on all sides they see and hear stories that portray us as bad, cruel, violent, and selfish. In the mass media, the focus of both action entertainment and news is on hurting and killing. Situation comedies make insensitivity, rudeness, and cruelty seem funny. Cartoons present violence as exciting, funny, and without real consequences.

To our youth, these pictures hold up a distorted mirror of themselves. And rather than correcting this false image of what it means to be human, some aspects of our education reinforce it. History curricula still emphasize battles and wars. Western classics such as Homer's *Iliad* and Shakespeare's kings trilogy romanticize "heroic violence." Scientific stories tell children that we are the puppets of "selfish genes" ruthlessly competing on the evolutionary stage.

If we are inherently violent, bad, and selfish, we have to be strictly controlled. This is why stories such as those mentioned, that claim this is "human nature" are central to an education for a dominator or control system of relations. They are, however, inappropriate if young people are to learn to live in a democratic, peaceful, equitable, and Earth-honoring way: the partnership way urgently needed if today's and tomorrow's children are to have a better future—perhaps even a future at all.

Youth futures are impoverished when their vision of the future comes out of a dominator worldview. This worldview is our heritage from earlier societies structured around rankings of "superiors" over "inferiors." In these societies, violence and abuse were required to maintain rigid rankings of domination—whether man over woman, man over man, nation over nation, race over race, or religion over religion.

Over the last several centuries, we have seen many organized challenges to traditions of domination. These challenges are part of the movement toward a more equitable and caring partnership social structure worldwide. But at the same time, much in our education still reinforces what I call dominator socialization: a way of viewing the world and living in it that constricts young people's perceptions of what is possible and even moral, keeping many of them locked into a perennial rebellion against what is, without a real sense of what can be.

Partnership Education

Partnership education counters this limited picture of human possibilities. It integrates three core, interconnected components. These are partnership *process,* partnership *structure,* and partnership *content.*

Partnership process is about how we learn and teach. It applies the guiding template of the partnership model to educational methods and techniques. Are young people treated with caring and respect? Do teachers act as primarily lesson-dispensers and controllers, or more as mentors and facilitators? Are young people learning to work together or must they continually compete with each other? Are they offered the opportunity for self-directed learning? In short, is education merely a matter of teachers inserting "information" into young people's minds, or are students and teachers partners in a meaningful adventure of exploration and learning?

Partnership structure is about where learning and teaching take place: the kind of learning environment we construct if we follow the partnership model. Is the structure of a school, classroom, and/or home school one of top-down authoritarian rankings, or is it a more democratic one? Do students, teachers, and other staff participate in school decision-making and rule-setting? Diagrammed on an organizational chart, would decisions flow only from the top down and accountability only from the bottom up, or would there be interactive feedback loops? In short, is the learning environment organized in hierarchies of domination ultimately backed up by fear, or is it a combination of horizontal linkages and hierarchies of actualization where power is not used to disempower others but rather to empower them?

Partnership content is what we learn and teach. It is the educational curriculum. Does the curriculum effectively teach students not only basic academic and vocational skills, but also the life skills they need to be competent and caring citizens, workers, parents, and community members? Are we telling young people to be responsible, kind, and nonviolent at the same time that the curriculum content still celebrates male violence and conveys environmentally unsustainable and socially irresponsible messages? Does it present science in holistic, relevant ways? Does what is taught as important knowledge and truth include—not just as an add-on, but as integral to what is learned—both the female and male halves of humanity as well as children of various races and ethnicities? Does it teach young people the difference between the partnership and dominator models as two basic human possibilities and the feasibility of creating a partnership way of life? Or, both overtly and covertly, is such a partnership presented as unrealistic in "the real world?" In short, what kind of view of ourselves, our world, and our roles and responsibilities are young people taking away from their schooling?

Partnership Education and the Transformation of Society

We need an education that counters dominator socialization—and its subconscious valuing of the kinds of undemocratic, abusive, and even violent relations that were considered normal and even moral in earlier, more authoritarian, times.

Partnership education includes education for partnership rather than dominator childrearing. Children dependent on abusive adults tend to replicate these adults' behaviors with their children, having been taught to associate love with coercion and abuse. And often they learn to use psychological defense mechanisms of denial and to deflect repressed pain and anger onto those perceived as weak by scape-goating, bullying, and, on a larger scale, conducting pogroms and ethnic cleansings.

Through partnership process, school teachers can help students experience partnership relations as a viable alternative. And partnership structure provides the learning environment that young people need to develop their unique capacities.[2] But partnership process and structure are not enough without partnership content: narratives that help young people better understand human possibilities.

For example, narratives still taught in many schools and universities tell us that Darwin's scientific theories show that "natural selection," "random variation," and later ideas such as "kinship selection" and "parental investment," are the only principles in evolution. As David Loye shows in *Darwin's Lost Theory of Love,* Darwin did not actually share this view; he emphasized that, particularly as we move to human evolution, other dynamics, including the evolution of what he called the "moral sense," come into play. Or, as Frans deWaal writes in *Good Natured: The Origins of Right and Wrong in Humans and Other Animals,* the desire for a *modus vivendi* fair to everyone may be regarded as an evolutionary outgrowth of the need to get along and cooperate.

Partnership education offers scientific narratives that focus not only on competition but also, following the new evolutionary scholarship, on cooperation. For example, young people learn how, by the grace of evolution, biochemicals called neuropeptides reward our species with sensations of pleasure, not only when we are cared for, but also when we care for others.

Awareness of the interconnected web of life that is our environment, which has largely been ignored in the traditional curriculum, leads to valuing of activities and policies that promote environmental sustainability: the new partnership ethic for human and ecological relations needed in our time.

Because the social construction of the roles and relations of the female and male halves of humanity is central to either a partnership or dominator social configuration, unlike the traditional male-centered curricula, partnership education is gender-balanced. It integrates the history, needs, problems, and aspirations of both halves of humanity into what is taught as important knowledge and truth. Because in the partnership model, difference is not automatically equated with inferiority or superiority; partnership education is multicultural. It offers a pluralistic perspective that includes peoples of all races and a variety of backgrounds, as well as the real life drama of the animals and plants of the Earth we share. Since partnership education offers a systemic approach, environmental education is not an add-on but an integral part of the curriculum.

Partnership education offers empirical evidence that our human strivings for love, beauty, and justice are just as rooted in evolution as is our capacity for violence and aggression. It does not leave young people with the sense that life is devoid of meaning or that humans are inherently violent and selfish. In that case, why bother trying to change anything?

Moreover, as the young people we have worked with through the Center for Partnership Studies' Partnership Education Program will attest, partnership education is much more interesting and exciting than the old curriculum. It offers many new perspectives, from partnership games, multicultural math, and a wealth of information about women worldwide to a new perspective on our prehistory and history; from the opportunity to talk about issues that really engage young people to ideas, resources, and social actions that can accelerate the shift from domination to partnership worldwide.

A NEW VIEW OF OUR PAST

From the perspective expressed in this chapter, much of young people's hopelessness stems from the belief that the progressive modern movements have failed, and that the only possibility is to either dominate or be domi-nated. Many factors contribute to this distorted and limiting view of possible futures. But a major reason is that our education does not show young people that, despite enormous resistance and periodic regressions, the movements toward a more just and peaceful world have in fact made great gains—and that these gains have been due to the persistence of small, unpopular, and often persecuted minorities.

Partnership education offers young people a clearer understanding of history—one that is essential if they are to more effectively help create a more equitable, peaceful, and sustainable future that cannot be constructed within the context of social arrangements based on domination and con-trol. This perspective argues that the struggle for our future is not between capitalism versus communism, right versus left, or religion versus secu-larism, but between a mounting movement toward partnership relations in all spheres of life and strong dominator systems of resistance and periodic regressions.

By using the analytical lens of the partnership/dominator continuum, young people can see that along with the massive technological upheavals of the last 300 years has come a growing questioning of entrenched pat-terns of domination. The eighteenth-century rights of man movement chal-lenged the supposedly divinely ordained right of kings to rule over their "subjects," ushering in a shift from authoritarian monarchies to more dem-ocratic republics. The eighteenth- and nineteenth-century feminist move-ment challenged men's supposedly divinely ordained right to rule over women and children in the "castles" of their homes. Antislavery, culmi-nating during both the nineteenth and twentieth-centuries in worldwide movements to shift from the colonization and exploitation of indigenous peoples to their independence from foreign rule, also challenged entrenched patterns of domination. The twentieth-century civil rights and the women's liberation and women's rights movements were part of this continuing challenge, as were the nineteenth-century pacifist movement and the twentieth-century peace movement, which was the first fully organized challenge to the violence of war as a means of resolving inter-national conflicts. The twentieth-century family planning movement has been a key to women's emancipation as well as to the alleviation of poverty and greater opportunities for children worldwide. And the twen-tieth-century environmental movement has frontally challenged the once-hallowed "conquest of nature" that many young people today rightly recognize as a threat to their survival.

But history is not a linear forward movement. Precisely because of the strong thrust toward partnership, there has been massive dominator sys-tems resistance.

Over the last 300 years, we also have seen a resurgence of authoritari-anism, racism, and religious persecutions. The United States has seen the repeal of laws providing economic safety nets, renewed opposition to reproductive rights for women, and periodic violence against those seeking greater rights. In Africa and Asia, even after Western colonial regimes were overthrown, authoritarian dictatorships of local elites over their own people have risen, resulting in renewed repression and exploitation. We have seen a recentralization of economic power worldwide under the guise of economic globalization.[3] Under pressure from major economic players, governments have cut social services and shredded economic safety nets—an "economic restructuring" that harms women and children worldwide particularly. The backlash against women's rights has been increasingly violent, as in the government-supported violence against women in fundamentalist regimes such as those in Afghanistan and Iran. We have also seen ever-more advanced technologies used to exploit, dominate, and kill—as well as to further "man's conquest of nature," wreaking ever-more environmental damage.

These regressions raise the question of what lies behind them—and what we can do to prevent them. Once again, there are many factors, as there always are in complex systems. But a major factor that becomes apparent using the analytical lens of the partnership and dominator social configurations is the need to fully integrate challenges to domination and violence in the so-called public spheres of politics and economics and in the so-called private spheres of parent–child and man–woman relations.

In Europe, for example, a rallying cry of the Nazis was the return of women to their "traditional" place. Stalin's Soviet Union abandoned earlier, feeble efforts to equalize relations between women and men in the family. When the Ayatollah Khomeini came to power in Iran, one of his first acts was to repeal family laws granting women a modicum of rights. And the brutally authoritarian and violent Taliban have made the total domination of women a centerpiece of their violence-based social policy.

This emphasis on gender relations based on domination and submission was not coincidental. Dominator systems will continue to rebuild themselves unless we change the base on which they rest: domination and violence in the foundational human relations between parents and children and men and women.

The reason, simply put, is that how we structure relations between parents and children and women and men is foundational to how we perceive what is normal in human relations. It is in these intimate relations that we first learn and continually practice either partnership or domination, either respect for human rights or acceptance of human rights violations as "just the way things are."

Young people need to understand the social dynamics, still generally ignored. They need to understand the significance of today's increased violence against women and children and of a mass media that bombards us with stories and images presenting the infliction of pain as exciting and sexy. If they are to build a world where economic and political systems are more just and caring, they need an awareness that these images normalize, and even romanticize, intimate relations of domination and submission as the foundation for a system based on rankings of "superiors" over "inferiors." At the same time, they need to understand the significance of the fact that child abuse, rape, and wife-beating are increasingly prosecuted in some world regions, that a global women's rights movement is frontally challenging the domination of half of humanity by the other half, and that the United Nations has finally adopted conventions to protect children's and women's human rights. With an understanding of the connections between partnership or domination in the so-called private and public spheres, young people will be better equipped to create the futures they want and deserve.

A NEW VIEW OF POTENTIAL FUTURES

I have seen how inspired young people become once they understand that partnership relations—be they intimate or international—are all of one cloth. I have seen how excited they become when they are shown evidence of ancient societies orienting to the partnership model in all world regions.[4] And I have seen how they move from apathy to action once they fully understand that there is a viable alternative to the inequitable, undemocratic, violent, and uncaring relations that have for so long distorted the human spirit and are today decimating our natural habitat.

Through partnership education—through partnership process, structure, and content—we can help young people understand and experience the possibility of partnership relations, structures, and worldviews. We can all use partnership education in our homes, schools, and communities to highlight the enormous human potential to learn, to grow, to create, and to relate to one another in mutually supporting and caring ways. I believe young people really care about their future, and that if their education offers the vision and the tools to help them more effectively participate in its creation, they will readily do so.

NOTES

1.   Johann Pestalozzi, *Leonard and Gertrude* (New York: Gordon Press Publishers, 1976; originally published in 1781); John Dewey, *Democracy and Education* (New York: The Free Press, 1966; original 1916); Paolo Freire, *Pedagogy of the Oppressed* (New York: Seabury Press, 1973); Maria Montessori, *The Montessori Method* (New York: Schocken Books, 1964; original 1912). These works foreshadow much that is still today considered progressive education.

2.   For a description of partnership process, structure, and content as the three interconnected elements of partnership education, see Riane Eisler, *Tomorrow's*

Children: A Blueprint for Partnership Education in the 21st Century (Boulder: Colo.: Westview Press, 2000).

3.   Some readings that contain materials that could be excerpted by teachers are Jerry Mander and Edwin Goldsmith, eds., *The Case Against the Global Economy and for a Turn Toward the Local* (San Francisco: Sierra Club Books, 1996); Hazel Henderson, *Paradigms in Progress: Life Beyond Economics* (Indianapolis: Knowledge Systems, Inc., 1991); David Korten, *When Corporations Rule the World* (San Francisco: Barrett-Koehler, 1995); Riane Eisler, David Loye, and Kari Norgaard, *Women, Men, and the Global Quality of Life* (Pacific Grove, Calif.: Center for Partnership Studies, 1995). For a short piece that has some good statistics and could serve as a handout, see also David Korten, "A Market-Based Approach to Corporate Responsibility," *Perspectives on Business and Global Change* 11, 2 (June 1997): 45–55. See also the Center for Partnership Studies' Web site, http://www. partnershipway.org to download "Changing the Rules of the Game: Work, Values, and Our Future," by Riane Eisler, 1997.

4.   Riane Eisler, *The Chalice and The Blade* (San Francisco: Harper and Row, 1988).

Chapter 5

Cultural Mapping and Our Children's Futures: Decolonizing Ways of Learning and Research

Francis Hutchinson

Those to whom the King had entrusted me, observing how ill I was clad, ordered a tailor to come next morning, and take my measure for a suit of clothes. This operator did his office after a different manner from those of his trade in Europe. He first took my altitude by a quadrant, and then with a rule and compasses described the dimensions and outlines of my whole body, all which he entered upon paper, and in six days brought my clothes very ill made, and quite out of shape, by happening to mistake a figure in the calculation. But my comfort was, that I observed such accidents very frequent, and little regarded.[1]

CHILDHOOD AND THE WESTERN CARTOGRAPHIC GAZE

Jonathan Swift in *Gulliver's Travels* brings a humorous reminder that our mental maps are often taken for granted. Swift takes a satirical look at the eighteenth-century world of European empire builders, explorers, and surveyors. He presents a dissenting voice to the Western cartographic gaze. Serious doubts are expressed about the universal applicability of Western methods for researching the world and mapping "the other."

In our time, how important are dissenting maps and multicultural journeys? When it comes to considering young people's views and images of the future, is this especially important? What assumptions do we bring with us in our cultural cartographies of "childhood" and "youth"? Do we value what young people are saying in inclusive, participatory and multicultural ways? Or do we tend to fragment, stereotype, and foreclose? Do we need to begin to unpack our cultural baggage and critically reflect on what we are doing? (See Table 5.1.)

TABLE 5.1 *Cartographies of Childhood: Images of Children through Western Eyes*

Some Major Cultural Sstereotypes	Related Educational and Psychologica Ideas	Period of Widest Acceptance
Children as naturally sub-ordinated "territories" and "male property"	Patriarchal	Sanctioned under ancient Roman law but with a major persistence into modern era
Children as a site of a lost Eden/children as "little innocents" corrupted in a sinful world	Feudal/patriarchal/Augustinian legacy	Medieval Europe/pre-sixteenth-century Christendom
Children as "little savages" needing to be "civilized" and "disciplined" in the journey to adulthood	"Ages of Man"/Darwinian competitive struggle/Galton and intelligence testing/Piagetian develop-mental stage theory	Sixteenth century to mid-twentieth century/major period of Western imperial expansion
Children as a site of "nat-ural living"	Rousseauian "noble savage"/A.S. Neill and Summer Hill/Rudolf Steiner/"new age" educa-tional ideas, late twentieth century	Eighteenth and nineteenth centuries/European romanticism/Industrial Revolution
Children as "resources," "assets," and "commodi-ties" for national progress and economic growth/children as future workers, soldiers, nurses, patriots, businessmen, etc.	Fordism/Behaviorist psy-chology/conditioned-child learning theory/machine images of schooling/utili-tarian assumptions	Nineteenth and twentieth centuries/Industrial Revolution/two world wars
Children and contested futures, e.g., dilemmas such as "passive, future shock" victims vs. "active, socially literate" global cit-izens; cyborg babies, designer babies vs. less mechanistic, technocratic, consumerist, and Western-centric futures	Increasing commodifica-tion as signifier of post-modern times/education as multi-media "infotain-ment." Contradictions which enhance the rights of the child/transformative learning/peace education/environmental education/futures education	Late twentieth century/early twenty-first century globalization/cybercul-ture/"grassroots" globalism

This chapter is an invitation to widely converse on the futures of future generations. Are there opportunities for choice and engagement, whether we are parents, teachers, youth workers, social researchers, or concerned citizens?

How actively do we listen to what our children are saying about the world and the needs of future generations? In resisting colonization of the future, are there alternative maps and alternative pathways?

Questioning Colonizing Maps: Researching in Whose Interests?

Conventional Western pathways for researching young people have been guided by colonizing methodological and epistemological maps.[2] Over many years, the younger generation's views have been sorely neglected. Rather than placing a high value on effective enfranchisement and solidarity across the generations, the research gaze has tended to focus narrowly on matters such as "youth problems" and "fitting young people for the future."

The bulk of research has tended to treat young people's hopes, dreams, fears, and aspirations as peripheral to dominant social and economic agendas and to major policy considerations.[3] With such research, the timeframe is usually short-termist, such as opinion polls that predict the likely political behavior of young people in the lead-up to an election. Advertising agencies widely employ focus groups, but they are interested in the more effective mapping and exploitation of "the elusive youth market."

Even the quality of academic research has been distinctly uneven. There has been a definite lack of critical awareness of the embeddedness of the research process in selective knowledge traditions and power relations. Critical matters of paternalism, ageism, gender-bias, social class discrimination, "racialized" hierarchies and Western-centrism are often left invisible. At the same time, there has been a tendency to decontextualize and psychologize young people's dilemma about their social worlds and the future, including worrying trends in adolescent male homicide rates and youth suicide rates in late industrial societies such as the United States and Australia.[4]

Such matters highlight the difficult dilemmas and challenges inherent in the choices we make and the pathways we take. If we are to value young people's voices on the future with wisdom, compassion, and foresight, what are some of the possible ways? Are there potentially empowering multicultural maps for our various journeys into the early decades of the twenty-first century? This chapter does not delineate a straightforward route, but it suggests several ways of resisting colonization of the future.

A New Global Ethic?

"Treat the earth well. It was not given to you by your parents. It was lent to you by your children." This Kenyan wisdom not only offers valuable insights into the need to care for our natural environment, but affirms the need for building compassionate solidarity with future generations. It implies a very different way of mapping our world and looking at our responsibilities to future generations than has been commonplace. It is a theme taken up over recent decades by movements of "grassroots globalism," such as the peace, environmental, and feminist movements, and a range of nongovernmental organizations (NGOs). Together with United Nations bodies such as UNICEF, these social change movements and NGOs have been active not only in affirming the rights of children but in seeking to extend the notion of rights and responsibilities to unborn generations. Maps of practical hope are affirmed rather than denied by such movements.

The Idea of Intergenerational Equity

Gandhi remarked that there is enough for everyone's needs but not everyone's greed. If this principle is to be extended to unborn generations, what does this imply? Is a paradigm shift toward less violent and more inclusive ways of intergenerational caring likely? Are there practical contributions that our teachers and schools may make to a new global ethic? Can we contribute in practical ways to journeys for our children and their children to making a better world? Or is this merely a traveler's pipe-dream?

As a peace educator, environmental educator, and critical futurist, I am the first to admit that the obstacles to any such shift are considerable. After all, there is a powerful push of the past. Business-as-usual practices often hide the real environmental and social costs of enterprises, especially on children, women, the poor, and the natural environment. Such culturally myopic practices are defined in mainstream economic theory as "externalities."[5] Attendant risks may be obscured in terms of how the futures of unborn generations are being mortgaged. Rather than attempting constructively to deal with trends in violence, such as the two million children who have been killed in wars over the past decade, or the increased pace of environmental destruction, we may assume such trends are destiny. Rather than prudential care and applied foresight, there may be the blind pursuit of short-term goals that ignores the interests of the "two-thirds world" and of generations to come. Rather than working together to help build a better world, in which unborn generations have the possibility to live, to laugh, to play, to share, to care, and to transform conflicts nonviolently, we may fatalistically accept a foreclosed future. Rather than building intergenerational partnerships, we may be stealing or colonizing the well-being of children today and of successive generations by our lack of quality responses.

SCHOOL CURRICULUM NEGLECTS FUTURE GENERATIONS

It has been commented that much of what happens in our schools is about driving into the future while looking in the rear-view mirror. This metaphor has been extended to picturing our young people as, in many cases, crash victims of "future shock." Even if we question the cynicism of this comment, we may see some truth in its description of reality and potential reality. Yet, is the situation more complex and open? Even if there is taken-for-granted knowledge about "perpetual" trends in direct, structural, and ecological forms of violence, are there opportunities for resistance? Notwithstanding foreclosed images or guiding metaphors about our schools and other social organizations, are there site-specific opportunities for our teachers and teacher educators to become practical futurists? Are there opportunities for choice and engagement to help to build cultures of peace and environmentally sustainable futures? Are there opportunities for civic engagement in our schools and other social organizations to challenge narrow notions of education and citizenship that fail to take seriously our children's rights and the needs of future generations?[6]

Schools, Cultural Editing, and Restricted Images of "the Future"

Our maps, metaphors, images, and assumptions about the world—about our schools and our children's futures and their children's—are likely to play an important part in what we do or do not do in the present. Such images not only may be taken for granted, but may rebound on whether we attempt to help create nonviolent futures. Even if we would like a less violent future, we may assume that the task is too difficult and, by our own inaction contribute to a self-fulfilling prophecy.

In this context, it is important to note that major traditions of thought tend to "edit out" schools as sites of much, if any, genuine possibility in resisting violent trends. Schools in some radical critiques may be relegated to a mechanistic reproductive function. Teachers may be seen as largely "authoritarian dupes" or "structural dopes." The predominant metaphors may be ones in which teachers are little more than technicians on a factory production line unthinkingly working for agendas set elsewhere, "quality control" on manufactured outcomes, and "a docile work face."

In more conservative or economic rationalist versions, there is also foreclosure of the future. The metaphors of teaching and schooling are likely to be couched in the language of "competitive excellence," restated myths of "the hidden hand of the market place" in a time of globalization and of "learning organizations" in which schools learn from businesses how to become entrepreneurial. Rather than seeing schools as potential sites for helping create nonviolent futures, they may be pictured more narrowly as places for adaptation to market-place demands, the quickening pace of technological change and "the future."

Critical futurists use the term "cultural editing" to describe processes within both formal and nonformal education that are likely to restrict imagination about social alternatives, including alternatives to violence, and to hamper action competence or skills in nonviolent democratic participation.[7] Our "maps" of the world and the future may foreclose on other ways of knowing, doing, acting, and relating. Dissenting voices may not be heard or may be marginalized.

Active Listening and Coparticipation with Our Children

In resisting cultural violence that denies the interests of future generations, a number of working principles may be cited. These principles are not intended to be exhaustive but are merely invitations for open-minded dialogue. If we are to enhance the prospects of moving in the twenty-first century toward more peaceful cultures and more environmentally sustainable ways of living, it is important to share ideas, to learn from other cultural lifeways, and to actively listen to our children's voices on the future.

As teachers, if we are to take seriously the notion that "our world has been lent to us by our children," is it enough to reconsider what we teach? Or do we need also to review how we teach? Are both the formal and informal curriculum crucial?

If we overconcentrate on the formal curriculum, we may neglect the powerful push of educational structures and pedagogical processes that works against lessening racial intolerance, gender violence, and ageist stereotyping. Ageism, for example, devalues the contributions of both young people and the elderly. Ageist myths deny the possibility that adults can learn much of value from listening to what children say about the future. Instead of learning environments that encourage coparticipation, democratic action competence, and partnership across the generations, short-sighted patterns of age segregation, dependency, and helplessness may be perpetuated:

> Given the age-segregated nature of [our] children's world, the further along they move in age, schooling, work experience, and socialization to adulthood, the more likely they are to reject their own wisdom and accept adult "wisdom" as the price of entry into adulthood. Conventional adult wisdom at present confirms a rather violent, inequitable and increasingly polluted world. Admitting children to co-participation in social thinking, dreaming and planning while they

are still free to draw on their own experiential knowledge of the world will help make the adult social order more malleable, and more open to new and more humane developments.[8]

The conventional mug-and-jug metaphor about teaching, in which the jug's contents of "expert knowledge" are poured into empty mugs, denies any childhood wisdom and the possible value of participatory and collaborative approaches. Greatly undervalued are the potentials of coparticipation and collaborative learning techniques in the classroom:

Hundreds of research studies have been done on the relative impact of cooperative, competitive and individualistic learning experiences. . . . The various studies of cooperative learning are quite consistent with one another . . . indicating very favorable effects upon students. They develop a considerably greater commitment, helpfulness and caring for each other regardless of differences in ability level, ethnic background, gender, social class, or physical disability. They develop more skill in taking the perspective of others, emotionally as well as cognitively.[9]

Conventional teaching forecloses futures rather than opens them. There is a likely foreclosure in what is meant by "literacy" or "the educational basics" and what are interpreted as valuable, worthwhile, or valid knowledge sources about times past, times present, and times future. Rather than having the teacher or the teacher educator as a practical futurist, the conventional approach to schooling is very much "business as usual." In terms of the sociology of knowledge, or as some feminist critics have preferred to describe it, "the sociology of the lack of knowledge," certain sources are likely to be strongly privileged in "the texts" of conventional pedagogies. Other sources, such as voices from the low-income or the two-thirds world and from women and children, are likely to find more difficulty getting a serious hearing for their views about war, peace, and the future.

RESISTING FATALISM: THE PRINCIPLE OF EMPOWERMENT

To recognize, however, that there are restricted "texts" on the future in conventional pedagogies, whether on gender relations, the institution of war, or other assumed social invariances, is not the same as fatalistically accepting such "texts" as the only true reading of potential reality. The partiality of such texts or cultural maps is both a challenge and an opportunity. There are signs of this in nonformal educational contexts in the futures work of a range of NGOs (nongovernment organizations), international NGOs (INGOs), and social change movements, as well as in varying formal educational efforts to negotiate preferable futures.

In critical futurist and peace research literature, the metaphor of the future as a fan highlights the varied potentials for nonviolent resistance to feared futures:

> At every present moment the future stretches out before us like a giant fan, each fold of which is a possible future. We can range these from total catastrophe on one side to the fulfillment of human potential on the other. To each segment we can assign a rough probability. . . .
>
> For some of us the range of decision is very small; for the prisoner in jail who has not served his term tomorrow will be very much like today—there is not much choice. For all of us, however, there is some choice and we cannot escape a moral responsibility to choose. . . . Every decision that any human being makes, changes, however infinitesimally, the probability of catastrophe . . . or betterment.[10.]

Are there crucial challenges to become practical futurists whether as teachers or teacher educators? Are important questions raised about personal choice, professional foresight, and responsibility? More particularly, what quality responses may be made to our children's fears of the future and safeguard the interests of posterity? Newly proposed social innovations, such as a bill of rights for future generations and the creation of ombudsmen, guardians, or spokespersons to represent future generations

TABLE 5.2   *Reconceptualizing "Literacy": What You and I Can Do for Future Generations*

Narrow curriculum focus "rear-view mirror" perspective	Broad curriculum focus "anticipatory driving" perspective
Learning conventional Rs, plus "hidden curriculum" Rs (e.g., reductionist computer literacy, social illiteracy about alternatives)	Learning beyond the conventional Rs, with active challenges to "hidden curriculum," business-as-usual Rs (e.g., critical multimedia literacy, skills in resisting "colonization of the future")
Restriction of social imagination (image illiteracy)	Recovery of social imagination (image literacy)
Resignation to an "inevitable" future (e.g., conflict resolution illiteracy, political illiteracy about democratic processes)	Resourcefulness about alternative futures (e.g., conflict resolution literacy, action competence in global civics, and democratic participation)
Rigidity in thinking rather than responsible foresight (e.g., global futures illiteracy)	Responsibilities relating to foresight and respect for the rights of successive generations (e.g., global futures literacy)

at the United Nations and at national levels, deserve strong support. However, consistent with the principles of active listening and coparticipation, should we be in our schools new ideas of "grassroots globalism" such as "our children as ambassadors for future generations"? The latter approach may help to more directly empower young people by seriously valuing what they have to say about the future.[11]

New Literacies Value Future Generations

In preparing for the future, our schools have an important part to play. The caricature of many of our schools as places for driving into the future while looking fixedly in the rear-vision mirror is just that—a caricature. There are institutional constraints but there are also opportunities that may be realized to a greater or lesser extent. Opportunities may be missed in our schools to help negotiate more sustainable, less violent futures that respect the rights of future generations. Perhaps what is crucial is that fewer opportunities are missed.

Schools have various opportunities to extend what might be termed "the foresight principle," and to encourage defensive or anticipatory practices. There are varying opportunities for our students to learn not only from past travels or hindsight but from developing new "maps" of potential reality, including less violent routes for would-be travelers into the early decades of a new millennium.[12]

In this context, there are arguably important considerations for ourselves as teachers and teacher educators. In a world that is becoming more interdependent but is confronted by violent trends, is there an increasing need to be more futures-oriented in what we do or do not do? In preparing our children for the twenty-first century, is more needed than the traditional 3Rs and the appeal of the apparent security of "the good old days," with a "back to basics" curriculum? Does the answer lie in adding the often proffered R or ROM of computer literacy? Or, in actively listening to our children's voices on the future, do we need to reconceptualize "literacy" in more optimal ways, such as skills of foresight, empathy, social imagination, and action competence in the nonviolent resolution or transformation of conflict? (See Table 5.2.)

Beyond Impoverished Social Imagination

To work effectively for more peaceful and environmentally friendly futures, how important is our students' ability to imagine what such futures might be like? Instead of the implicit R of Resignation to a feared, violent future, do we need to encourage skills of social imagination about nonviolent alternatives and an explicit futures dimension across the curriculum? Do we need what Elise Boulding has described as "image literacy"? With the latter there are the Rs of Resourcefulness in envisaging peaceful futures and of Respect for the rights of future generations.[13] Research approaches that actively listen to children's views on the future are among the strongest evidence of such needs.[14]

Broadened notions of literacy relate closely to practical considerations of whether our children are primarily empowered or disempowered by their learning experiences. In what we do in our communities, our classrooms, our schools, our colleges, and our universities, is active hope about more peaceful futures made more convincing than despair about "perpetual" trends in violence? Can we make practical contributions to lessen illiteracy about cultural editing and foreclosed visions or maps on the future? For what you and I can do, the challenges are great, but there are site-specific opportunities for constructive choice and engagement that celebrate multicultural maps and decolonize learning journeys.[15]

NOTES

1. Jonathan Swift's *Gulliver's Travels* (1726) is a satirical account on the theme of intellectual arrogance and psychological pride, including reductionist assumptions about measuring or mapping reality and potential reality.

2. See Allison James and Alan Prout, eds., *Constructing and Reconstructing Childhood* (London: Falmer Press, 1997): passim. As used in this chapter, the concepts of "cultural mapping" and "cultural cartographies of childhood" extend the argument of critical futurists, such as Fred Polak and Elise Boulding, about the importance of developing critical image literacy in resisting foreclosed futures.

3. For further discussion of related issues, see, for example, N. Wyn and R. White, *Rethinking Youth* (St. Leonards: Allen & Unwin, 1997); N. Pearce and J. Hillman, *Wasted Youth: Raising Achievement and Tackling Social Exclusion* (London: Institute for Public Policy, 1998); R. Davis-Floyd and J. Dumit, eds., *Cyborg Babies: From Techno-Sex to Techno-Tots* (London: Routledge, 1998).

4. For a more detailed discussion of these issues, including colonizing and decolonizing research methodologies, see Francis Hutchinson, "Young People's Hopes and Fears for the Future," in *World Yearbook of Education: Futures Education*, eds. David Hicks and Richard Slaughter (London: Kogan Page, 1998): 133–148.

5. For a critical discussion of the concept of "externalities," see Johan Galtung, *Peace by Peaceful Means* (London: Sage, 1996), 154–176.

6. See K. Knutsson, "A New Vision of Childhood," *Future Generations Journal* 21 (1996), 27–30; K. Bickmore, "Preparation for Pluralism: Curricular and Extra Curricular Practice with Conflict Resolution," *Theory into Practice* 36, 1 (1997): 3–10.

7. The concepts of "cultural editing" and "cultural violence" are discussed in Johan Galtung, "Cultural Violence," *Journal of Peace Research* 27, 3: 273–889;

Francis Hutchinson, *Educating Beyond Violent Futures* (London: Routledge, 1996): 32–36.

8.   Elise Boulding, "Image and Action in Peace Building" in *The Future* (London: Sage, 1995).

9.   Morton Deutsch, "Educating Beyond Hate," in *Education Beyond Fatalism and Hate,* ed. E. Boulding and K. Boulding (Malmö, Sweden: School of Education, Lund University, 1994), 8.

10.   Kenneth Boulding, *Human Betterment* (Beverly Hills: Sage, 1985), 214–5.

11.   Allen Tough, "What Future Generations Need from Us" *Futures,* 25, 10 (December 1993): 1041–1050.

12.   Francis Hutchinson, *Educating Beyond* . . . . :195–273.

13.   See Elise Boulding, *Building a Global Civic Culture: Education for an Interdependent World* (New York: Teachers College Press, Columbia University, 1988), for a discussion of the need for new social literacies in educating for responsibility toward future generations.

14.   See, for example, David Hicks, "A Lesson for the Future: Young People's Hopes and Fears for Tomorrow," *Futures* 28, 1 (1996): 1–14.

15.   See, for example, Birgit Brock-Utne, "The Challenges for Peace Educators at the End of the Millennium," *International Journal of Peace Studies* 1, 1 (1996): 37–55; Rupert Maclean and John Fien, *Learning for a Sustainable Environment: Innovations in Teacher Education Through Environmental Education* (Australia: Griffith University and UNESCO-ACEID, 1995).

Chapter 6

From Youth Futures
to Futures for All:
Reclaiming the Human Story

Marcus Bussey

I recently watched the 1960 Academy–Award winning movie *The Time Machine* with my boys (aged ten and thirteen). We enjoyed ourselves, and they felt quite inspired by how the time traveler helped the young Eloi take on the evil Morlock. This got me thinking about how the relationships between adults and youth are framed in our culture. What lessons had my boys learned by watching this movie? Well, I looked at what H. G. Wells had written in his original story and found that what had changed between the two versions—a lapse of sixty-five years—was a real escalation in the level of agency exhibited by the time traveler in the movie. The original book was more philosophical and speculative and owed a real debt to Darwinism. The movie version was more romantic and offered a thoroughly modernist manifesto for change.

The Time Machine, in its movie form, is a parable rich in the ambiguities and tensions that define and sustain the modernist enterprise. Essentially, Wells is describing, and the movie amplifies this considerably, the tensions between utopian and dystopian systems of governance. Utopia leads to weakness and decay, dystopia to brutalization and degeneration. The movie version brings in romance and revolution, which give hope—thank you, Hollywood!—while Wells's text leaves the Eloi and Morlock to their manifest Darwinian destiny of further decline. In both the book and the film, the young are at the mercy of an adult world gone wrong, but it takes Hollywood to actually turn the time traveler into an archetypal hero with the qualities necessary to galvanize action and energy into the young Eloi. Revolution follows and leads to the overthrow of generations of servitude to the machines and the Morlock. From this struggle between utopia and dystopia, a new world order will emerge: a utopia or good society.

So to answer the question about what my boys learned by watching this movie, they learned that tension—the struggle or dialectic—is a hallmark of civilizational progress and should be acknowledged as a painful but healthy mechanism within the modernist dynamic. They also learned that young people are important in the struggle against adult mores as they generate new energy and new visions within the dominant paradigm. The message here is clear: the young are essentially naive and need adult direction but—and here the romantic view comes through—they are somehow innocent and graceful, as both book and movie confirm. They are also idealistic, and this idealism has but to be shaped by a "good man" like the time traveler to bear fruit.

Of course, the movie (not Wells) goes on—the foundation stone of idealism (and modernism) is sacrifice. The Eloi sacrifice their innocence in order to throw off the Morlock. Youth must let go of their simple, carefree ways to become adult. They need to accept Wells's maxim that: "Strength is the outcome of need: security sets a premium on feebleness."[1] In declaring their independence, they lose their idyll and are, like Adam and Eve, cast out of the garden. To compensate them for this loss, the time traveler also sacrifices his own present, by returning to them as a latter-day Nelson Mandela or Moses, and, we assume, leading them to safety.

Implicit to the story is that the young need such a figure. Thus we end up with the myth of the savior: the quintessential "good man." Such a figure embodies culture and is strong, solitary, visionary, and deeply compassionate. Here we find the modernist formula for the creative (but safe) revolution. The good man (Obi-wan Kanobi) with the good machine (light saber) and an army of young idealists (Luke Sky Walker, et al.) can overthrow the evil empire. Once again, thank you, Hollywood.

CRITICAL SPIRITUALITY

In this chapter I argue that if we are to reclaim a youthful culture that honors all players—the young and the old—and addresses the central concerns of both aware youth and adults, then we need to take a critically spiritual lens to the processes of culture and enculturation as they occur within the family, school, and society. Such a lens moves analysis from a horizontal discourse of empirical studies and populist rhetoric to a vertical discourse that offers a critical appreciation of the layered nature of human action. Such a "spiritual empiricism" allows for mystery, silence, and meditative reflection to broaden human perception and values while maintaining the centrality of critical theory and practice as it functions within a poststructural context.[2] This approach allows for an analysis to emerge that describes the role of youth futures as an integrative practice. Along with other subsets of futures like feminist, postcolonial, and indigenous futures, it is seeking to reclaim a broader human story that will function as an antidote to the highly toxic narrative of hypercapitalism and its handmaiden, globalization.

My argument begins with an examination of some of the obfuscations inherent to modernism and its expansion and how they often have limited the effect of the critical tools of youth futures. The idealism and vigor of the young is then described in terms of a coherent way of knowing and experiencing the world. I then look at how adult civilization is framed within the current episteme, exploring how this frames adult responses to the young and also steers the work of many youth futurists today. From there I proceed to look at what a youthful civilization might be and how youth futures might transform and be transformed.

DUALISM

At the heart of the narrative of Western civilization is the assumption that the dualist tension (young-old, utopia-dystopia, matriarchy-patriarchy, good-evil, and so on. . . .) defines reality. This is a modernist subterfuge that is amplified in postmodern discourse to embrace a center-less world. *The Time Machine* describes the playing out of this tension in such a way that it maps our lived experience. On the micro level, each day is a day when we face moral choices, we struggle with the Morlock within—we stare down the numbing machine of quotidianity, and spirit triumphs over matter. On the macro level, our world is constantly under threat, but these forces in the universe will ultimately end on the side of "good."

The modernist worldview, by posing dualism as a defining feature of reality, keeps synthetic processes from coming to grips with its core assumption that everything is a resource if you are powerful enough to take it. It prevents us from thinking our way out of our global problematique because it has offered us the seductive "red herring" of choice between utopia or dystopia, between youth or maturity, plenty or poverty, primitive or developed, weak or strong, individual or collective, matriarchy or patriarchy, and so on. In this way it keeps even the most profound criticism on horizontal rather than vertical trajectories. It thus keeps its heartland safe, allowing the ultimate survival of the machine/dominator model even though we can name it and deconstruct it. Such is the centralizing force of modernism that criticism fails to have more than superficial results. Modernism is a hermetically sealed unit. Thus the cultural critic and futurist Zia Sardar points out that "it is not possible to think our way out of modernity with the philosophical system of thought and language supplied by modernity."[3]

The temptation in depicting youth futures is to romanticize youth—just as early Marxists romanticized the working class and romantic poets romanticized rural life. Thus we put a lot of energy into giving shape and form to their dreams and fears, to mapping their perceptions of reality and truth so that the adult world can hear in their voice validating statements about a preferred reality and thus find our way towards better and richer more plural futures. There is nothing wrong with this, except that it tends to miss the possibility of situating youth, and youthfulness, within the broader tale of human progress from birth, through growth, to maturity and decline. Furthermore, romanticism leads to sentimentality, which continues the "othering" that is so frustrating and disempowering for the young.

This desire to advocate, to give voice and create a meaningful space for the young can put youth futurists into the same category as other agents of peak bodies who lobby the "halls of power" for a slice of the cake. It does not alter the power balance. Nor does it challenge the roots of that power nor the inequities and misinformation at the heart of the system of dominance.

Thus we remain trapped in a labyrinth of mirrors that define reality by surface and reflection. The postmodern nightmare is upon us. Reality, as the movie *Matrix* elegantly portrays, becomes nothing more than a collectively shared illusion. This can be mapped, as youth futurist Frank Hutchinson points out, either with our linear intellects, in which knowing becomes a highway and knowledge bullets and bytes, or as a landscape which is the map itself. Our consciousness can then inhabit and map such a space in "alternative, deeply spiritual ways."[4]

The Failure of Adult Civilization

Young people know that the adult world has let them down. They may be the future but the future is tenuous. Schools, as Jim Dator reminded the Hawaiian Board of Education some years ago,[5] promise to prepare young people for the one thing that will not exist in the future: Jobs!

Furthermore, the nuclear family, ensconced in its neat suburban home in any-place Down-Town west, is lonely and empty because both parents now need to work to keep up with the mortgage. There is no community, no collective dream other than more consumption. It is not surprising that first-world youth are angry and frustrated. They have seen through the Big Lie and they want to get off the roller coaster of "progress" and breathe fresh air.

It is against this backdrop that what is unique about the young, their idealism and vision, stand out. Young adults in general have a special vision. They see what the adult world has lost touch with. They inhabit a world of ideal dimensions. They get angry at us. They protest by being difficult, passively resisting, challenging through a variety of behaviors, joining subcultures that either express or ease their pain and disillusion. Parents weep. So do their children.

One young woman summed up her experience in these strident words
of condemnation:

Actions Speak Louder
Listen, with your closed ears
To cries and pleading words.
Hear me, with your closed heart.

For I have much to say.
I see a world of madness,
I dream of future visions.
Yet there is no one who can hear me
Above the din of angry words.

You talk of changes made,
You talk of future peace.
You talk and talk, until I scream.
You'll talk us all to death!

—Mathilda Element, nineteen

Youth futurists all agree that our culture is letting young people down.
Our education system is caught up in archaic modes of organization and
learning.[6] Consumerism has latched onto youthful cynicism and despair
and fostered a flight into headlong hedonism and denial.[7] The young are
now seen as, and actively identify with, a highly profitable niche market,
and youth itself has become a commodity to be striven for through style,
fashion, and all the arts of illusion.

At fifteen, Jennifer Fitzgerald sees the falsity of the capitalist god:

Poor people,
They do not know Life,
We are free (in our own chains)
Free to buy our own homes
Says our "marvelous" democracy.

And the emptiness spills over into ennui. With no valid and validating
futures, what's the point? Here we find young people torn between emptiness and the drive—their central function—to create meaning that goes
beyond the mundane. Another young voice, Star Hungerford, age fourteen,
sums her feeling up with these words:

I admit I am bored
Lost, life and loveless maybe

But that doesn't explain
How little excitement I see.

Spit in the gutter,
Smoke a lung cancer stick
Say something, mutter
Think of a mission to do

AND THINK IT DAMN QUICK![8]

The Youthful Paradigm

The young are learning the world through their hearts. Heads follow later and often confuse the messages with "shoulds" and "oughts," with comparison and diminution, with the gray that seemingly engulfs the adult world. The difference between youth and maturity can be summed up in an old East Asian metaphor that says we can see the moon reflected in a puddle or choose to see the mud. Similarly, the romantic poet William Wordsworth idealized the enchantment of youth, "when blessing spread around me like a sea," and lamented the decline of the adult world, which was trapped in a "melancholy waste of hopes o'erthrown" in which the adult "sneers on visionary minds."[9]

Some young adults in the West are rediscovering what they need. They are listening to their hearts. Youth futurists have been skillful at isolating the main features of Western youth's preferred visions of the future. Such a worldview has much in common with that of women and non-Western cultures. It has, as a result, suffered a similar fate to these in our industrial and materialist age when the egalitarian, interpersonal, empathic, environmental, and compassionate consciousness inherent in these worldviews has been perceived as inimical to Western civilization.

Many Western youth are therefore returning to their romantic roots and discovering what is authentic and desirable beyond the materialist mirage of hypercapitalism. In this they are moving counter to many non-Western youth who (as Sohail Inayatullah demonstrated in his earlier chapter), are still called to the cities in the hope of freeing themselves from the tyranny of poverty, thereby supporting the maintenance and expansion of consumerism and globalization.

The temptation of studying an innately romantic way of knowing is to lose sight of the deeper forces at work within the paradigm itself. Frequently, young people's descriptions of preferred futures are expansive and very willing to sacrifice for a perceived "greater good." But such energy is intrinsically blind. It can therefore be hijacked by charismatic or cynical adults and turned either toward violence or individual aggrandizement and selfishness.

This allows us to see the ironic tension at the center of the youthful experience of reality. The young, thinking with their hearts, frequently balk at what they correctly see as the limited nature of most adult constructions of reality. On the other hand, they are vulnerable to manipulation and brutalization because of their relationship with adults, who, for better or worse, play the role of mentor. The reciprocity implied by this relationship has great implications for the generation and implementation of positive, future-oriented action.

The Adult Response

Standard adult responses to youth tend to fall within a narrow belt of expression. Its main characteristics are at the level of litany in which:

- the media bewails the follies (violence, crime, drugs, sex, apathy, laziness, and so on . . .) of youth;
- politicians take moral high ground (where the votes are) on youth issues, pushing for more police, harsher punishments, less money, more "responsive" schools;
- community members feel fear and suspicion;
- business capitalizes in a variety of ways on dissatisfaction by promoting "youth" industries, from smoking to violent video games.

Much of this derives from the primal human response of "shoot the messenger." Young people press our adult buttons. They show up our inconsistencies by refusing to play the Game. Because they are less powerful, they are ideal targets in the ongoing struggle to maintain a vulnerable hegemonic structure that bases its power and wealth on the exploitation and manipulation of the vast majority of life and resources on the planet.

There is growing pressure for this male, white, thirty-five-plus dominance characteristic of modernism to change. Fear is in the air and needs to be focused on groups who, like the young, are marginal and relatively powerless. Youth activist Mike Males explains:

> Fear of the young is enthusiastically embraced by modern economic and political interests busy dismantling the public sector, promoting unprecedented concentration of wealth, and building an enclave/prison society to manage the inevitable conflict such inequality creates.[10]

Futurist Riane Eisler put it this way: "There are today signs of massive dominator systems' resistance and regression."[11] She points out that all marginal groups—young, old, nonwhite, female—are under increased pressure from a conservative, dominator backlash that is sweeping the planet. The dynamic here is one of confrontation, a digging in. Negotiation is out. In her analysis, the tensions of millennia of habit lie at the heart of the current crisis.

From a youth futures perspective, this tension has also been played out over the years wherever authority has been the domain of a conservative, suspicious, and jealous oligarchy of elders. To illustrate this point, it is salutary to note that the conservative ancient Greek poet Hesiod (eight century BC) felt he had his hands full with the young too. In fact, he was so concerned that he lamented that there was "no hope for the future of our people if they are to be dependent upon the frivolous youth of today, for certainly all youth are reckless beyond words."[12]

A YOUTHFUL CIVILIZATION

For the young living at the cutting edge of postindustrial civilization, an adult civilization of hierarchy and fragmentation, the response is to yearn for that which is missing. This yearning, as framed in the findings of much of the youth futures research in this book, is for everything their world currently lacks. Futurist David Hicks has drawn seven themes from his work with students, which suggest a "base-line" future consisting of no discrimination, a sense of community, locally produced foods, soft technology, peace, green ethics, and celebration.[13] Such a worldview is not dissimilar to those of women and the non-West who share with youth positions of relative powerlessness within our global system. Those on the periphery of power tend to seek definition in the negative by reference to what is currently accepted practice. It should be noted that issues, such as those listed by Hicks, subscribe to a horizontal analysis of social and cultural problems. They are useful as indicators but fail to go to the heart of the problem.

For a youthful civilization to emerge—a civilization that not only honors a base-line future but also tells the story differently—power has to be drawn into accepting the new set of definitions inherent to that civilization. Such a project is not going to result from checking through a list of preferable scenarios; instead, it can arise only from fundamental relocations of will and identity involving deep shifts in consciousness. Such a relocation requires the kind of critically spiritual method[14] described earlier that shifts the focus from horizontal analysis to vertical methodologies that accommodate the pluralism of globalism within an ethical and spiritually responsive commitment to self-development through service to the whole: community, culture, environment, and planet.

To this end, futurists are looking beyond the dominant Western discourse to gain distance from the present. This search is leading us in two directions. First we engage in what Confucian futurist Weiming Tu calls "inter-civilizational dialogue."[15]

Here we access ways of knowing that can realign and redefine what is intelligible and appropriate: the Imam of Islam, the Tapu of Polynesia, the

Dreaming of Indigenous Australians. Second we can engage in a dialogue with the underbelly of Western civilization. Such a dialogue would involve accessing the nondominant cultures referred to by Nandy: youth culture, female culture, aged culture, migrant culture, and so on. . . . Both directions risk further commodification as cultural artifacts that can only lead to a superficial redrawing of the current map. Yet to engage deeply with the processes implicit within these various ways of knowing is central to weaving a vigorous alternative to current discourse.

This is where youth futures has real relevance. It is seeking to give voice to the young, to advocate for cultural and systemic change, to engage with the broader society in meaningful ways that engage both the heart and the head, while seeking to provide young people with the skills to define and engage with their own futures. In short, it seeks to take the cap off human potential and generate a meaningful story that acknowledges the intrinsic difference that effectively constitutes youth and its unique way of knowing and interacting with the world.

Reclaiming Our Story

This youthful way of knowing is diminished by current civilizational values that have become, I believe, incorrectly associated with an adult worldview. We cannot seek to reclaim the validity of uniqueness of youthfulness without doing the same for both maturity and old age. We are in a position now to reestablish the relevance of the entire human story, the life cycle itself, which now becomes charged with a renewed sense of meaning and purpose. Thus Neil Postman calls for "shared narratives"[16] and Eisler reminds us that: "We all hunger for stories. . . . [I]t is from the stories we are told that we in turn unconsciously fashion our own life scripts."[17]

Story unifies human action by bringing meaning to the whole. Inspiration is to be had from this meaning-making. Materialism has bled meaning from the lives of many young people. Yet there is room for confidence. An emerging critically spiritual consciousness, a neohumanistic groundswell, is sweeping the planet. Change, as critical educationist Paolo Freire reminds us, comes in the wake of movement in the hearts of humanity.[18]

The core of a vigorous youth futures is in reclaiming and activating a valid human story. Central to this is a vision of continuity and relationship in which everyone has an intrinsic meaning within the whole. Such a cohesive vision has always been part of non-Western cultures where, for instance, in traditional Indic culture the life cycle was seamlessly understood as a time to learn (0 to 25), a time to practice (25 to 50) and a time to reflect (50-plus). Throughout this cycle, an intrinsic respect for the qualities of each group combines with a sense of purpose and mission.

Each age group is defined by a specific way of knowing and experiencing the world. It is the desire of the adult world, bound and currently confined to the modernist structural worldview, to impress its way of knowing on the young, particularly via the schooling system, that has led to the deep alienation of so many young people throughout their schooling years.

A new story is emerging. To look find it, youth futurists rightly turn to the young, who have the story within them. They are the true romantics who hold the torch of idealism high. The adult world needs to combine and support this idealism with the strength, skill, and vigor that marks their adult place in the life cycle.

Implications

Such a redrawing has wide implications for youth, youth futures, and Western civilization. With the rise of a critically spiritual mentality, knowledge becomes something other than discrete packages of information. Learning thus becomes a real process of discovery and recovery. Spirituality in turn becomes a valid way to interpret and experience reality and allows for a reclamation of the heart for both the young, who have been denied it, and for adults, who have lost touch with it. From this will arise a loving economics of knowledge that leads to a new emphasis on knowledge as action.

The young do not want to read about life, they want to live it. Both Western and non-Western commentators point to desire as a central component of any new transformative learning praxis. "To change the world through work," observes Freire, "to "proclaim" the world, to express it, and to express oneself are the unique qualities of human beings. Education at any level will be more rewarding if it stimulates the development of this radical, human need for expression."[19]

Prabhat Rainjan Sarkar, mystic poet and political commentator, points out that this engagement of body, mind, and spirit with the world is a glorious thing. "The beauty that is writ large on the sweating body of a person who is on the move has no comparison."[20] Meaning is to be had only from this engagement; it is a spiritual activity, not simply movement for its own sake. Thus he advises that we perform more work but also, and in tandem with this, more meditation.[21] The critically spiritual action of reflecting on our actions is central to the transformation of our culture and our consciousness. Without it the materialist roots of the global civilizational project cannot be effectively challenged or transformed.[22]

Learning partnerships will become increasingly common; they will actively incorporate the new communications technologies as groups develop global learning networks which shift the focus from self—the isolated individual—to other, as learning-in-action becomes service to all. In concert with such a dramatic shift, a new family ethos will also spring up that sees not the end of the nuclear family but the expansion of the meaning of *nuclear* to include the local and the relational. In this way, learning relationships for young people will expand and incorporate a wide and diverse series of interactions.

Finally, such futures see young people and adults engage in relationships that shift the parameters of power to include, acknowledge, and actively develop their inherent natures. All ages have a part to play and a purpose intrinsic to themselves. Thus the elderly offer wisdom, the adult provides the basis of effective action in the world, and the young provide inspiration and raw energy. In the current context of deep contestation, we can remember the words of the Mozambican activist Graca Machel who points out, "One of the historic responsibilities of the oppressed is to liberate the oppressors."[23] Youth can be seen as messengers of the heart to the adult world. Their clear vision is needed to engage and focus adults on meaningful change. This process is absolutely essential if we hope to loosen the bonds of habit and fear that hold many adults in check, while we can still remember how to dream and see the cracks in the system.

Beyond "Youth Futures" Research

In the light of such possible developments, youth futures as a field of research stands to lose its identity and purpose in the process of synthesis—but not before it has defined, interpreted, and articulated the voice of the young to the present so that we may generate stories of hope for future generations. Youth futures has an important function to perform, along with feminist, non-Western, and indigenous futures. It is about making a unique way of knowing the world become relevant in the collective process of, as futurist Sohail Inayatullah puts it, "undefining" the future[24] so that we can free ourselves from the pervasive monocultural trajectory of Western civilization.

In doing this, we are likely to see:

- a broadening of the youth futures lens to include cross-cultural and civilizational research;
- more critical practices emerge that make use of layered methodologies;
- a shift from a romantic (horizontal) to a critically spiritual (vertical) appreciation of the meta story;
- the application of critically spiritual neohumanist practices to expand the definition of liberatory education and cultural literacy to include spiritual literacy;
- a focus on the entire human story so that youth futures become futures for all.

It is evident in many of the chapters of this book, that this transition has already begun.

NOTES

1. H. G. Wells, "The Time Machine," in *The Complete Science Fiction Treasury of H.G. Wells* (New York: Avenel Books, 1978), 23.

2. Marcus Bussey, "Critical Spirituality: Neo Humanism as Method," in *Journal of Futures Studies* 5, 2 (2000): 21–25; Sohail Inayatullah, "Causal Layered Analysis: Post-structuralism as Method," in *Alternative Futures: Methodology, Society, Macrohistory and the Long Term Future* (Taiwan: Tamkang University, 1999).

3. Zia Sardar, "Surviving the Terminator: The Postmodern Mental Condition," *Futures* (March 1990): 204.

4. Francis Hutchinson, *"Learning Journeys and Future Generations: Towards Cultures of Peace?,"* (paper presented at the International Peace Research Associations Conference, Tampere, Finland, August 5–9, 2000).

5. Jim Dator, "Is There a Future for Public Education in Hawaii?," Governor's Commission on the 150th Anniversary of Public Education in Hawaii (July 26, 1991). http://www.soc.hawaii.edu/future.

6. See Jim Dator, op cit.

7. See Willis Harman, *Global Mind Change: The Promise of the Last Years of the Twentieth Century* (Indianapolis, Indiana: Knowledge Systems Inc., 1988), 141.

8. All poetry is from the author's private collection unless otherwise indicated by a separate footnote.

9. William Wordsworth, "The Prelude: Childhood and School-Time," in *The Oxford Library of English Poetry*, vol. 2 (Oxford University Press, 1986), 281–282.

10. Mike Males, *Framing Youth: Ten Myths about the Next Generation* (Monroe, Maine: Common Courage Press, 1999), 10.

11. Riane Eisler, *Sacred Pleasure: Sex, Myth, and the Politics of the Body* (San Francisco: Harper, 1996), 363.

12. Mike Males, *Framing Youth . . . . :*338.

13. David Hicks, "Identifying Sources of Hope in Postmodern Times" in *World Yearbook of Education 1998: Futures Education,* eds. David Hicks and Richard Slaughter, (London: Kogan Page, 1998), 223.

14. Marcus Bussey, "Change or Progress?: Critical Spirituality and the Futures of Futures Studies," *Futures* (2002).

15. Weiming Tu, "Confucian Humanism and the Dialogues among Civilizations," (paper presented at International Conference on World Civilizations in the New Century: Trends and Challenges, April 25–26) (Taipei: National Library, 2000). http://www.inpr.org.tw/inprc/event103.htm.

16. Neil Postman, *The End of Education: Redefining the Value of School* (New York: Vintage Books, 1996), 18.

17. Riane Eisler, *Sacred Pleasure . . . . :*373.

18. Paolo Freire, *The Politics of Education: Culture, Power and Liberation* (South Hadley, Mass.: Bergin and Garvey, 1985), 40.

19. Paolo Freire, *The Politics . . . . :*21.

20.   Prabhat Rainjan Sarkar, "Druva and Adruva," in *Sabhastita Samgraha,* part 21 (Calcutta: A.M. Publications, 1994), 2.

21.   Prabhat Rainjan Sarkar, "Incantation and Human Progress," in *Sabhastita Samgraha,* part 24 (Calcutta: A.M. Publications, 1997), 110.

22.   Ibid., 95.

23.   Graca Machel, "The Dignity of the Enemy," in *Shared Values for a Troubled World: Conversations with Men and Women of Conscience* (San Francisco: Jossey-Bass Publishers, 1994), 91.

24.   Sohail Inayatullah, *Alternative Futures,* 3.

Youth Essay 1

Optimistic Visions from Australia

Raina Hunter

When I try to imagine how I would like the future to be, I tend to romanticize, to idealize. I concoct a perfect world in my mind. A world filled with love, with peace, with happiness. A world free from prejudice and discrimination, from hate and destruction, from sickness and starvation, from poverty and crime. A world that would epitomize all my hopes and dreams yet contain none of my fears.

I am lucky that I can view the world so optimistically. Born in Australia and brought up by hard-working parents, I've always been healthy and have never wanted for anything in my life. Millions of others around the world aren't so lucky. Some are born into famine or poverty, some into civil war, some with debilitating or incurable diseases. Some of these people live lives filled with hunger and suffering, never even getting a chance to break away from the hand of fate that has been given to them. Still others are subjected to lifelong discrimination and prejudice if they are born into a lower class in a class-ridden society such as the "untouchables," or lowest class, in India. Even if these people are able to provide for themselves and their families to an extent, they are condemned to their social position for life, as are their children and grandchildren. All because of where they were born!

I hope that in the near future, all of the above will become irrelevant. In my preferred future, all people worldwide will be born with equal opportunities in life and the chance to make of it what they will. Although these social justice issues are of utmost concern to me, I also have hopes and dreams for the future on other issues, such as the environment, war, relationships, politics, and work.

I don't believe we are doing anywhere near enough in Australia or worldwide at the moment to protect and sustain our natural environment. This environment in which we live is absolutely crucial to our health and survival as people today. The effects of our actions or lack of action today will have even more crucial effects on future generations. Will they still have clear air to breathe and clean water to drink? What of the world's rainforests that are being logged at an alarming rate, for example, the Otways forest in Victoria? What about the increasing proximity of nuclear dumping and testing to areas inhabited by people, for example, Lucas Heights in New South Wales or the current dumping in South Australia? I believe that if we are to have a future, we must act now to stop the degradation of our environment, as well as pro-actively strive to make our environment better. My preferred future for the environment is a place that is respected by people so that it can be enjoyed safely.

What can I say about my hopes for the future of war and conflict? Of course I don't want to see any more war or conflict anywhere in the world, especially closer to home, as we are all most concerned about what goes on in our own backyards. But I think that now and into the future, with the increasing development of nuclear weapons, it is more important than ever to sort things out without resulting to warfare. Nuclear warfare is terrifying due to the sheer immensity of damage that can be caused so easily. We are already at the stage where someone in a remote corner of the world can create havoc worldwide with the push of a button. Such technology is also terrifying because it places such enormous power in the hands of individuals or small groups. If people in extremist groups got their hands on such technology, the world would be answerable to them. What would happen if someone like Hitler had the chance to kill people so easily? The terrible deaths of millions at his hands without this technology illustrate what could result.

Increasing advances in science and technology are impacting on all areas of our lives in Australia and worldwide, and I believe these impacts will continue to increase into the future. We can already see a kind of distancing occurring in communication, both in personal relationships and in the workplace. Many people even in the same office prefer to e-mail each other than talk to each other over the phone. I believe this is because e-mail is less personal and requires less effort and imagination than real, face-to-face, two-way communication. We are also seeing the development of an "answering machine society" where people will tend to call at "off-times" of the day when the caller doesn't expect anyone to be at the phone. Leaving a message, as opposed to having a conversation, means that the caller can get the message through without having to listen to the receiver of the message. It requires less time and saves the effort of having to talk to a real person. Sadly, many of us are simply too lazy to engage in real communication any more.

We also see trends away from personal contact in the workplace, with the development of computer technology that allows people to work from home rather than commuting to the workplace. Since real communication is becoming less common in the workplace, someone can participate almost as well from home, or even from another country. Technology is also changing the entire face of the workforce, as many jobs previously done by people can now be done by computers and more advanced machinery. This makes redundant not only many people, but also the entire industry in which they worked. I really hope that personal communication is regained in the future, as interacting with other people is a necessary and important part of everyone's fulfilling life.

I have many hopes and dreams for the future of politics in Australia. I am disappointed that the recent republican referendum was defeated but have faith that becoming a republic is the way forward for Australia, and it will only be a matter of time before enough people realize this. I work as a volunteer for the Australian Democrats because it is forward-looking, and reflects and stands for everything I believe in, and is much more up to date with the way society is is the way it is changing than the old parties who in many ways are still stuck back in the past. On a worldwide basis, I hope that politics will become more diplomatic and honest, with an elimination of corruption that is so rife in many governments around the world.

So many hopes and dreams for the future, yet it remains to be seen whether any of them will become reality. I believe that the ability to hope and dream about our own future and the future generally is invaluable, and can lead to achievement of those dreams. As the old saying goes, prophecies can be self-fulfilling. But we must also take ownership of our future and empower ourselves to actually help make a difference and change our future into a place where we want to live. Although it might be quite a mission (although not impossible by any means!) for one person to change the world, I believe it is quite possible to make a world of difference within our own lives and for the individuals we come into contact with.

Part II

Comparative Research from Around the Globe

Chapter 7

Japanese Youth: Rewriting Futures in the "No Taboos" Postbubble Millennium

David Wright

JAPAN'S "NO TABOOS" MILLENNIUM

According to a young interactive multimedia technologies (IMMT) entrepreneur[1] for Japan, this is the century of "no taboos" (*tabuu nashi*), setting Japan up as a new frontier—no rules, tradition is dead, all is possible, all dials set to zero, the slate wiped clean. Although a simplistic metaphor, it does point to the overall mood of Japan and, in part at least, sets the agenda for the following critique. The young have come to perceive Japan increasingly as an open text onto which they must inscribe their own futures.

The sociopolitical and economic bubble period in Japan helped accelerate the fragmentation of youth cultures from the singular post–World War II youth cultural prototype that was characterized by its singular mission to rebuild the nation, restore Japan to its former glory, and achieve economic status commensurate with those of the victors of war. Bubble affluence in turn gave rise to the exponential fragmenting and birthing of new cultural youth types. Although alarming to Japanese cultural purists, from a biological perspective, this would appear as an inevitable byproduct of the social evolutionary trajectories of the organism we know as youth, adults in progress, as they grapple with inherited social realities and resist, unwittingly adopt and shape their own futures.

The objective of this chapter is to articulate something that is strangely missing from the conventional discourses on Japanese youth futures, namely, a transformative future-oriented vision for a start-up environment of Japanese youth in order to create future possibilities that transcend current postbubble Japanese social realities. Ultimately, the objective of worthwhile and justifiable futures thinking activity lies in the task of articulating the types of start-up environments required from which new futures can be imagined, concretely articulated, and implemented into real-world social contexts. This may be a task of transforming the natural future-oriented human imagination into articulated future images—in essence, a problem of good design.

LAYERED OVERVIEW OF JAPAN'S PERCEIVED YOUTH PROBLEMATIC

> *To know the truth partially is to distort the Universe. . . . An unflinching deter-*
> *mination to take the whole evidence into account is the only method of preser-*
> *vation against the fluctuating extremes of fashionable opinion.*
> —A. N. Whitehead

There is a tradition in Western culture, and by implication in contemporary Japanese culture, to perceive adolescence and youth as a period of storm and stress, marked by difficult behavior, a rebellious outlook, and a great deal of internal conflict and suffering.[2] And yet, "field studies among primitive peoples show that adolescence is by no means always a period of storm and stress. In some societies it is traversed with a calmness quite at odds with our own expectations. The problems of adolescence are highly relative to the values of the culture."[3] To establish for the reader an overview effect, we now turn to a context-setting exercise using a cursory causal layered analysis.[4]

Official metadiscourses on Japanese youth concern the perceived lack of social skills to assume the roles of responsible successors to the nation's postbubble future. There simultaneously exists a generous compendium of pathologies relating to contemporary Japanese youth. Violence has escalated; school truancy (*futou-kouji*) is almost fashionable; school bullying (*ijime-mondai*) is rampant; respect for traditional culture and the time-honored reverence for elders is fast becoming extinct; youth are lawless and rude, self-serving, lazy, unfocused, ultraconsumerist, and ultimately out of control.

At another level—the perceived social causes that contributed to the problematic—we find a suite of discourses emphasizing the collapse of the bubble economy, the systemic effects of ongoing globalization and the meddling influences of outside world (usually the United States), the new media technologies' negative influences that push youth away from the traditional modes of Japanese cultural expression, assimilation, and values-making that have come to constitute the nation's mood.

Delving to deeper levels, the worldviews and discourses in which the problematic is situated, we excavate the profound role of Japan's "catch-up and overtake the United States and Europe" guiding image of the future and its agenda to set Japan on the path of economic might, a trajectory of national development that culminated in the unstoppable bubble economy and all its well-documented excesses.[5] The Japanese people's recognition of the imperative to actively dismantle the self-destructiveness of this now obsolete model and replace it with more appropriate futures images has been gradual and shrouded in a national mood of denial. It is at this level of worldview and discourse that the futures researcher finds the greatest potential for preferred futures transcending the limitations of historical visions.

At the deepest of human social levels, the burdens of maintaining cultural myth in Japan is a significant futures-influencing factor for today's Japanese young people. Cultural uniqueness and superiority weigh heavily on the ability of the nation and the young in particular to position themselves within the larger global context of the world's culture areas and exacerbates the problem of dealing with new global social realities and articulating alternative states of Japanese-ness. The unmasking of this Grand Myth necessarily plays a part in subverting the apparent naturalness of Japan's postwar linear trajectory of economic progress, in which youth are prewritten as the successors (*koukeisha*) of history and the continuation of the artificial successes achieved in the bubble economy.

EMERGING AGENTS OF TRANSFORMATION

> . . . [I]t is important to perceive what I have called "the seeds of change," those aspects of society that are in the process of developing and that require new modes of understanding that go beyond the rational and work at the levels of intuition and emotion.
>
> —Masini[6]

> The change points in society are found on city streets, on school playgrounds, in the privacy of the home, and in all kinds of little-recognized civic spaces, from neighborhoods to global organizations.
>
> —Boulding and Boulding[7]

Postbubble Japan is typified by an abundance of identifiable transformative seeds of change. I now isolate and explicate some of these concrete manifestations of change significant in the construction of everyday realities for Japanese youth.

Japanese Youth and the Unspoken "Cool Resistance"

The first seed of change is the emergence of a resistant young Japanese refusing to inherit the ways of his parents' generation, a form of resistance that one youth-oriented magazine has embodied in the term "cool resistance."[8] Born as much as the mother of necessity after the postbubble socioeconomic environment in Japan, the cool resistance youth, as the early adopter of a partially diffused subculture, is based on the imperative of living with less because of the prolonged depression's negative economic impact on the young. This cool resistance phenomenon is further developed in later sections.

Ko-gyaru and *Tame-guchi:* The Language of Subversion

Another emerging seed of change are the so-called *ko-gyaru*, a subculture of young Japanese women renowned for outlandish, eccentric, and un-Japanese social attitudes and nonconforming personal aesthetics. *Ko-gyaru*—literally the "girl-girls"—to the consternation of linguistic purists, deploy their own linguistic forms, which they refer to as *tame-guchi*. This *ko-gyaru* dialect systematically banishes all forms of honorific Japanese, effectively subverting the hierarchical social stratification of traditional Japanese society and interpersonal communication modes (1999, *Tamori ii to mo*, Channel 7).

New Languages of Bit Valley, J-Phone, and DoCoMo

Increasingly savvy telecommunications companies are acutely aware of the latent power for instigating social change by strategic deployment of communications and new communications technologies. In 1999, J-Phone ran an ingenious national television commercial campaign which insightfully brandished the slogan "the other standard has come." In this series, a middle-aged salaryman suddenly and for the first time confesses to his wife, "I love you." Shrugging off her husband's unfamiliar advance, he repeats the confession two more times until she recognizes his seriousness. Both appear personally transformed by the outward expression of one's true feelings—a communication style of significant un-Japanese-ness.

A recent *Time* magazine special issue[9] on technologies, language, and social change also explicitly refers to the transformative potential latent in changing the historical dynamics of Japanese communication modes. The writer notes that: "The cell phone has become the weapon of Japan's rebellious new generation, who are fed up with the hierarchies and formalities of their parents' era. In the *i*-mode world, there is no bowing to superiors or lengthy, roundabout language." If these claims were to become a new social reality for the Japanese, the ramifications for the social super-structures would be irreversibly significant.

Jiyuu no mori gakuen: Self-Learning Center

In Saitama Prefecture, the Jiyuu no Mori Gakuen—literally the Freedom Forest School—has challenged the legitimacy of conventional schooling and educational arrangements. In microcosmic form this institution, which practices new ways of learning, represents the experimentally inclined attitude from which new social learning paradigms and arrangements are potentiated.

Television Celebrities (*tarento*) and Their Transformative Potential

Despite the relative apolitical nature of much Japanese television, it appears that postbubble Japanese realities in the form of disgraced politicians, the fall of the salaryman, company restructuring, and the general loss of Japanese confidence has proven too seductive a range of comic material to resist. High-profile Japanese comedians, among them George Tokoro, Beat Takeshi, and Terry Itoh, have all recently published books giving the comic's view on Japan's future and how to transform the nation. Among the infinite variety of mechanisms for undermining dominant images, humor, a strategy Polak refers to as the "comic mirror," can be deployed as one of the most powerful of tools for social transformation.

> Humor is the oldest weapon in the arsenal for attacking the social order and appears in many forms. . . . The main goal of the comic mirror is not amusement but annihilation and, afterwards, reconstruction (though this may not easily be discerned).[10]

Gai-atsu (External Foreign Pressure)

Many influential Japan-watchers have opined that Japan is incapable of change from within. Future-oriented economist Tadashi Nakamae[11] suggests in a concluding section of his book, *Three Futures for Japan,* that in order to facilitate the positive image embodied in the crash and rebirth scenario, "foreign pressure"—*gai-atsu*—will be a primary influence. It is also suggested that Japan's national characteristics of resilience to crisis situations, the samurai spirit, and social solidarity will facilitate transitions to a preferable future society. Elsewhere, it is opined that Japan lacks the ability to transform itself. The author notes that even the changes brought by the Meiji Restoration directly resulted from foreign pressure in the form of the "black ships."[12]

Zainichi gaikoku-jin (Foreign Residents in Japan)

One other form of "foreign pressure" is exerted from within, namely, the increasing numbers of non–Japanese residents in Japan. As their populations increase, cluster into interpretive communities and develop politically effective Japanese language skills, they begin to exert, sometimes consciously but also unwittingly, pressure for social change. There is even a weekly television show, *koko ga hen da yo nihon!* (Japan . . . This Is Really Strange!), that is run like a freak show, yet captures a significant television audience, acting as a rare venue for Japanese and non–Japanese to debate contentious issues of life in Japan.

Furthermore, children from mixed marriages (Japanese to non–Japanese) are beginning to not only significantly alter the Japanese gene pool and the physical topology of the Japanese, but gain recognition as the subtle but powerful agents of change. Although they frequently are the brunt of schoolyard harassment because "they are different," increasingly, it is becoming fashionable to look different, even foreign. Greater acceptance of physical difference may prove to assume a mediatory function in ushering in the acceptance of different ways of being.

The Home-Coming Japanese Youth *(Kikoku-shijou)*

There is an increasing population of Japanese youth returning home from overseas upbringings and educational experiences. These *kikoku-shijou* were recently the subject of investigation on an NHK television series exploring their uniquely formed ideas pertaining to their sense of identity as Japanese, their capacity to fit back into Japanese society, and their own idiosyncratic ideas on the future of Japan. One episode featured these young returnees' life experiences and difficulties assimilating back into Japanese culture, having grown up in non–Japanese environments. It is through this de-familiarizing visual experience that Japan–eared Japanese citizens are encouraged to consider the nature of Japanese uniqueness and the ramifications of the time-honored notion of an original Japanese cultural essence.

Seductive Change Agents

Of all the agents of change in contemporary Japan, time may demonstrate that the most powerful and pervasive have been the new entertainment icons, the modern-day strange attractors, exemplified by the *enfant terrible* of Japan's literary world, Murakami Ryu, and by the New York–schooled singer-songwriter Utada Hikaru, whose biggest-selling CD of all time (at the age of sixteen) has inspired young Japanese to aspire to a new kind of dream, a living example that Japan is capable of producing its own symbols of success. These new change agents who have become famous and wealthy by pursuing their own life plans, are significant influences on Japan's younger generations, who are in search of role models appropriate to the times.

A New Elite/Equality Awareness

It is premature to refer to the emerging social awareness as a movement, but an NHK Television series has been instrumental in highlighting the inherent elitist nature of Japanese social life. Conventional social discourses seldom refer to such elitism. To the contrary, surveys show that most Japanese feel themselves to be middle-class and egalitarian. This simplistic self-perception is easily shattered with even a rudimentary understanding of Japanese social structures. Language, the primal organizer of social realities itself, is exceptionally hierarchical. Deviating from one's place in this hierarchy can have devastating effects on the individual's capacity to cope in society.

The previous list of emerging agents of transformation is by no means exhaustive, nor has it been included according to any preconceived order of personal preference. It illustrates significant awareness of the transformation imperative, and the social forces emerging in direct response to this imperative.

I now turn to a semiotically-dense term mentioned earlier—cool resistance—which I have isolated from the youth specific literature because it displays the characteristics that best describe the social strategies Japanese youth employ to rewrite the futures already colonized by the parent culture. I conclude that this singular terminology harbors the most powerful catalyst for authentic transformative change for today's Japanese youth.

ARTICULATING A TRANSFORMATIVE VISION OUT OF THE PROTOTYPE METAPHOR "COOL RESISTANCE"

Societies cannot safely put off finding collective national goals. A divisive selfishness that makes democracy fragile is the natural condition of a society that has no larger common vision.

—David Calleo[13]

We cannot build a future we cannot imagine. A first requirement, then, is to create for ourselves a realistic, compelling, and engaging vision of the future that can be simply told. If our collective visualization of the future is weak and fragmented, then our capacity to create a future together will be commensurately diminished. Without a strong sense of the future and meaningful orientation for our lives, we can lose confidence in ourselves, our leaders, and our institutions.

—Duane Elgin[14]

Metacriteria for a Future-oriented Social Environment

No transformative vision should attempt perfection or completion; it should be the outline for a set of initial conditions that make the future possible. As previously stated, my ultimate aim in futures thinking is to envision and commit to tangible form something creative, new, not entirely articulated before, possessing transformative power yet firmly grounded in both theory and extensive fieldwork. Japanese youth, no longer satisfied to be the passively "written" social formations of the parent culture and inherited social constructions of reality, are beginning to "write" themselves, in a language exemplified by a new metaphor, *cool resistance*, a term I borrow from Yasumasa Sekiguchi[15] and develop in this chapter. Cool, because it refers explicitly to a new social style. Resistant, because it rejects the cultural paradigm inscribed on the national psyche embodied in the cliché, Japan Inc.

The principle components of the cool resistance vision are the notion of cool itself, and its wider interpretation as a form of beauty/design-driven, minimal living. Resistance, on the other hand implies new communication styles, the macrocatalyst in producing new meanings, new types of discussions, new openings of possibility, new meanings of Japanese-ness, and alternative modes of self-construction and identity creation.

But more than being pure negation of extant social realities and social signification assigned to Japanese society by the parent culture, cool resistance is subtlely creative. To understand how it is creative, it is useful to think of Japan as going through what I call a postnarcotization period. Narcotization is a term from communication theory that refers to a negative effect or dysfunction of the mass media in which mass communications are seen as inducing apathy and political inertia among the mass audience. As Lazarsfeld and Merton have suggested: "increasing dosages of mass communications may be inadvertently transforming the energies of men from active participation into passive knowledge."[16]

Cool resistance represents the linguistic embodiment of defiance toward ready-made social realities. This aesthetics–derived variety of resistance is a pattern that has emerged from the youth in search of meaning and a way of contextualizing their existence from the perspective of their own lives, which no longer seem to be coherent. The current stage of cool resistance may be pre-articulative, which precedes concrete and realizable visions for creating new and better futures.

Therefore, this section presents four metacriteria as the future-oriented super-structure. These four criteria, extant in embryonic form, suggest one conceptual framework for imagining, articulating, and implementing an authentically transformed future that transcends the limitations of inherited future images guiding Japanese youth. The four metacriteria are: (1) cool as philosophical producer of new social meanings; (2) the practice of new modes of communicative-ness that do not contravene indigenous communication styles; (3) strategies for dispelling inherited Japanese myths of uniqueness in order to facilitate the normalization of difference and function as catalyst for alternative forms of self-construction; and (4) a brief reconceptualization of space-time dynamics as a potentiating factor in opening up future possibilities.

(1) **Cool** *as philosophical producer of meaning.* The term *cool* is no arbitrary terminology. *Cool* is the style of the generation, the "means by which cultural identity and social location are negotiated and expressed."[17] Robert Farris Thompson isolates the notion of coolness and develops it into an articulated "aesthetic of the cool" by illustrating its philosophical implications for "right living," especially as it is manifest within the context as a West African/Afro-American metaphor of moral aesthetic accomplishment.[18]

In Japanese terms, contemporary usage and applications of *cool* can be traced to other notions deriving from sophisticated Japanese aesthetic traditions such as *sabi*[19] (rustic beauty), *aware*[20] (the sadness of things, the sensitivity of things), and *yuugen*[21] (tranquility and elegance; the mark of supreme attainment in all of the arts and accomplishments). *Cool* celebrates a modern revival of neglected yet deeply-rooted Japanese aesthetic sensibilities, overwhelmed by the primacy of postwar Homo Economicus. Implied in the original manifesto of contemporary Japanese, *cool* is the philosophy of minimal lifestyle. To his parents, this youth with hair dyed blond and pierced ears is a freak violating the salaryman code of personal style, whereas to himself he is merely demonstrating and living out the innate human proclivity to aestheticize—"make special"[22]—an external world rendered mentally and geographically de-aestheticized by his modernistic parents. *Cool,* too, in the Japanese youth usage, is closely related to Dissanayake's general theory of beauty and making special, in which the human tendency to beautify our environment is more than superficial embellishment—it is a biological imperative.

The fundamental importance of environmental aestheticization is insightfully explained by James Hillman's account on the greater implications of a world that marginalizes beauty. Consider the relevance of these words to Japan's hyperindustrial landscape.

> [A] practice of beauty is economic. . . . Contrary to this usual view, ugliness costs more. What are the economics of ugliness: what is the cost to physical well-being and psychological balance of careless design, of cheap dyes, inane sounds, structures, and spaces? To pass a day in an office under direct glaring light, in bad chairs, victim of the constant monotonous hum of machine noise, looking down at a worn, splotched floor cover, among artificial plants, making motions that are unidirectional, push-button, sagittal in and out that repress the gestures of the body—and then, at day's end, to enter the traffic system or the public transportation system, fast food, project housing—what does this cost? What does it cost in absenteeism; in sexual obsession, school drop-out, overeating and short attention span; in pharmaceutical remedies and the gigantic escapism industries of wasteful shopping, chemical dependency, sports violence, and the disguised colonialism of tourism? Could the causes of major social, political, and economic issues of our time also be found in the repression of beauty?[23]

In the future-oriented communicative social world, there is a shift away from a top-down imposed Homo Economicus way-of-living to an emphasis on maintenance and beautification of the physical environment, crafts-manship, and design orientation. In a Japanese context, one imagines a nationwide re-enchantment with an extraordinary scope and breadth of expressivity in Japanese aesthetics, the underrecognized source of much that is futures-positive, socially constructive, and globally respected about Japan.

(2) The practice of communicativeness. Expanding upon the seminal work of Stevenson and Lennie, I propose the need for a new kind of communication climate, what the authors term a Communicative Age model.[24] I call this a Future-Oriented Communicative Paradigm (FOCP). Building on their work and that of theorists such as Yoshikawa[25] specializing in Japanese communication modes, I suggest a new type of communicative environment that transcends communication as a tool for maintaining current social constructions of meaning.

The future-oriented communicative paradigm facilitates the production of alternative texts through authentic ongoing dialog between the genera-tions and the holders of disparate power relations. By reconceptualizing traditional Japanese power relations—mediated through little-recognized linguistic hierarchies—Japanese youth are re-empowered to participate in the communicative processes leading to new social meanings and trans-formation-potentiating situations. For example, one Japanese communica-tion mode is *awaseru,* a conformist or fitting-in-with-the-other-person mode of communication. As two or more communicants enter a commu-nicative event, it is common to avoid disagreement with the other by sup-pressing one's true feelings (*honne*). With neither communicant communicating honestly, frustration and resentment compile, conversation is perfunctory. Transformation through communication is denied. Pathologies are spawned and proliferate in the communication life-world.

If we re-install a futures-facilitating communicative paradigm in the above communicative event, top-down communication is dislodged from its former naturalized status. If it is now socially acceptable that communi-cation can proceed despite difference and that the ultimate objectives of communication transcend the reiterations of that-which-is-already-known; communication itself assumes new social meanings. In current Japanese social communication, arrangements dictate that communicating to tran-scend, to open up new possible futures which necessarily contest the pre-sent, contravenes Japan's top-down communication mode, a product of a modernistic communication paradigm in which subordination to superiors' commands was the inevitable method for achieving economic rationalist objectives. No argumentation, no dissent—consensus through the fear of humiliation and excommunication from an unforgiving and totalizing corporatist worldview.

Fear of communication is at the heart of many of the social problems perceived to characterize contemporary Japanese youth. By dismantling the fear-producing features inherent in recently constructed communication modes—honorific language, *awaseru* conformity—the threat of excommunication from one's peers if socially unaccepted self-truths are disclosed disappears. This may be instrumental in the prevention of Japan's youth from retreating into the privately controllable worlds of their own bedrooms and into the increasingly artificialized worlds mediated by new communications technologies. Has this deep fear of communicating forced high-schoolers into pathological overreliance on mobile telephones because the consequences of face-to-face contact are too terrible to contemplate?

(3) Dispelling myths of uniqueness and the normalization of difference

The social view of man needs to be balanced by the biological view, in which living organisms are perceived as themselves centers of force.

—Robert W. White[26]

Technologies of the self . . . permit individuals to effect by their own means or with the help of others a certain number of operations on their own bodies and souls, thoughts, conduct, and way of being, so as to transform themselves in order to attain a certain state of happiness, purity, wisdom, perfection, or immortality.

—Michel Foucault[27]

Another prerequisite is the fostering of a future-oriented youth capable of critically dispelling the myths of Japanese cultural uniqueness in order to normalize difference and its negative byproducts. To some extent, exposure to global information has to partly dispelled notions that Japan is unique or superior. Global information access has also brought about a new skepticism about the legitimacy of Japan's past successes and economic miracle. Youth are questioning themselves and the inherited meanings of nation in previously unthinkable ways.

No society obsessed with finicky differentia is a mature society, nor can it offer fair opportunity to pluralistic ethnic social groups. In order to establish a societywide essential "allrightness" of being and doing differently, there needs to be a new understanding about Japan's own cultural roots. Japan is far from a homogeneous uniracial nation of pure Japanese; the simplest analysis of Japan's national evolution reveals the multicultural, multiethnic trajectory of the nation, giving new meanings to the ongoing accelerated ethnicization of the Japanese peoples.

(4) Reconceptualizing space-time.   In a space-time–squeezed environment, as is much of contemporary life for young Japanese, impaired critical thinking and reflective skills diminish abilities to choose between options. This is significant, as White notes, because from "such choices come the individuality that makes each of us a unique person."[28] A future-oriented communicative social milieu would inevitably lead to a systemic questioning and re-evaluating of the other fundamentals of human existence, including space and time, both of which are in short supply to Japanese youth. They are hurried by overschooling and an overscheduled daily timetable, often with time unfolding in confined physical locations with scant regard for human ergonomics.

If we refer to the Japanese words for *human, time,* and *space* (*ningen, jikan, kuukan*), we notice that the second *kanji* character is the same. This *kanji,* simultaneously pronounceable as *kan, aida,* or *ma,* assumes a multiplicity of meanings, anything from interval, space between, time, distance, pause, rest (in music), space (in theater, painting, or architecture), and even leisure. The *kanji—kan—*is especially semiotically dense in Japanese aesthetics, manifest in the imperative of allocating and depicting space in Japanese painting, calligraphy, Noh theater, and architectural spaces. Without appropriate allocation of space and time, the design configuration, whatever medium, is aesthetically unsatisfying. The same concept of space can also be extended to the notion of "leeway," the kind of conceptual social space that allows for error, forgives mistakes, and makes conflict resolution and reconciliation possible.

One paradox of the human condition is the desire to balance the company of others with solitude and time to ourselves. Swamped in the crowd, squashed into confined spaces, deluged by an unrelenting flow of messages, we experience a disorientation as though discommunicated from our true selves. Time alone, we return to our self, we can once again reengage in spontaneous play, be creative—in short, we refind the initial conditions that allow us to be future-oriented. Time is no inconsequential factor in futures dynamics. In postwar Japan, time is salaryman time, corporatized time, CEO time, overtime with compensation time, industrial time, Quality Control time, bullet train hyperscheduled time, cram school after school time. Where is the *ma*—the space-time so important to Japanese aesthetic sensibilities?

I leave this section with the thoughtful theorizing of Maria-Therese Hoppe on how the "ownership of time" is necessarily tied to how a society sees and organizes itself, and that when "a society changes, it is only with changes in the ownership of time that the new society reaches its full effect."[29] The creative resistance of Japanese youth indicates the intensity of will to regain ownership of both space and time with new purposes in mind for the future.

CONSEQUENCES OF A *SHOU GA NAI* FUTURE

The communication of values from one generation to the next takes place under circumstances that favor strong, lasting but uncomprehending acceptance. Thus values become enshrined, and it is far from easy to secure their rational examination in later life.

—Robert W. White[30]

In Japanese, the expression *shou ga nai*, meaning "there is nothing I/we can do about it" or "that's just the way things are," is an utterance so frequent and so internalized by the linguistic paradigm that it subconsciously shapes the cognitive mood of the Japanese nation. It is the linguistic residue of a fatalistic and passive attitude toward life events and the future.

In this current *shou ga nai*–legitimized communication climate—one can expect that in the future, Japanese youth could become more emphatic versions of their current selves. If contemporary futurecratic discourses on Japan's futures, mainly economic futures, continue along present trajectories without public demonstration of willingness to legitimize alternative futures discourses, we can imagine a broad range of negative long-term social effects. Among these might be the widespread infection of social withdrawal, unsustainable intergenerational divisiveness, diminishing employability opportunities for youth, a rapid loss of youth vitality, negative and self-disempowering resistance against the established order of Japan, Inc., and an increasingly chronic lack of workable alternative strategies to replace the obsolete.

Just as in the end of a tragic movie, it takes little to envisage an intensification of the out-migration of Japan's creative youth, departing in search of better personal futures.

NOTES

1. Akira Ujihara, LOGICOM Corp., personal communication with Osaka, May 2000.

2. Robert W. White, *Lives in Progress,* 3rd ed. (Austin, TX: Holt, Rinehart and Winston, 1975): 16.

3. Ibid., 17.

4. Sohail Inayatullah, "Causal Layered Analysis," *Futures* 30, 8 (1998): 815–829.

5. Christopher Wood, *The Bubble Economy: The Japanese Economic Collapse* (Tokyo: Tuttle, 1993).

6. Eleonora Barbieri Masini, in *Rescuing All Our Futures: The Future of Futures Studies,* ed. Ziauddin Sardar (Westport, Conn: Praeger, 1999), 41.

7. Elise Boulding and Kenneth Boulding, *The Futures: Images and Processes* (Thousand Oaks, Calif.: Sage Publications, 1995), viii.

8.   Yasumasa Sekiguchi, "Cool Resistance," *Barfout* (August 1999).

9.   Gregory Beals, "DoCoMO Conquers All," *Newsweek* (July–September 2000): 56.

10.   Fred Polak, *The Image of the Future*, trans. Elise Boulding (New York: Elsevier Scientific Publishing, 1973): 104.

11.   Tadashi Nakamae, ed., *Three Futures for Japan: Long Hollowing or Rebirth—Views from 2020* (Tokyo: Nihon Keizai Shinbunsha, 1999): 256.

12.   Ibid., 260.

13.   Harvey Franklin, *Cul de Sac: The Question of New Zealand's Future* (Urwin Paperbacks: Wellington, NZ, 1985), 163.

14.   Duane Elgin in *Visions of the Future: Why We Need to Teach for Tomorrow,* eds. David Hicks and Catherine Holden (London: Trentham, Books, 1995).

15.   Yasumasa Sekiguchi, "Cool Resistance."

16.   P. F. Lazarsfeld and R. K. Merton, "Mass Communication, Popular Taste and Organized Social Action," *Key Concepts in Communication*, eds. Tim O'Sullivan, John Hartley, Danny Saunders, Martin Montgomery, and John Fiske (London: Routledge, 1994), 194.

17.   Tim O'Sullivan, John Hartley, Danny Saunders, Martin Montgomery, and John Fiske, eds., *Key Concepts in Communication* (London: Routledge, 1994), 305.

18.   Robert Farris Thompson, "An Aesthetic of the Cool," *Uncontrollable Beauty,* eds. Bill Beckley and David Shapiro (New York: Allworth Press, 1998), 371.

19.   Theodore de Bary, ed., "The Vocabulary of Japanese Aesthetics II," *Sources of Japanese Tradition,* vol. I (New York and London: Columbia University Press, 1964): 280.

20.   Ibid., 172.

21.   Ibid., 282.

22.   Ellen Dissanayake, *Homo Aestheticus: Where Art Comes From and Why* (Seattle and Washington: University of Washington Press, 1995).

23.   James Hillman, "The Practice of Beauty," *Uncontrollable Beauty,* eds. Bill Beckley and David Shapiro (New York: Allworth Press, 1998): 265.

24.   Tony Stevenson and June Lennie, "Emerging Designs for Work, Living and Learning in The Communicative Age," *Futures Research Quarterly* (Fall 1995): 5–34.

25.   Jay Muneo Yoshikawa, "Japanese and American Modes of Communication and Implications for Managerial and Organizational Behavior," *Communication Theory: The Asian Perspective,* ed. Wilmal Dissanayake (Singapore: Mass Communication Research and Information Center, 1996).

26.   Robert W. White, *Lives in Progress.*

27.   Michel Foucault in *Reading Foucault for Social Work,* eds. Adrienne S. Chambon, Allan Irving, and Laura Epstein (New York: Columbia University Press, 1999), 18.

28.   Robert W. White, *Lives in Progress*, 128.

29.   Maria-Therese Hoppe, "The Owner of Time has the Power," *Foresigh* 1, 4 (August 1999): 362.

30.   Robert W. White, *Lives in Progress.*

Chapter 8

Reflections Upon the Late-Modern Transition as Seen in the Images of the Future Held by Young Finns

Anita Rubin

I want the future to give me a good job, a family, a flat of my own, a car, a dog and a summer cottage.

This statement was declared by a fifteen-year-old boy in an interview that formed one part of a study into images of the future held by Finnish youths. The research consisted of two surveys and structured theme interviews. This chapter describes some of the results gained from that research and discusses the meaning of those images in the light of the present period of social transition.[1]

The first part of the research was carried out in 1994 and 1995 as a survey at twelve schools and educational institutes situated in different parts of the country—cities, small towns, and the countryside. However, Lapland and the island province of Åland were left out of the study. The surveys were carried out in the schools, and the questionnaires were answered under the supervision of teachers. The respondents were divided into three groups according to age and school level (Table 8.1).

The results of the analysis reveal that young Finnish people share a clearly dichotomic image of the future. When the respondents deal with their own personal futures, the images are bright and full of hope and show a great deal of confidence in their own possibilities for influencing their own futures. However, the further the images go from a personal level, the gloomier and the more hopeless they become, resulting in feelings of having reduced possibilities for affecting the future on the broader national and world levels.

This dichotomy results from the confusion in, and the lack of, social and political direction characteristics of the present time of social transition. In some aspects, the contents of future images rise from the concept of

TABLE 8.1 *School Levels and Students' Age Groups*

School level	Number of schools	Age	Number of survey answers	Number of thematic interviews
Comprehensive schools	4	11, 12	198	10
High schools	3	12, 13, 14, 15	78	10
Vocational institutes and AMK institutions	5	over 17	78	4

modernity and reflect the needs, expectations, and presumptions of industrial rationality. In other aspects, they already reflect the qualities of change toward late modernity and the late industrial age in society. It is further argued that the concepts of late modernity, late industrial socioeconomic rationality, and the information society have an explanatory power consistent with the empirical findings of young people's images of the future.

INDIVIDUALIZATION AND INCONSISTENCY AS LATE-MODERN CHARACTERISTICS

According to Peter Berger and Thomas Luckmann, society manifests itself to individuals both as a subjective and an objective reality.[2] While the objective reality is composed of organisms such as society and its institutions, the subjective reality is composed of individual experiences of everyday life—the experience of reality. Knowledge about this reality is transmitted and constructed in social processes.

One of the main features of the present late modern information age[3] is the confusion produced by the mixture of simultaneous but contradictory aspects—old and new, modern and "postmodern."[4] Completely antagonistical incidents and processes take place simultaneously, yet do not eliminate each other.[5] Paradoxically, while the transition has brought about a number of technology-originated changes that have resulted in the collective foundations of social life becoming more obscure, the powerful frameworks of modernity—such as education systems, school, and the principles guiding their development—still affect both society and individual people.

For instance, young people have to spend much longer periods in a state of semidependency than before. Even though the variety of lifestyles and possibilities has grown, it has become economically more difficult for young people to start living on their own. Many young people in Finland cannot find a permanent job comparable to their long years of studying, at least not very easily. The labor market does not offer steady jobs readily. Youth unemployment seems to have become more a permanent than merely a temporary state of affairs that can be dealt with by better social decision making. The educational phase has become prolonged because jobs require more specialized skills. The "youth" life stage is therefore becoming longer through a combination of increased economic dependency on the family and prolonged education.[6]

A young person probably cannot improve upon the quality of life of his parents, although, according to many studies, a high standard of life, better education, and material welfare still today benefit those young people whose parents have had the same qualifications.[7] It is possible that this generation is the first one for many centuries that cannot attain a better life and more material goods than their parents did, although the social structures and institutions still reflect this as their basic, modern task.[8]

Young people today are caught up in these transitory pressures and conflicting demands. They find themselves left alone in a society that increasingly emphasizes individuality and places responsibility on the individual self to build a happy and prosperous life. Furlong and Cartmel speak of the illusion of individuality created by the breakdown of collective youth transitions—again a sign of conflicting social phenomena.[9] It has brought about completely new forms of vulnerability. Lifestyles are increasingly shaped by certain actors behind the markets and thus do not necessarily express true individual choice. Instead, those who lack resources to participate in consuming "lifestyle products" might end up in financial as well as cultural exclusion.

It seems that the traditional division of time into past, present, and future is breaking down for the benefit of the enlarging present. Youth cultures and lifestyles emphasize phenomenal and immediate, real-time sensations. Thus the experience of the present is taking space from the past and also perhaps from the future, that is, it is reducing young people's knowledge of the past and the future.

Concurrent with social transition is the growth of individualization—the concepts of how to build a life are changing and multiplying. Young people are breaking loose from the institutional ties and constructing their lives rather as personal "self-projects."[10] Social interaction and communication with others continuously renew the reality of everyday life, both on an individual and a social level.

However, the process of individualization separates young people into small units, or tribes, within society, and during this process they cease to understand, or even care for, large social systems.[11] On the other hand, society can also be seen as restructuring into larger, even global, and network-like entities, bound loosely together by economic or cultural factors.[12] Thus the collective ways of thinking, which derived from society as it used to be—arbiters of guidelines or terms for everyday decision-making and activities—do not guide young people in their choices anymore. Instead, they adapt their actions and decisions to their current variety of social situations and to the needs those alternative situations seem to evoke.[13]

Ulrich Beck says that the people who live in this period of change have to plan, write, arrange, darn, and patch their own biographies, and act, stage, show, and direct their own stories, identities, social networks, commitments, and ideologies.[14] Therefore, young people are urged to create themselves unaided by, but in communication with, others, thus forming their identity via the dialogic process of accepting and abandoning the views of oneself created by others.[15] This is a growing paradox for a young person trying to be successful in the information age.

This social interdependency brings a heavy burden of responsibility on young shoulders to deal with such necessities as choosing an economically and socially successful education line and career, adopting the right kind of values, and so on.

All this brings social responsibility as well as confusion and moral problems back into our discussion because they can put the aim of an individual in conflict with aims of wider society. Finnish society has long valued strong stamina and the ethos of coping. However, the present Finnish trend is the withdrawal of a collective ethos[16] as social structures are replaced by information structures and the old, traditional collectivity disappears. Young people feel more and more insecure and confused, powerless when facing social and political phenomena, especially on the global level.[17] Morals and values become private matters and norms fluctuate and become indefinite,[18] while social ties loosen and young people's social integration weakens in the process.

This means that among young people, features from both "postmodernity,"[19] and modernity (and sometimes even premodernity) are merging.

The Dichotomic Images of Future: Empirical Results

The following generalizations about images of the future held by young Finns are made from their personal, national, and global imagining of what the future will be like in some fifty years from the present day. Their general images are constructed from answers to the first questionnaire and the theme interviews.[20]

Young people's images of their personal future in Finland are rather conventional by nature and reflect the generally accepted values and attitudes.[21] The image is a success story of a wealthy suburban family living happily in a beautiful private house not far from the city, but not in the countryside, either. The family is composed of the parents—that is, the young themselves in the future—and two children, a daughter and a son. The parents have just retired and or are about to retire, own a summer cottage, a boat, and two cars. (The only truly future-related phenomenon is the description of the two cars as electric.) The house is made of bricks or wood and is very much like normal Finnish family houses today.

The couple has been happily married since their youth. Both parents have had successful and upwardly mobile careers: they are now in good positions as lawyers, doctors, teachers, or private entrepreneurs. The country youth describe themselves as running a well-to-do farm. The parents have also managed to give their children a similarly sound education and thus provide future society with still more well-to-do doctors, lawyers, and so on. Unemployment has not really touched them personally, although it is clearly recognized as a future-related problem. The image occasionally includes short periods of personal unemployment right after graduation, but this is regarded as important only in very general terms, not as forming a possible future course for one's own life.

However, when the focus turns from the personal future to the future of society and the world, the story changes into a tale of horror. Finland's future is described as a society of corruption, unemployment, growing environmental problems, drugs, and dirty urban centers full of poor people struggling for their livelihood. The population has swelled with economic and environmental refugees, especially from Eastern Europe and Russia, and this growth has caused the welfare state and its administration to collapse.

An alternative image indicates that the population in Finland has sunk—all those who could afford to have gone away to wealthier lands, and only the poor and those with less initiative have stayed. Corruption, crime, and uncontrollable violence have taken over, and the use of drugs and alcohol brings the only escape from the gloomy reality. There has been some kind of an environmental disaster quite close to the Finnish borders—a nuclear power plant has exploded or a war has broken out—and that has spoiled the lakes and forests so that one cannot swim, ski, hike, hunt, camp, or pick berries and mushrooms anymore.

The future of the world is described as a devastating mess of hunger, wars, overpopulation, and pollution, with no hope or sign of any improvement in sight. The oceans have become huge pools of oil waste and dirt; the rain forests have been destroyed and global warming has caused huge droughts; the wars have driven millions of hungry people to wander from their homes westward or northward, and famines and large AIDS-like epidemics have burst out everywhere.

While the views of the future of Finland and the world are oppressive and threatening, one's personal future is envisioned as a fulfillment of personal dreams. At the end of each interview session, the interviewees were asked

how they would find it possible for their own bright futures to become true
in the gloomy world they just presented. How could they live a happy life
and carry on with their successful careers in this kind of disastrous world? At
this point, the interviewees became puzzled and had no answer. The same
dichotomic dilemma can be seen in the questionnaire answers written down
by a seventeen-year-old high school girl student, who was asked what she
would say as a retired person to her grandchildren:

> Important events: Wars, leaks from nuclear power plants, explosive population
> growth which has to be controlled, new and different diseases, many new
> inventions. . . .
> Personal Achievements: Started a family, worked, and started own small
> animal clinic.

A twenty-one-year-old woman studying at a vocational school answers
the same question:

> Important events: People have messed everything up, the waters are polluted
> causing animals and nature to die. The ozone layer has thinned so that it is not
> possible to live outside. . . .
> Personal Achievements: Started my own business, which was successful. Got
> married and started a family.

A large number of young people in Finland seem to have lost the long-
lasting belief in the ideal of economic growth and in the value of the constant struggle for increased welfare. Life in the future in general was
regarded by 50 percent of the female respondents and 40 percent of the
male respondents as not as good as the present. The old idea of the parents struggling for a better future for their children does not seem realistic
anymore to the little brothers and sisters of the previous decade's
Generation X,[22] even though they still cherish the very same ideal for their
own children. In addition, 47 percent of the female and 38 percent of the
male respondents saw the future as more or less predestined and saw the
lives of individuals determined and steered by forces which they cannot
affect.

It must be remembered, however, that the research was carried out
during the recession in Finland. This colored the tone of the images as well
as some big national and international issues, such as joining the European
Union (EU). In addition to the historical facts and phenomena, the
dichotomy needs explanation from a wider social level.

Discussion

The future has a two-way effect on human decision-making and planning processes. First people are aware that their current decisions and

actions affect the future by narrowing the variety of possible future alternatives. At the same time, the image of a specific future state in the given question has an impact on a person's present decision-making, at the individual as well as at the social level. Thus, the individual idea of the future, together with the prevailing social ideas of it, influence the general direction of decision-making and actions in the present day.[23] This reciprocal process is dialectic as well as interactive in character.

Results of some previous studies in Sweden and Finland show that people tend to cast current visible problems into the future, and then construct their life strategies accordingly, that is, they plan for the future, but do not have foresight.[24] This easily leads to a reactive life strategy instead of a proactive one, in which people give up self-management, and control over their own future gets lost. Young people who feel they can affect the future also find the future as controllable and encompassing, and are able to foresee. Their actions are goal-directed and purposeful; they strive to create strategies to plan their own future to make it the best possible.[25] On the other hand, those young people who do not feel that they can affect the future find it confusing, impossible to outline, and often preordained and inflexible. When facing this kind of a future, they continuously return to their original aims and strategies, but instead of seeing a new way forward they reinterpret the present situation over and over again. That way, they never end up in dealing with or changing their actual image of the future.[26] As a result, they give up a large part of their ability to affect the forces of transition because they are unable to imagine alternative futures. This limits their freedom of choice and reduces their proactive abilities.

The contradictory expectations and models, derived partly from the fading industrial age and partly from the emerging information age, conflict to the point where young people are now left with difficult personal selections and decisions to make regarding their own future. This moment may come, for instance, when a person has to choose a main study subject, profession, start a family with a girlfriend or boyfriend, or search for a job. In this situation, the dilemma becomes visible. The social environment, its institutional structures (e.g. school system, social system, and so on), or personal experiences do not necessarily support a young person in this decision-making process anymore, at least not as clearly as they used to.

The dichotomy, antagonism, and discontinuities in the images young Finnish people envision of the future indicate that the images derive from different—but simultaneous—time interpretations. It seems that the personal positive images are based on and interpreted from the processes of primary socialization, which still strongly lean on the needs and values of the industrial, modern era. At the same time, the images of the future that deal with issues away from one's personal life and possibilities reveal features based on the late-modern, late-industrial era.

It is apparent that there exists an unchanging picture of what a good and happy life is or should be like. The high expectations for a personal future take the form of happiness and success that reflects the way young people understand those values, interpret social expectations, and translate them into the language used to define success and happiness for decades. Finnish youth's expectations of their own future, evaluations, and objectives have changed very little in recent years, while the social context in which these objectives and expectations should come true has changed rapidly.[27]

Youth's prevailing images of the future on a personal level are based on the ideas and values of the welfare state model and its basic social unit, the nuclear family, which are the focus of the social and educational functions of the industrial phase. These functions answer to the needs and expectations typical of the industrial era. Thus the idea of how to define success and happiness also derives from this model—the positive expectations derive from an optimistic strategy that promotes a straightforward drive for success.[28] These ideals and this model are deeply rooted in the minds and expectations of the youth, as can be seen in the contents of the images.

On the other hand, young people's images of the state-level future and global future are based on diversified, but not profound, information about global problems with such as the environment, diminishing resources, and population growth. These images derive mainly from the various phenomena caused by the constant inflow of new information and from the values at the center of the problem-centered education and forms of production of the transitional information society. In this aspect, the images of Finnish youth are very much like those of young people elsewhere.[29]

Does this mean that young people will feel themselves failures if they are not able to reach the standards of a "good life" or "success," which still prevail in their minds and anticipations? Or, to the contrary, are they going to blame society for failing to provide the welfare they see as their birthright? The contradictory situation might result in an inability to act, indifference, reluctance to make decisions for one's future, or passive and negative reactions to decision-making and cynical, indifferent, or even hostile attitudes to the functions and practices of society. It can also increase the tendency toward heedless use of alcohol and/or drugs, as well as induce depression and psychosomatic and physical symptoms of illness, such as eating disorders. The situation also can push young people to searching for somebody else to blame for their oppressive feelings and unsatisfactory life conditions. Moreover, it might spur support for various antisocial, religious, or extremist groups, which are more able to provide young people with a clear worldview, strict value structure, sense of right and wrong, and an authoritarian model to which it is easy to adjust in these days of confusion and change. In the worst case, all this can end up in alienation from society and its processes.

Therefore, the present strategy for the future should be based on alternatives—on recognizing possible alternative futures and then on choosing the best and the most preferable for all. This, naturally, calls for an ability to assess values and discuss them. However, this is still a more challenging task in these days when value structures lose the authority of their content; the knowledge of alternative values offers new life opportunities; and cultural habits, practices, and ways of living pour in from the mass media and new technology.

The transition thus poses a great challenge to educators, parents, and decision-makers in their efforts to increase young people's optimism. This requires new methods to help young people in their struggle for personal growth. Emphasis should be turned to young people's coping strategies in order to make their aims and images of the future more realistic—reachable, but still positive. This viewpoint in education and youth policy will encourage a proactive attitude toward the future by showing real possibilities to affect the world and increase faith in the future on national and global terms.

NOTES

1. The research has been fully reported in Anita Rubin, *The Images of the Future of Young Finnish People* (Turku: Turku School of Economics and Business Administration, 1988).

2. Peter L. Berger and Thomas Luckmann, *The Social Construction of Reality,* trans. T. Aittola and V. Raiskila (Helsinki: Like, 1995).

3. For example, Manuel Castells, "The Information Age: Economy, Society and Culture," vol. I, *The Rise of the Network Society* (Oxford: Blackwell Publishers, 1996); Manuel Castells, "The Information Age: Economy, Society and Culture," vol. III, *The End of Millennium* (Oxford: Blackwell Publishers, 1998).

4. Andy Furlong and Fred Cartmel, *Young People and Social Change: Individualization and Risk in Late-Modernity.* Series Sociology and Social Change. (Buckingham, U.K.: Open University Press, 1997).

5. Paul Davies, *The Cosmic Blueprint: New Discoveries in Nature's Creative Ability to Order the Universe* (New York: Simon & Schuster, 1988).

6. Gary Pollock, "Individualization and the Transition from Youth to Adulthood," *Young* 5, 1 (1997): 55–68.

7. Andy Furlong and Fred Cartmel, *Young People;* see also Jari-Erik Nurmi *Whose Training Routes? Widening Higher Education and Selection* (translated from Finnish) (Turku: University of Turku, 1997).

8. Douglas Coupland, *Generation X: Tales for an Accelerated Culture*, trans. M-L. Tirkkonen (Juva: Art House, 1991.)

9. Andy Furlong and Fred Cartmel, *Young People,* 41–44; 109–111.

10. Kai Ilmonen, "Is Finland Bbreaking Up?" *Tiedepolitiikka* 1 (1996): 21–28.

11. Michel Maffessoli, *The Time of the Tribes: The Decline of Individualism in Mass Society,* trans. D. Smith (London: Sage Publications, 1996).

12. Manuel Castells, *The Information Age . . . .*

13.   Erik Allardt "Science and the Fundamental Questions," (in Finnish) *Tiedepolitiikka* 20, 4 (1995): 5–12.

14.   Ulrich Beck, "The Reintervention of Politics: Towards a Theory of Reflexive Modernization," in *Reflexive Modernization: Politics, Tradition and Aesthetics in the Modern Social Order* (Cambridge, U.K.: Polity Press, 1994): 1–55.

15.   Charles Taylor, *The Ethics of Authenticity* (Cambridge and London: Harvard University Press, 1991).

16.   Kai Ilmonen, "Is Finland Breaking Up?"

17.   Charles Taylor, *The Ethics of* . . . .

18.   Zygmundt Bauman, *Postmodern Ethics* (Oxford, Cambridge: Blackwell, 1993).

19.   Modernity and postmodernity are understood as varying aspects within present reality. As concepts, they offer ways of differentiating and grouping together contemporary social phenomena that co-exist and that can result from each other in a dialectic process, the latter appearing from the maturing process of the previous. See e.g., Zygmundt Bauman, "A Sociological Theory of Postmodernity," in *Intimations of Postmodernity* (London: Routledge, 1992).

20.   For more details, see Anita Rubin, *The Images of the Future* . . . .

21.   For similar interpretations, see Helena Helve *"The Worldview of Young People: A Follow-up Study Among Finnish Youth Living in a Suburb of Metropolitan Helsinki"* (in Finnish) (Tutkimuksia ja selvityksiä 1/87, Kansalaiskasvatuksen keskus: Helsinki, 1987).

22.   In the way Coupland (1991) described it in his famous novel.

23.   Helena Helve, *The World View*, 154; Sohail Inayatullah, "From 'Who Am I?' to 'When Am I?' Framing the Shape and Time of the Future," *Futures* 25, 3 (1993): 235–253; Anita Rubin, *The Images of the Future* . . . .

24.   Åke Bjerstedt, "Conceptions of Future Threats and Developments: Psychological Starting Points and Educational Possibilities," in *Society and the Environment,* eds. U. Svedin and B. Aniasson (Netherlands: Kluwer Academic Publishers, 1992), 229–255; Pirkko Remes, *Futures Readiness in Vocational Adult Education* (Jyväskylä: Research Institute of Pedagogy, 1992).

25.   Åke Bjerstedt, "Conceptions of. . . ."; Jari-Erik Nurmi "Aims, Means and Illusions—A Human Being as the Maker of His/Her Future," *Tiedepolitiikka* 1 (1995): 5–12.

26.   Jari-Erik Nurmi, "Aims, Means . . . ."

27.   Maarja-Liisa Rauste, "Young People's Concept of the Human Being and the Images of the World II: Girls' Concept of the Human Being," (in Finnish) *Turun yliopiston psykologian laitoksen tutkimuksia* 14, Turku (1974); Maarja-Liisa Rauste-von Wright and Riita Kinnunen, "Young People's Concept of the Human Being and the Images of the World VII: Young People's Time Perspective as the Outliner of the Image of the World," *Turun yliopiston psykologian laitoksen tutkimuksia* 55, Turku (1983).

28.   Jari-Erik Nurmi, "Adolescent Orientation to the Future: Development of Interests and Plans, and Related Attributions and Affects, in the Life-Span Context,"

Commentationes Scientarium Socialium 39, (Helsinki: The Finnish Society of Sciences and Letters, 1989).

29. Richard Eckersley, "Young Australians' Views of the Future," *Youth Studies Australia* 15, 3 (September 1988): 11–17; David Hicks and Cathie Holden, *Visions of the Future—Why we Need to Teach for Tomorrow* (Staffordshire: Trentham Book, 1988).

Chapter 9

Imagining the Future:
Youth in Singapore

Alfred L. Oehlers

CONFORMITY AND DISSENT ACROSS SOUTHEAST ASIA

Following the outbreak of the financial crisis, young Thais took to the streets of Bangkok to protest the government's mishandling of developments. Largely because of their agitation, the government subsequently fell and was replaced by an administration more closely representing their aspirations and visions for the future. Similarly, in Indonesia, young student protesters were at the forefront of the popular revolt against the Suharto presidency. Acting in concert with other sections of Indonesian society, these students eventually forced the resignation of Suharto and set their country on a new path of evolution.

These recent events in Thailand and Indonesia are extremely momentous and noteworthy in themselves. For present purposes, though, they are also highly significant in one other important regard: they clearly demonstrate that youth in Southeast Asia are an increasingly potent force, capable of instigating major social, economic, and political change. Increasingly, youth in the region are articulating independent visions of the future, very often at odds with established wisdoms. Moreover, they are fully prepared to agitate in support of these views, despite the evident risks to life and limb. An increasingly vocal, articulate, and committed force is taking shape in Southeast Asia, capable of fundamentally altering the futures of countries in the region.

The strength of such youth, of course, varies considerably from country to country, with Indonesia and Thailand perhaps representing one extreme of the spectrum. At the other end, one may identify countries such as Singapore, conspicuous by the distinct lack of any form of youth protest, organization, or movement, despite recent upheavals in the region. In sharp contrast to their brothers and sisters in neighboring countries, youth in Singapore appear to be content to conform to visions of the future elaborated by the ruling Peoples' Action Party (PAP), rather than articulating and pursuing their own. Many, indeed, appear to subscribe fully to the conservative values championed by the PAP and which will lie at the foundation of a PAP-defined future.

This high degree of conformity and compliance to PAP-defined ideals may seem somewhat puzzling. If the readiness of Singapore youth to embrace the latest global fads and fashions is any indication, Singapore must surely rank as one of the most open societies in Southeast Asia. Given this, it may be reasonable to expect youth in that country to be influenced by alternative ideas, and through their exposure to global popular culture, to be perhaps even slightly rebellious in this respect. Singapore youth, moreover, are one of the most affluent, highly educated, and articulate in the region, easily qualifying as one of the most capable of forming a vision independent of the established order. Indeed, on the basis of these qualities, observers have long held high expectations for Singapore youth. Believing them to be "a force for . . . political change," seeking "greater autonomy from the PAP state in an attempt to take more control over their lives,"[1] many were convinced Singapore youth possessed a "strong desire for participation and a high level of political awareness"[2] and were capable of posing challenges for the ruling party.

This chapter attempts to shed some light on this puzzle. As it will be suggested, the high level of conformity to a PAP-defined future among youth in Singapore is largely a product of the pervasive social and political controls exercised by the state in that country. Through such controls, the PAP has successfully cultivated and reproduced in youth those key conservative values lying at the center of its future vision, while at the same time, suffocated the emergence of any competing alternative.

To begin, the following section briefly reviews the vision of the future most recently elaborated by the PAP and the extent to which youth in Singapore subscribe to the conservative values underpinning this. In Section 3, the discussion considers the various social and political controls operating in Singapore that cultivate and reproduce these values. Section 4 concludes the chapter by commenting on some likely implications for Singapore.

The PAP Vision and Youth in Singapore

The task of defining a future vision for Singapore is not something new to the PAP. Since coming to power in 1959, the party has issued a succession of edicts on the future of the tiny island republic, each accompanied by meticulous plans providing extensive support and defining precise roles for citizens. In the early 1960s, for example, as part of a broader effort to win entry to the Malayan Federation, the vision that was articulated espoused a "Malayanised" Singapore. Supported by a broad range of measures in education, language, culture, and the arts, citizens were exhorted to embrace Malayan identity, customs, and way of life. Following Singapore's expulsion from the federation and emergence as an independent republic in 1965, this vision was drastically altered. Together with a strategy that sought to develop Singapore into an international manufacturing and financial center under the umbrella of Western capital, it was envisioned that Singapore's future lay in an open, competitive society, much along Western lines. In keeping with this, Singaporeans were encouraged to be individualistic and materialistic go-getters, pursuing economic achievement above all else.

The PAP's most recent effort at to define a future vision has its origins as far back as the early 1980s. At that stage, having exhausted the opportunities for labor-intensive export-oriented industrialization, the PAP was seeking to launch Singapore on a new path of development, with skills, knowledge, and high technology as the new pillars of economic development. While there was little dispute about the economic foundation for the future, considerable apprehension existed over the sort of moral values that would guide the future behavior of citizens. The PAP was concerned that the individualism and materialism of Singaporeans it had once encouraged had reached excessive proportions. A new set of values was sought to replace these now undesirable qualities and to underpin the new society to be created.

Around this time, cultural explanations for the economic rise of East Asia were coming into vogue. Both internationally as well as locally in Singapore, a variety of commentators increasingly asserted that it was East Asia's common Confucian heritage that lay behind the region's economic dynamism. Tapping into this line of reasoning, the PAP began to suggest that traditional Confucian values perhaps offered the most appropriate foundation for Singapore's future development. As they were responsible for the past success of the region, such values, it was reasoned, virtually guaranteed Singapore would remain economically vibrant into the future. Further, given the inherent conservatism of such values, they would serve as a highly effective check against the perceived moral decay of Singaporeans and the dangers of creeping liberalism.

Subsequent discussions during the 1980s would refine official thinking on these issues, eventually culminating in the adoption of the following five shared values in 1991 as a guide for Singapore's future social and political development.

1. Nation before community and society before self;
2. Family as the basic unit of society;
3. Community support and regard for the individual;
4. Consensus, not conflict, as the basis of national decision making;
5. Racial and religious harmony.[3]

Though the PAP argued otherwise, it was clear that Confucian thinking strongly influenced elements of these shared values. The first, for example, drew heavily on Confucian notions of hierarchy and political order in asserting the primacy of society over the individual and all that this implied for civil rights. Similarly, the second value, elevating the traditional family as the preferred unit of social organization, has long been recognized as a hallmark of Confucian tradition, with its emphasis on marriage, patriarchal family structures, and filial piety. Last, the insistence on orderly, consensual decision making under the fourth value was clearly related to the Confucian abhorrence of conflict in civil society and the attendant dangers of disorder and turmoil.[4]

To what extent were these shared values and their Confucian foundations accepted by Singaporeans? Judging by the muted protests and limited discussion these prompted, one might conclude the population generally concurred with the overall tenor of these values. A variety of survey findings lends some support to this interpretation. With particular reference to youth, these clearly indicated a vein of support for the sort of Confucian thinking lying at the root of the entire shared values project.

With respect to the primacy of society over individuals and the concomitant curtailment of individual rights, for instance, surveys suggested Singapore youth were quite comfortable with this loss of civil liberties, as evidenced by the low ranking consistently accorded to such rights as the freedom of expression. Moreover, as one survey showed, as many as half (47 percent) agreed with the statement, "Personally, I don't care about human rights issues."[5] Similar sentiments were echoed in other studies. In a survey conducted by David Hitchcock, for example, none of the Singapore respondents considered personal freedom or individual rights to be of critical significance.[6] In yet another survey, respondents displayed a high level of tolerance of official censorship. On average, more than 60 percent approved of government controls on newspapers, television, cinema, and the Internet.[7]

This conservative bent in Singapore youth was also very evident in their thinking about marriage, family, and filial piety. For many, marriage remained the predominant basis of cohabitation, with very few entering into de facto relationships or living as single parents.[8] Many young Singaporeans also continued to subscribe to traditional gender roles within marriage. As a national survey of recently married couples revealed, three-quarters believed that husbands should remain the main provider, while two-thirds accepted that women should do more household chores than men.[9] Yet another survey revealed that many couples continued to hold traditional views on the purpose of marriage. A vast majority of respondents (72 percent) accepted that the main reason was procreation and the continuation of the family line. Less than a third (29 percent) mentioned companionship or love.[10] For many, the issue of filial piety was also highly significant. In a study of youth attitudes and beliefs, an overwhelming 91.8

percent of respondents believed in being filial to their parents, while an equally impressive 92.4 percent indicated they would support their aged parents.[11]

Finally, mention should be made of young Singaporeans' attitudes toward consensus and the avoidance of conflict and disorder. Studies have shown a strong tendency among Singapore youth to compromise whenever major differences in opinion arise. Reflecting this trait, nearly half (46.1 percent) the respondents in a study strongly disagreed that one should fight rather than compromise in a given situation.[12] Many, moreover, held a profound regard for law and order, with as many as 62 percent strongly agreeing that authority must be respected without question.[13] At the same time, there seemed to be little tolerance of those who failed to honor this: more than three-quarters of respondents approved of the harsh punishment customarily meted out to convicted criminals in Singapore.[14]

To summarize, in sketching its vision of a future Singapore, the PAP drew heavily on traditional Confucian values to establish a moral foundation to guide the future behavior of citizens. It would appear, moreover, that most young Singaporeans readily identified with the conservative values the PAP was seeking to cultivate. But why was this the case? How may this close correspondence between the views of the young and those of officialdom be explained? If Singapore's outspoken former prime minister and current senior minister, Lee Kuan Yew, is to be believed, the answer to these questions is quite straightforward. According to Lee, the values pursued by the PAP were already culturally ingrained in the young; they were the "software," so to speak, of young Singaporeans, inherited from the past and immutable despite their extensive exposure to the West.[15] While there may be some truth to Lee's remarks, it must be recognized that a number of other processes at work in Singapore contributed to the cultivation and perpetuation of such conservative values among young Singaporeans. The state's pervasive social and political controls were some of the most important of these, and shall be discussed in the following section.

ENFORCING THE VISION

It is by now well known that the state has an ubiquitous presence in Singapore. Through a variety of instruments, the ruling PAP influences virtually all aspects of citizens' lives.[16] The array of instruments at the state's disposal is quite extensive. In what follows, the discussion focuses only on a small sample of the more significant and interesting of these, through which conservative values have been cultivated in the young.

The Education System

By far the most important in this regard must be the education system. By manipulating the curriculum, the state has introduced material that is explicitly supportive of traditional, conservative values. A good, and by no means isolated, example of this was the introduction of Confucian studies during the 1980s.[17] Beyond the curriculum, however, it should also be pointed out that the highly competitive nature of the education system serves as a fertile breeding ground for conservative attitudes. As many observers have noted, quite apart from encouraging "rote learning, cramming, lack of creativity and the breeding of obedient technocrats and bureaucrats,"[18] the intense competition engendered by the system produces a uniquely Singaporean trait: *kiasu* behavior.[19] Translated from the local Hokkien dialect, the term *kiasu* means, quite literally, "a fear of losing." This unusual trait sheds considerable light on the conservatism of Singaporeans, both young and old alike. Accustomed to high standards of living—a product of existing social and political arrangements—most Singaporeans would balk at doing anything that might remotely jeopardize these arrangements. Many consequently tend to frown on liberal Western social and political values. As these may precipitate the wholesale unraveling of society and the destruction of everything that the people's prized prosperity rests upon, they are rejected completely.[20]

National Service

This bias toward retaining the existing framework of social and political relations is reinforced by another key instrument of control: national service. In Singapore, all males attaining the age of eighteen are required to perform at least two years of military service. During this time, they are immersed in a hierarchical and authoritarian that cultivates an intense nationalism, as well as discipline and an unswerving obedience to authority. Emerging from this stint in the military, most young males would identify strongly with the prevailing set of social and political relations. They would, as well, have a deep respect for authority (both military and civilian),[21] and given their strong sense of nationalism, a greater preparedness to place society's interests above those of the individual.

Legislation

Beyond the education system and military service, a wide range of statutes and government policies encourage the retention of traditional values. Singapore, for example, is unique among countries by having an explicit law that makes children responsible for the care of aged parents (the Maintenance of Parents Act, passed by Parliament in 1994). Under its provisions, "deserted" parents may sue children for compensation and maintenance. Several other policies also encourage the preservation of traditional intergenerational ties. The state's housing policies, for instance, accord extended family units priority in housing allocation. In a country where more than three-quarters of the population live in public housing, this is a powerful instrument ensuring the respect of traditional customs.[22]

The Mass Media

Any discussion of social and political control in Singapore would be seriously lacking if it failed to mention the mass media. Given the state's complete control over the print, television, and radio media, it has at its disposal an extremely powerful instrument to influence public opinion and values. The media has been used extensively in the past to popularize traditional values.[23] During the push to inculcate Confucian or "Asian" values, for instance, it was a matter of course to see, hear, and read messages extolling the virtues of such values and cajoling citizens to adopt them. From television, radio, and newspaper commercials, to billboards in subway stations, to banners strung across streets, these inescapable messages probably played no small role in influencing the thinking of the young. Apart from these traditional values, the media has also been used to promote nationalism, and most particularly, an attachment to the status quo. It is not uncommon, for example, for catchy songs and jingles singing the praises of the existing order to be given extensive airtime. On television, these same jingles are accompanied by footage that highlight grand achievements, a towering city skyline, and the like.[24] While debatable, it would be reasonable to presume that such catchy tunes and impressive imagery would have had some impact on the young, perhaps contributing toward their more conservative disposition. Finally, before leaving this discussion of the media, mention should also be made of one other stage-managed event that has profoundly affected on the consciousness of young Singaporeans: the annual National Day Parades. As a recent study shows, these are spectacular events that are carefully choreographed and managed to instill awe and admiration of the prevailing order.[25] For many young Singaporeans, they have precisely that effect, while also raising their nationalistic fervor and willingness to sacrifice for the good of "Singapore." These parades, as such, are yet another device through which conservatism in the young may be cultivated and any desire for fundamental change forestalled.

Consequences of Dissent

Pervasive as these social and political controls in Singapore are, they do, however, occasionally fail. Instances have arisen in the past where young Singaporeans have emerged to challenge the received wisdom and ideological hegemony of the PAP. University student movements have been prominent in this regard, especially during the late 1960s and up to the mid-1970s. More recently though, it has principally been young Christians drawing on Liberation Theology or strands of fundamentalist evangelical thought.[26] In all these cases, the state has invoked the notorious Internal Security Act to crush these movements. Activists have been arrested and subjected to grueling interrogation, through which signed "confessions" have then been obtained criminalizing their activities.[27] For other young Singaporeans, the lessons to be learned from these well-publicized affairs are abundantly clear. Any attempt to criticize or challenge the existing order would not be tolerated and would be dealt with severely by the state. At a general level, the resulting climate of fear ensures that the young will be unwilling to entertain or express opinions contrary to the established wisdom. As a result of the intimidation exercised by the state, a conformity to traditional conservative values is enforced.

To summarize, there exist in Singapore a wide range of instruments that both cultivate and perpetuate traditional conservative values. Even when these instruments fail, the state has available to it punitive measures to ensure compliance and the destruction of any alternatives. In light of this, it should not be surprising that the young in Singapore subscribe so fully to the conservative values and visions espoused by the PAP. This is, ultimately, a product of deliberate and conscious social engineering by the state.

TOWARD A MORE LIBERAL FUTURE?

In comparison with their contemporaries in some other Southeast Asian nations, youth in Singapore show a remarkable readiness to conform to visions of the future elaborated by their ruling government. As this chapter has suggested, this should not be surprising. Singapore youth have internalized the core conservative assumptions underpinning this state-defined vision. This process of internalization, in turn, may largely be attributed to the pervasive social and political controls in Singapore that have cultivated and reproduced such values while stifling the ability of youth to freely elaborate any alternatives.

These extensive controls on youth in Singapore are likely to have some negative repercussions. As the PAP itself has begun to realize, the numerous constraints on youth may well prove counterproductive to Singapore's high-tech future. Using the education system to illustrate this point, it is increasingly evident to the PAP that its controls on education retard independent thinking, imagination, and creativity in students—characteristics which are essential to develop a knowledge and technology-based economy.[28] More widely, the party has also recognized that its extensive political and social controls have alienated a considerable proportion of the citizenry and eroded many citizen's commitment to the nation. The consequent proclivity of Singaporeans—especially the younger and more talented—to emigrate is looked upon by the party with increasing alarm.[29]

Singapore 21

In an attempt to reverse these negative effects, the party has adopted a variety of measures. In education, for example, an overhaul of the school curriculum was recently undertaken to create more space for students to develop independent and creative thinking skills.[30] Further, in what amounts to an abandonment of the conservative and restrictive Shared Values vision, a new vision for the future has just recently been launched to coincide with millennium celebrations. Termed Singapore 21,[31] this latest vision is considerably more liberal than its predecessor; it allows far greater space for debate and the articulation of alternative viewpoints by individuals or groups in civil society. Under the umbrella of Singapore 21, a new form of "social tripartism" is to be forged between the people, government, and private sector. Through a Singapore 21 Facilitation Committee, both individuals and civic groups are to be encouraged to step forward and venture their opinions on all aspects of Singapore society. By allowing such a process of dialogue and debate, the PAP hopes to reverse the alienation afflicting many young Singaporeans—to make Singapore, in the words of Prime Minister Goh Chok Tong, more of a "home," where in addition to economic and material pursuits, they may also find "intellectual, emotional, spiritual, cultural and social fulfillment."[32]

Creativity with Limits

Whether these and other changes are sufficient remains to be seen. For example, while the recent education reforms are certainly commendable, it is extremely interesting to note that the encouragement of independent creative thinking extends only to subjects related to the sciences and technology. A similar level of encouragement in slightly more contentious subject areas such as economics and politics is difficult to discern. It would appear, therefore, that the PAP is seeking to encourage independent thought only in areas that may support its vision of the future. It is not yet prepared to fully equip students with the necessary skills to arrive at a holistic understanding of society and perhaps embark on a more extensive critique of existing policies and practices. Further, while on the surface, the Singapore 21 vision allows far greater opportunities for discussion, it must be remembered that the party still very much remains firmly in control. It alone is in a position to define the boundaries of such debate, and, most critically, the hazy line between what is acceptable political discourse or seditious criminal activity. As critics have pointed out, the Singapore 21 project is simply another means for the PAP to neutralize any opposition. Through various mechanisms under the project, the party is able to depoliticize sensitive issues and channel discussion into less harmful pursuits.[33] On the whole, therefore, it would appear there is still a long way to go before youth in Singapore may enjoy the full opportunity to independently imagine a future. This undoubtedly will have significant implications both for themselves and for the future of Singapore.

NOTES

1.   Garry Rodan, "Singapore: Emerging Tensions in the 'Dictatorship of the Middle Class,'" *Pacific Review* 5, 4 (1992): 370.

2.   E. Kuo and H. T. Chen, "Toward an Information Society: Changing Occupational Structure in Singapore," *Asian Survey* 27, 3 (1987): 369.

3.   Government of Singapore, *"Shared Values"* (white paper) (Singapore: Singapore National Printers, 1991).

4.   For a fuller discussion of these links, see e.g., Michael Hill and Kwen Fee Lian, *The Politics of Nation Building and Citizenship in Singapore* (London: Routledge, 1995); Christopher Lingle, *Singapore's Authoritarian Capitalism: Asian Values, Free Market Illusions and Political Dependence* (Barcelona: Edicions Sirocco, 1996); Joseph Tamney, *The Struggle for Singapore's Soul* (New York: Walter de Gruyter, 1996); Christopher Tremewan, *The Political Economy of Social Control in Singapore* (New York: St. Martin's Press, 1994).

5.   "Value Judgments," *Far Eastern Economic Review* (August 8, 1996): 40.

6.   David Hitchcock, *Asian Values and the United States: How Much Conflict?* (Washington: Center for Strategic and International Studies, 1994).

7.   *The Straits Times* (June 29, 1996): 29.

8.   Dang Rajakru, "The State, Family and Industrial Development: The Singapore Case," *Journal of Contemporary Asia* 26, 1 (1996).

9.   Cherian George and Hui Ling Wang, "Singaporeans Not Ready Yet For Complete Equality of Sexes," *Straits Times Weekly Edition* (December 31, 1994): 14.

10.   Stella Quah, *Between Two Worlds: Modern Wives in a Traditional Setting* (Singapore: Institute of Southeast Asian Studies, 1988).

11.   Soon Beng Chew, Gwo Jiun Lee, and Kim Heng Tan, *Values and Lifestyles of Young Singaporeans* (Singapore: Prentice Hall, 1998), 13.

12.   Ibid., 19.

13.   Ibid., 16.

14.   Ibid., 16.

15.   Fareed Zakaria, "Culture is Destiny: A Conversation with Lee Kuan Yew," *Foreign Affairs* 73, 2 (1994).

16.   John Clammer, "Framing the Other: Criminality, Social Exclusion and Social Engineering in Developing Singapore," *Social Policy and Administration* 31, 5 (1997); Christopher Lingle, *Singapore's Authoritarian Capitalism* . . . ; and Christopher Tremewan, *The Political Economy.* . . .

17.   Khun Eng Kuah, "Confucian Ideology and Social Engineering in Singapore," *Journal of Contemporary Asia* 20, 3 (1990).

18.   Wei Ming Ho, "Value Premises Underlying the Transformation of Singapore," in *Management of Success: The Molding of Modern Singapore,* eds.

Kernial Sandhu and Paul Wheatley (Singapore: Institute of Southeast Asian Studies, 1989), 686.

19.   David Brown and David Jones, "Democratization and the Myth of the Liberalizing Middle Classes," in *Towards Illiberal Democracy in Pacific Asia*, eds. Daniel Bell, David Brown, Kanishka Jayasuriya, and David Jones (New York: St. Martin's Press, 1995); David Jones and David Brown, "Singapore and the Myth of the Liberalizing Middle Class," *The Pacific Review* 7, 1 (1994); Barry Wilkinson, "Social Engineering in Singapore," *Journal of Contemporary Asia* 18, 2 (1988).

20.   David Jones and David Brown, "Singapore and the Myth . . . ."

21.   In Singapore, civilian and military authority are virtually indistinguishable given the high level of interpenetration between the PAP and officer corps, as well as extensive militarization of society (see e.g., Christopher Tremewan, *The Political Economy of Social Control*). The current deputy prime minister, Lee Hsien Loong, for instance, apart from being Lee Kuan Yew's son, is also a brigadier general in the army.

22.   Michael Hill and Kwen Fee Lian, *The Politics of Nation* . . . .

23.   For a discussion of the Speak Mandarin campaign, see e.g., Eddie Kuo, "Mass Media and Language Planning: Singapore's 'Speak Mandarin' Campaign," *Journal of Communication* 34 (Spring 1984).

24.   Lily Kong, "Music and Cultural Politics: Ideology and Resistance in Singapore," *Transactions, Institute of British Geographers* 20 (1995); Siew Chye Phua and Lily Kong, "Ideology, Social Commentary and Resistance in Popular Music: A Case Study of Singapore," *Journal of Popular Culture* 30, 1 (1996).

25.   Lily Kong and Brenda Yeoh, "The Construction of National Identity Through the Production of Ritual and Spectacle: An Analysis of National Day Parades in Singapore," *Political Geography* 16, 3 (1997).

26.   Joseph Tamney, *The Struggle for* . . . .

27.   Christopher Lingle, *Singapore's Authoritarian Capitalism*; Christopher Tremewan, *The Political Economy of* . . . .

28.   Barry Porter, "Learning to Think as Future Leaders," *Sunday Morning Post* (August, 24 1997).

29.   "Stressed Citizens Eager to Emigrate," *South China Morning Post* (August 16, 1997).

30.   "Pupil's Workload Cut to Develop Creativity," *South China Morning Post* (March 21, 1998).

31.   *Singapore Bulletin* (May 1999).

32.   Ibid., 1–2.

33.   James Gomez, "The Singapore 21 Report: A Political Response," *Viewpoint* (May 21, 1999).

Chapter 10

The Future Orientation of Hungarian Youth in the Years of the Transformation

Eva Hideg and Erzsebet Novaky

Tracing the future orientation of Hungarian society in the years of the transformation is of utmost importance. The future orientation of the young people and the changes it undergoes are vital to shaping the future of Hungary; the success and speed of the transformation hinge greatly on these changes. For futures researchers to be able to exert a positive influence on the future orientation of young people, they must become familiar with the youth's attitude to the future.

> Future orientation is the characteristic and the capacity, unique to human beings, which enable thinking to be regulated by the past and present, but also to reflect continuously assumptions regarding the future. . . . Humankind has a historical view and also has a future attitude, which is expressed in future orientation. The decisions and actions of the future-oriented person are guided more by his or her intentions, goals and desires for the future than by his or her experiences of the past. The future inspires the driving force of human activity."[1]

Since 1992, the Department of Futures Research of the Budapest University of Economic Sciences has regularly surveyed the future orientation of Hungarian society in groups of varying composition and size. We have endeavored to learn the components of future orientation through the following criteria:

1. **Interest in and thinking about the future**
   - why is the person interested in the future
   - why are others interested in the future
   - what does the person think about (family, place of residence, country, world) and in what timespan

2. **Activities carried out in the interest of the future**
   - what does the person do for his/her own future
   - what does the person do for the future of his/her loved ones
   - what does the person do so that the situation in his/her place of residence, his/her country, and the world will be better in ten years time
3. **Expectations for the future**
   - how does the person expect to live in ten years time
   - how does the person expect his/her loved ones to live in ten years time
   - what will the situation be like in the person's place of residence, country, and the world in ten years time
   - can certain specific events be expected to happen before the year 2000 or 2020

Working in an academic environment, we have for many years been able to survey the attitude to the future of various cohorts of young people. Analyzing the outcome and changes over time of the empirical surveys we conducted between 1992 and 1996—the initial years of the transformation in Hungary—has been particularly informative.

We relied on questionnaires, one of the time-honored methods used in futures research, to review the attitude to the future, future orientation, and how future orientation has changed among:

- secondary modern school pupils between fourteen and eighteen;
- university economics students of the Budapest University of Economic Sciences; and
- engineer-economists (undergraduates between twenty-five and thirty who had to abandon their engineering studies for studies of economics).

THE FUTURE ORIENTATION OF HUNGARIAN YOUTH AND THE TRANSFORMATION

The young people polled in Hungary represent three different types of future-orientation. Most future-oriented and ambitious are the university economics students, while the engineer-economists have a troubled future orientation, and secondary modern school pupils have the most underdeveloped (and probably the least elaborated) attitude to the future.

University economics students. They tend to be the most future-oriented because they do not fear the future and wish to influence it in keeping with their individual goals and interests. Although the future is uncertain, they believe that by thinking about it the uncertainty can be lessened. Beyond their own personal future they are equally interested in that of their families and the world. The future of the country and their place of residence, however, carries less weight for them. They are more and more concerned about the five- to ten-year timespan and the future beyond forty years ahead.

They are increasingly convinced that with their activity they can influence and shape the future, especially their own and that of their loved ones. This is the motivation that makes them study and preserve their health. They have less power to influence the future of their country, the world, and their place of residence. They have progressed from the passive backing of good causes to recognizing the importance of environmental protection, saving and taking on active political roles.

They are less optimistic in their expectations for the future. Although quite sure of their own personal future, because they are preparing for a career that is prospering in Hungary, they tend to see the future of their broader surroundings in an increasingly pessimistic light. Yet they are still more optimistic than the other two young age groups polled. They do not trust that the situation in Hungary will improve significantly because they fail to see how the process of impoverishment and the deterioration of the state of the environment can be halted even in the long run—but they considered Hungary's accession to the European Union before the year 2000 impossible too. They were more optimistic about these questions at the outset of the transformation.

Engineer-economists. They account for a still young generation that has amassed more experience in life but has had its share of failure too. Their future orientation is laden with a number of problems. They fear the future but will not admit it, and they are disillusioned with the transformation, as they had to retrain themselves early on in their careers. They have realized that they must think about the future not only for their families but for their own future and a better standard of living. While the future of their families and the world (after their own personal future) used to be equally important for them, now it is the future of their families and their country that carry equal weight. The future of their place of residence still does not really interest them. Their attitude has shifted from a short-term to a medium-term view, and their need to think about the long-term future has increased.

Many of them, though in a decreasing proportion, think that they can do nothing for the future. Those who believe they can consider their own retraining most important. Furthermore, many of them believed in investment and entrepreneurialism following the transformation, but moonlighting has again become important. Economizing and taking out insurance policies have surfaced as a new field of activity from the point of view of their own future and that of their loved ones alike. Early on in the shift of system, they did not consider their task to be doing something for the future of their place of residence, the country, and the world—they expected that from the state. Today, however, they believe they can make their mark felt in environmental protection, work, tax-paying, and taking on active political roles.

The optimism of their expectations has also decreased significantly. However, they expect their personal circumstances to improve more than the situation of their wider environment. The majority showed uncertainty when judging the situation of the country and their place of residence. Fewer and fewer expect the situation to improve within ten years. They manifested similar uncertainty concerning the halting of the process of impoverishment and the improvement of the state of the environment, though they tend to believe more in the latter than the former until 2020.

Secondary modern school pupils. These young people, who will obtain their final certificates of vocational training within a few years, had the most unformed future orientation. A great many of them had not even thought about why they and others might be interested in the future. Those who had thought about it were interested in the future primarily to attain a better living standard. They are not particularly interested, however, in continuing their studies or in their future workplace. They are the most materialistic, or perhaps the most honest, because they express the value judgement—so forcefully present in Hungarian society today— that the future is interesting because they'd like to make a lot of money. They do not fear the future, but at the same time, they do not think of the future in relation to their eventual happiness. Beyond their own future, they are interested in the future of their families and their place of residence. They do not know how to handle the future of the country and the world. For them, the future is important in the short and the medium term. They display no long-term conscience of the future, though they watch and read a lot of science fiction.

They also fail to perceive the future and its dimensions concerning their activities. Studies, sports, and helping in the home are important for them, and work also emerges as a priority. Generally, they do not think that they are or will be able to do anything for the well-being of others, the community at large, beyond their own well-being and that of their loved ones. The only exception is their place of residence. They believe they could, in fact, do something for the future of that by protecting the environment and undertaking a role in public life.

Their expectations for the future are also unformed and uncertain. Only half of those polled believe that their situation will be better in ten years time, while the other half think their situation will remain unchanged. They are completely unsure of the future of their place of residence, the country, and the world. They are unsure about the country because they see both the halting of the process of impoverishment and the improvement of the state of the environment as impossible to solve until 2020. Yet it is this group that believed in the greatest proportion that Hungary can become a member of the European Union before the year 2000.

Naturally, all young age groups embrace atypical opinions of the future, but the number of those holding such contrary views is insignificant. This may, in our opinion, be due to the fact that the surveyed age-groups are closely linked to certain types of schools, and the Hungarian school system is still rather closed from the point of view of social mobility.[2] School and schooling fundamentally influence people's future orientation. This is also corroborated by studies of the future orientation of different adult groups in Hungary.[3]

THE FUTURE OF THE TRANSFORMATION AND THE FUTURE ORIENTATION OF YOUNG PEOPLE

The picture unfolding from the samples is not favorable for accomplishing the transformation process in Hungary. At the outset of the shifting, especially the young technical professionals starting out in their careers, and even the university economics students of the time, expected fast and sweeping favorable changes not only in the political system but in living conditions. Their hopes of fast and positive changes both in their living conditions and of everyday life in general have been disappointed, however. By no means did they expect their situation and that of the country to further deteriorate. Pessimism now prevails more and more in Hungarian society, even among the younger generations.

The future orientation of young people who will have a secondary school and vocational certificate and who will comprise the majority of the future society is unformed and underdeveloped. Hungarian schools provide a limited foundation for the development of their future orientation because they still teach only specific knowledge and are past-oriented. Even education fails to turn them toward the future; instead, it emphasizes the values of the past. The future orientation of young people is, therefore, mostly shaped by impressions and information gathered from the social environment and the mass media. And because the latter are characterized by disillusionment, a worsening standard of living, being money-minded and workaholics, as well as by a feeling of impotence and pessimism, the young people cannot but follow suit.

Although university economics students studying for an elite career have a developed and active attitude toward their own future, they do not consider the Hungarian environment promising. They apparently accept the fact that in order to become the elite in society, they have to accomplish their own positive expectations. Although in that social position they could do something for the future of their wider environment too, they are becoming more and more unsure about just what results their efforts will bring.

This unfavorable picture of the future orientation of the young people is, however, changing and can be changed too. This is proved by the fact that more and more people realize that they must think about the future because of its growing uncertainty and not in order to find out what the future holds. Passive future orientation is gradually being replaced by an ever-widening circle of activities that can be carried out for the future. Growing activism in the field of environmental protection with a view to shaping the future of the place of residence, the country, and the world is a particularly welcome feature of this trend. The importance of the future for the individual—its individualization—tends to overshadow the importance of the future from the point of view of smaller and larger communities. The future is more and more ruled by our desire to acquire material things and the growing feeling that these desires are frustrated. Postmaterialist values have failed to emerge with the intensity that certain signs indicated at the outset of the shift in the system.

The future orientation of the young people shifted both in a positive and a negative direction during the short period under scrutiny, which also underscores the unstable and chaotic nature of the transformation. In our earlier surveys this appeared only in connection with socioeconomic macro indicators.[4] The instability of the socioeconomic environment and of future orientation means not only that they are changing but that they can be changed and influenced too. This gives us hope that the social transformation can eventually successfully renew Hungarian society's attitude to the future.

We believe that positively influencing young people's approach and attitude to the future is far more important today than achieving spectacular economic results in Hungary in a short time. If society accomplishes those results under duress or the pressure of outside forces, and not through its own consciously undertaken efforts, the results cannot be lasting and cannot serve as the basis of meaningful lives. Nor will they solve the ambivalence and pessimism inherent in the attitude of people, particularly young people, toward the future. Unless the importance of the future, the variety of activities that can be achieved for the future, and a well-founded optimism harmonize in people's expectations, the most human and abstract goal of transformation will be lost, namely, creating living conditions and everyday existence befitting human beings—in other words, the goal of reaching individual happiness.

In our opinions, the young people's attitudes toward the future can be positively influenced by developing teaching and education, and by futures researchers taking on new social roles. The latest reform of the Hungarian education system provides an appropriate basis for a view embracing future orientation to emerge in the fields of teaching, education, and vocational training alike through the reshuffling and elaborating of curricula and the more vigorous linking of academic knowledge with real life. The earliest possible introduction of futures research in secondary schools would be useful. To this end, the research and amassed educational experience of our department would provide great help. Yet the systematic formation of a positive attitude to the future in all walks of teaching and training is but a dream right now. It is no dream, however, that the further training of teachers can help them embrace relatively quickly a way of thinking open to the future and to the methods of introducing futures-oriented thinking into teaching and education.

ENRICHING FUTURE ORIENTATION
FOR TRANSFORMATION

We envisage a new role for futures research and researchers: the futures researcher, a maintenance worker and developer of society's future orientation, can positively influence and take further the process of systemic change. This can be done by elaborating futures research products that focus on those environmental conditions and well-aimed activities that can help expose and reinforce certain dimensions of the future. Such future studies must be widely publicized and included in the process of teaching so that young people have the means to reproduce them creatively. This type of future education can enrich future orientation and harmonize the various components (interest, activity and expectation), which can exert a positive influence on changes in young Hungarians' future orientation, and thus promote the earliest possible emergence of the positive components of the systemic shift and the subsequent transformation of the whole.

NOTES

1. Erzsébet Nováky, Éva Hideg, and István Kappéter, "Future Orientation in Hungarian Society," *Futures* 26, 7 (1994): 759.

2. See some details in Éva Hideg and Erzsébet Nováky, *Vocational Training and the Future* (in Hungarian) (Budapest: Aula Kiadó, 1998).

3. See some details in Éva Hideg and Erzsébet Nováky, "Our Attitude to the Future," *Magyar Tudomány* 1 (in Hungarian) (1998).

4. For some details and further information on social and economic chaos in Hungary, see Erzsébet Nováky, Éva Hideg, and Katalin Gáspár-Vér, "Chaotic Behavior of Economic and Social Macro Indicators in Hungary," *Journal of Futures Studies* (in Hungarian) (May 1997).

Chapter 11

Citizens of the New Century: Perspectives from the United Kingdom

Cathie Holden

I hope that all the children and grown-ups who are dying of hunger get some food and live.

—girl, age seven

I want to see more solar power and more green power.

—girl, age thirteen

I'm worried that war, nuclear weapons will destroy the world.

—girl, age fourteen

The late 1990s has seen much discussion in the United Kingdom about our values as a postmodern society, with fears that young people are growing up with no moral code, cynical and disillusioned about the part they can play in society as adults. The changing roles of men and women in the workplace and in the family, the advent of new technology, and the role of schools are all part of this debate. One outcome has been the proposal for a new subject, education for citizenship, for all pupils aged eleven to sixteen, with the intention that young people should be "informed, critical, and responsible" and thus "able to participate in society as active citizens of our democracy."[1]

However, in all the debate about how we should educate children for their role as citizens of the next century, there has been little discussion of what young children themselves think and feel, and how they see their future and the part they would like to play. Often only the voices of adults are heard. If we are to understand what the citizens of tomorrow value and are prepared to work for, then we need to listen to the children now in our schools. This chapter aims to assist with this process, drawing on the findings of a major UK research project in which children, as the decision-makers of the next century, were asked about their hopes and fears for the future, the kind of society they would like, and the role they might play in bringing this about.[2] The findings are then set in the context of the current debate on education for citizenship.

EXPLORING THE FUTURE

Images of the future play a central role in social and cultural change both at personal and societal levels. Peoples' hopes and fears for the future will influence what they are prepared to do in the present and what they are prepared to work towards for the future. The images that people hold may optimistically be of a better society, or of a pessimistic dystopian future.

Research over the past twenty years indicates that while children's images of the future are affected by current concerns in society at the time, some fears and hopes appear universal and timeless. For example, Toffler and Johnson found that most young people had a conventional, but optimistic view of their own personal future.[3] The great majority hoped to be married with children, to own a home and car, to be richer than their parents, and to be happy. Pupils' views of the future of their own country were less optimistic, with many expecting more crime, drug abuse, and poverty. They were equally pessimistic about the future of the world; they are being concerned about the depletion of natural resources, pollution, and the danger of nuclear war.

Brown's work, with sixteen- to eighteen-year-olds in Britain, recognized that young people's views of the future were bound up with contemporary issues of social change.[4] Common themes that emerged in their descriptions of the future were violence, boredom, unemployment, high technology, poverty, inflation, material prosperity and pollution. Nonmaterialistic values were expressed far more often than materialistic ones. Notable gender differences emerged: girls were more likely than boys to reject a technological future and were more likely to favor either a "rural paradise" scenario or a future characterized by greater equality in society, assistance for third-world countries, and advances in medicine.

Hutchinson's study of Australian teenagers revealed a high degree of negativity, helplessness, and despondency about the problems facing society.[5] They saw the probable future as being uncompassionate, physically violent, highly technological, corrupt, and environmentally unsustainable. In contrast their preferable futures emphasized "technocratic dreaming," a greening of science, making peace with people and the planet, and a greater concern for future generations. The belief that technology can solve all problems was especially popular among boys.

The most recent study by Oscarsson of 900 Swedish pupils' views of the future found the youths to be fairly optimistic, and those given the opportunities to practice democracy in school were likely to have a more "active, optimistic future orientation."[6] Gidley's work with Steiner-educated pupils endorses this: she found that pupils who had had a holistic and creative education, with opportunities for values-based experiences, were much more likely to feel they could work for change.[7]

THE VOICES OF BRITISH CHILDREN

With our research we wished to establish whether children in Britain in the 1990s had the same visions, hopes, and fears for the future as children in earlier surveys, and to determine what action they felt able to take, both in school and as individuals, toward creating a better future. Such data, we felt, could help policy-makers and teachers involved in the new initiatives on education for citizenship.

The research involved nearly 400 pupils from the southwest of England. Eight state primary and secondary schools were chosen to represent a range of socioeconomic backgrounds with a considerable number of ethnic minority children in the inner-city schools. Pupils were drawn from four age groups: seven, eleven, fourteen, and eighteen, with an equal number of boys and girls. Our research used both questionnaire and interview and notably included children as young as seven. The questionnaire included a variety of closed questions with multiple-choice format, as well as open-ended questions where pupils could write freely. They were followed up by in-depth interviews in which pupils were asked to elaborate and explain their thinking on some of the answers they had given.

A major focus of the study was the hopes and fears of young people. Pupils were asked to write freely on their hopes and fears for their personal futures, the future of their local area, and the future of the world. These responses were illuminated by further questions on particular social and economic issues such as pollution, unemployment, violence, families, the role of women, and poverty. Pupils were then asked what information they had received on these issues (via, for example, the school curriculum) and what action they took to create a better future. Initial findings, discussion of gender differences, and children's views on economic and social issues have been reported elsewhere.[8] The purpose of this chapter is to give a summary of the key findings for an international audience and relate this to current proposals in the U.K. for education for citizenship.

HOPES AND FEARS: REFLECTION AND ACTION

Neither the socioeconomic background of the school (e.g., rural or inner city) nor the ethnic background of the child appeared to be statistically significant. Gender and age were the only variables significantly influencing pupils' responses.

Hopes and Fears for the Personal Future

Around 75 percent of all pupils felt optimistic about their personal future. The themes most commonly emerging were a desire for:

- a good education;
- a good job;
- material success ("the good life");
- fulfilling relationships (children, partner);
- lack of health problems (cancer, AIDS, and so on);
- happiness per se.

Some of the seven-year-olds shared the concerns of the eleven- to eighteen-year-olds, but many were at a conceptually different level of understanding. For example, while one seven-year-old talked clearly about her desire to work "with blind people" when she was older, another wanted a future with "three cats and two guinea pigs" and "sunny weather."

Young people between eleven and eighteen were much more similar in their responses. A good job, material success, and good relationships were most often mentioned, along with the importance of a good education. Boys prioritized "the good life" and material success and worried about ill health, whereas girls were more likely to worry about personal violence (attacks, rape) and to prioritize education. Both boys and girls saw good relationships with families and partners as important. An eleven-year-old boy commented, "I'd like to have a good family and a supporting friend."

The oldest pupils' comments revealed an awareness of the emotional complexities of adult life and of the difficulties of establishing secure relationships. An eighteen-year-old girl wrote, "I hope that I obtain the career that I wish to have. That I remain healthy and live for a long time. That I settle down with someone when I wish to."

Hopes and Fears for the Local Future

The most commonly emerging themes were a desire for:

- less pollution;
- better amenities;
- less crime;
- greater prosperity.

Again, only a few of the seven-year-olds showed an emergent understanding of social and environmental conditions, with one girl mentioning
"people living in boxes" and another mentioning pollution in the local
river. By contrast, eleven-year-old children had a much firmer grasp of the
nature of their local community and, together with older pupils wanted
better amenities, ranging from a desire for "more bins, more hospitals,
more hostels" to "more playing areas and shops" and leisure facilities for
young people. One fourteen-year-old girl thought ahead and wanted, "a
clean area for my children to play in. A nice place where my children can
go outside and be safe."

Pollution was a concern and was blamed on "cars and exhaust pipes"
and emissions from factories. Pupils wanted "less graffiti, litter, and dog
dirt" and more emphasis on protecting the countryside (including wildlife)
and environmental awareness. Many hoped for a community free of crime,
"violence and robbery." They related crime to unemployment and to inad-
equate policing. An eleven-year-old girl wanted "the racism, bullying,
drunkenness and crime to stop." One eighteen-year-old was concerned
that "the local school will close; the bus route will stop," while another
worried "that the countryside [would] become the home of humans rather
than animals." They were not particularly optimistic that the future would
be better in their local area.

Hopes and Fears for the Global Future

Pupils were the least optimistic about a better global future. The main
themes emerging for all age groups were:

- a desire for no war, or peace;
- no poverty/hunger;
- good international relationships;
- less pollution or more environmental awareness.

The youngest children again illustrated how some at this age still have
a naive and limited worldview, while others can appear surprisingly aware
of global issues. On the one hand a seven-year-old boy wanted "a clown
to make all the people laugh," while on the other a girl hoped that "all the
children and grown ups who are dying of hunger get some food and live."

A few of the seven-year-olds mentioned war as a concern, but by the
age of eleven nearly three-quarters wanted a global future with peace or
no war. Many linked war with poverty, including this eleven-year-old:
"There will be no more hunger. No more wars and fighting. No more
killing and crime and also animals set free from zoos."

However, discussion was often unfocused, and it appeared that children
from eleven to fourteen were less well-informed about global concerns

than they were about local issues. They had no clear idea of how wars might come about and often blamed technology for increased unemployment and poverty. Countries were stereotyped into "poor" or "high-tech" with little understanding of the variations existing within one country or even a whole continent. The eighteen-year-olds had a broader understanding of environmental issues, with some aware of the dangers of global warming, the depletion of the ozone layer, and deforestation, but many still confused about the underlying causes of poverty and possible solutions. One boy thought there would be more poverty in the third world as "there's not much contraception" while another saw technology as the cause of unemployment.

Action for the Future

Finally, the research focused on the information young people had received and action they had taken to create a better future. Obviously, action taken varied with age. The youngest children said that not dropping litter was important, whereas older pupils saw their contribution in terms of environmental action, influencing people by sharing ideas, or caring for those less fortunate.

Twice as many girls as boys felt they could do something to bring about a better world. Boys of eighteen were the most cynical or disillusioned, although they were more likely than girls to mention the possibility of political action: "I'm pessimistic, because I think by the time we've got it right it'll be blown up or so polluted it'll be uninhabitable. It makes me want to be more political."

When asked what their schools did to help pupils create a better future, the response was mixed. Many eleven-year-olds thought the curriculum needed to be adjusted to include more "discussion classes" and that they needed more information about "environmental things and things we could do." Older pupils often praised their schools' efforts to raise money for charity but otherwise did not feel their schools did much to help them be actively involved in local or global action. As one fourteen-year-old said: "We learn the facts about what's happening but we don't learn what you can do."

An eighteen-year-old thought the problem was that teachers were "not allowed to talk about politics," while others said that the current curriculum was a constraining factor.

WORKING FOR CHANGE

Some conclusions can be reached. First, young people do appear to have a strong sense of morality and justice: they are not the careless and carefree individuals some would have us believe. They are grappling with social and economic issues and want to be more involved in creating a better future both locally and globally, but feel that they have had little assistance with this at school. Second, boys and girls hold different values, with some girls placing more emphasis on people and relationships and some boys more likely to hope for material success and good health. Our work endorses Brown's findings that girls are more likely than boys to reject a technological future. However, Brown worked only with secondary school children,[9] and we have shown that these differences are already established in primary school. Third, as with previous studies, young people appear to be more optimistic about their own future than that of their local community or the wider world. The older they are, the less they feel they can do, and the less optimistic they are about the future.

Our work indicates that young people would welcome more discussion of contemporary social and economic issues and that they need accurate information to inform their judgments. This needs to be linked to discussion of values, based on universal human rights, so that children have a moral basis for their decisions.[10] Many children indicated that they wanted to be more involved in their local community and wished to be active participants in working for change. This work needs to start in the primary school because children of this age were beginning to grapple with contemporary issues and were the most optimistic about their role in the change process: we need to ensure that the keen eleven-year-old does not become the cynical adolescent. The differing views of boys and girls also have implications: from an early age boys and girls need to be encouraged to listen to each other's views, learn from each other, and challenge assumptions.

OPPORTUNITIES AND EXAMPLES: EDUCATION FOR CITIZENSHIP

In the UK, there is now a chance that pupils may have the opportunity to become involved in the kind of work, which the above research has indicated is needed. Education for citizenship is to be introduced as a new area of the curriculum, mandatory for all pupils aged eleven to sixteen and recommended for all of primary age. This is a landmark in British education as pupils must be taught about "the world as a global community and the political, economic and social disparities that exist" and in so doing, learn how "to make themselves effective in the life of the nation, locally, regionally, nationally, and internationally."[11] Moreover, for the first time in ten years, there are a set of learning outcomes rather than specific programs of study, and teachers are free to choose how to help their pupils achieve these outcomes. This new curriculum is intended to help schools combat racism and promote equal opportunities by teaching about fairness, justice, rights, and diversity. There will be opportunity for teachers to address young people's hopes and fears and to help them become better informed, better prepared, and more optimistic about the future.

This innovation has implications for teaching styles: children cannot learn to debate, discuss, and participate in democratic processes if the teaching style is teacher-led, content-driven, and didactic. Teachers will need to consider their teaching styles, just as schools will need to consider the degree to which children are involved in the democratic processes of the school. The content will need to relate to contemporary issues and to children's concerns, and will need to look forward as well as backward. With such a focus, children will then need to be taught the skills of listening, discussing, and respecting the rights of others so that they can reflect critically and can relate their opinions and action to a values framework. The role of the teacher is not to encourage pupils to join campaigns to save the village green or even the world, but to provide opportunities for critical thinking and participation in a variety of authentic contexts. Jensen and Schnack point out that it "is not and cannot be the task of the school to solve the political problems of society." Its task is to provide opportunities for reflection and action where "the crucial factor is what the pupils learn from participating in such actions."[12]

The two following examples illustrate how schools can start providing meaningful opportunities for young children to think about the future and to understand a local controversial issue. These examples meet the needs voiced by the children in our research and also fulfill many of the learning outcomes of the new education for citizenship.[13]

Example One: Planning the Future

The teacher of a class of eight- to ten-year-olds extended a geography project on the local area to look at the future.[14] After a class discussion on the aspects they thought needed improving and the kind of community they would like, groups of children worked together to plan the kind of world in which they would like to live in 2030. Some focused on the local town while one adventurous group decided to replan the world. Each group had to think about the concerns the class had voiced earlier about future developments and to consider the housing, energy and transport needs of the community. Elaborate maps and plans were made. They then had to decide how people would look after their community and the rights of the citizens and the rules that might be needed to safeguard those rights. After much discussion of what would be desirable in a new community and how one could ensure that people would look after it, the group redesigning their town drew up these rules:

- help plant trees
- keep within the speed limit

- pick up all your litter and put it in the bin
- do not smoke
- use bike tracks when you can
- you must not have people without seat belts in your car
- do not pull down old houses
- do not pollute the river

If you do not go with the rules, you will be fined 500 Euros.

Another group tackled global issues and decided that the world would be much improved if governments could get together and agree:

- no skyscrapers above eight stories high
- talk through arguments instead of having wars
- stop all poaching and only hunt in a kind way if you really have to
- stop the fur trade and buying fur
- give some cars from the United States to poor countries, like Africa

The role of the teacher in clarifying and extending children's thinking within such a project was important. This teacher was able to take the children's thinking forward, helping them realize that solving local or global problems is a complex process. Jodie (age eight) was introduced to the idea of a futures wheel, where one proposition is placed at the center of the page and all possible repercussions are mapped, with links made where possible. She took "give some cars from the United States to poor countries like Africa" as her central statement from her group's list of solutions (above) and then wrote linking statements. One train of thought linked "less cars in the United States" to "less pollution" to "people are more healthy" to "less jobs for doctors" to "poor doctors." Another line linked the central statement to "more pollution in Africa" to "ill people" to "doctors needed" at which point she was able to say she would "send some doctors from the United States to Africa." Other lines from the central statement indicated that "Africans will be poorer" and "need more money." At the end of the exercise, she conceded that it was "a confusing business" and concluded:

> Well, giving cars to Africa could be a good idea because in one way you'd have less doctors and they could go to Africa. So in one way it's good. But then there's a bad thing—it would still be the same pollution. In the end I think it's good in some ways and bad in others. It's better to walk by foot.

The exercise had given her a structure for looking at alternative solutions and allowed her to appreciate the complexity of many current issues. The children's understanding of the complexities of working for change was further assisted by visits from local counselors and action groups, and by literature from national organizations such as Greenpeace and Global Action Plan. Such information helped them understand how change is brought about and the part they could play as children now and later as adults with voting rights.

Example Two: Dealing with a Controversial Issue

A few months ago, the staff of a small primary school in the southwest of the UK found itself with a road-building scheme on their doorstep, complete with a group of protesters and the national press. The staff were aware of the children's interest in what was going on and their apparent sympathy for the young protesters, many of whom had ensconced themselves in trees or tunnels. Rather than ignore this controversial issue, the staff decided to build on the children's interest and use it as a focus for the term's work in drama and geography.

Because teachers felt that children should learn about the many aspects of the situation, as a first strategy they asked the children to devise a questionnaire for parents. Questions included:

- Are you for the road improvement?
- Do you think people should have more say about the building of the new road?
- What do you think of the protesters?
- Did the police handle the situation properly?
- What should the police do with the protesters?
- Would you protest if you had to?

The variety of responses immediately alerted the children to the complexity of the issues. Second, people involved with the road building were invited to the school so the children could question them. In so doing, they realized as the head teacher said, "that what they hear on the radio or see on the TV is not the whole story and that they need to take time to consider what their own response might be." The third strategy for ensuring a balanced perspective was to dramatize the event in such a way that enabled all voices involved in the dispute to be heard. The play featured the displaced animals, counselors, local people, and the protesters. This enabled parents to see the approaches the school had taken to teach about the controversy.

Interviews with pupils at the end of the project showed how their thinking had developed since the early stages:

> More roads may mean that there will be more cars. The protesters did not have the right to trespass but I do think that they have the right to protest.

I have learnt you can protest in different ways, for example by writing a letter. Protesting can be very civilized, through talking and negotiating. You don't have to use force to stop something.

Having had children the opportunity to engage in a controversial issue relevant to them, these children began to have insights into the nature of democracy and to consider their own values, without feeling pressured to respond in a particular way. This provided a model for approaching similar situations in the future: encouraging children to appreciate the importance of considering both sides of the story, taking into account people's different perspectives, and thus reaching an informed decision before giving an opinion or taking action.

CHILDREN AS ACTIVE CITIZENS OF THE NEXT CENTURY

As indicated at the beginning of this chapter, children from a young age are already asking hard questions about their own lives and the lives of others in an unjust society and fragile environment. They are concerned about the future and wish to take an active part in working toward improving it, for themselves and the wider community. Education for citizenship may provide opportunities to address such concerns and to harness children's interest in the future. Such education will be effective when children are encouraged to voice their own concerns and opinions, ensuring that the issues under discussion have relevance for them. It may not be possible for every child to be involved in community action, but certainly all children can engage in informed debate about key concerns and contemporary issues. Global concerns can also be discussed, if not acted on, as in the example of the town planning and futures wheel. Such an approach that encourages children to discuss, debate, and listen to others' points of view is essential if we are to have well-informed young people, able to make their own judgements and optimistic about the part they can play as active citizens in the next century.

NOTES

1. Qualifications and Curriculum Authority, *The Secretary of State's Proposals* (London: QCA, 1999), 28.

2. David Hicks and Cathie Holder, *Visions of the Future: Why We Need To Teach For Tomorrowm* (Stoke-on-Trent: Trentham Books, 1995).

3. Alvin Toffler, *Learning for Tomorrow: The Role of the Future in Education* (New York: Vintage Books, 1974); L. Johnson, "Children's Visions of the Future," *The Futurist* 21, 3 (1987): 36–40.

4. Mary Brown, "Young People and the Future," *Educational Review* 36, 3 (1984): 303–15.

5. Francis Hutchinson, *Futures Consciousness and the School* (Ph.D. thesis) (Armidale: University of New England, 1992).

6. Vilgot Oscarsson, "Pupils' Views on the Future in Sweden," *Environmental Education Research* 2, 3 (1995): 261.

7. Jennifer Gidley, "Prospective Youth VisionsThrough Imaginative education," *Futures* 30, 5 (1998): 395–408.

8. David Hicks and Cathie Holden, *Visions of the Future* . . .; Cathie Holden, "Tomorrow's Citizens: The Differing Concerns of Girls and Boys," *Children's Social and Economics Education* 2, 2 (1997): 80–93; Cathie Holden, "Growing Up Today: Children Talking about Social Issues" in *Values Education,* eds. M. Leicester, C. Modgill, and S. Modgill (London: Falmer, 1999).

9. Mary Brown, "Young People and the Future . . . ."

10. Audrey Osler and Hugh Starkey, *Teacher Education and Human Rights* (London: Fulton, 1996).

11. QCA, *The Secretary of State's Proposals* . . . :28.

12. B. Jensen and R. Schnack, eds., "Action Competence as an Educational Challenge," *Didaktiske Studier: Studies in Educational Theory and Curriculum* 12 (Royal Danish School: Copenhagen, 1994): 6.

13. QCA, *The Secretary of State's Proposals* . . . :28.

14. Cathie Holden and N. Clough, *Children as Citizens: Education for Participation* (London: Jessica Kingsley, 1998).

Chapter 12

Longing for Belonging: Youth Culture in Norway

Paul Otto Brunstad

To elaborate on the subject, longing for belonging, I refer to my doctoral dissertation called "Youth and World View: College Students' Faith and Expectations about the Future"[1] as a point of departure. The study was based on a qualitative research method using essays and in-depth interviews. The dissertation focuses on one hundred secondary school students, aged eighteen to twenty, and their longings, dreams, hopes, and fears about the future in Norway.

REGRESSION AND PRIVATIZATION

My young informants seem in many ways to have lost their faith and hope in a meaningful global future and in the notion of a perpetual progress that will solve our present problems. Progress is no longer a living hope, but more a fate to which they feel condemned. Children have traditionally been seen as guarantors of a better future. The understanding of children has dramatically changed among some of my informants. A Danish study of college students' view of the future focuses on the same problem. In this study, 39 percent of them didn't want to bear children because the future was too insecure and risky.[2] In his essay, an eighteen-year-old boy wrote this to me about children and the future: "When it comes to the future, the only thing I can say is that I'm glad I'm not my children. The world will soon be a hell of a place. I belong to the last generation who could grow up surrounded by fresh air and in prosperity."

The next generation will be born into a world drained of important resources. We are eating the bread of the unborn generations. An almost apocalyptic expectation is imprinted upon this view of the future. This apocalyptic vision is formed not by a religious, but by a secularized and scientific understanding of the future. The potential and possibilities that children traditionally have represented contribute to nothing in the wake of coming technological and ecological disasters. The world inherited from previous generations is their fate. Therefore, to bear children is a risky enterprise best avoided. An eighteen-year-old girl wrote: "In my opinion, the world will become worse than today. Humankind becomes more and more greedy and selfish. People don't care about others, and most people are left alone."

My informant's visions of the future differ from a traditional Judeo-Christian view of the end of time. They replace a sovereign God with a sovereign humankind ruled by greed and selfishness and with an inherited ability to destroy the world. The end of time is not understood as a cosmic catastrophe caused by divine forces, but is more a result of humankind's own devastating activities. It's interesting to notice the same perspective in contemporary apocalyptic films like *Waterworld* and *Twelve Monkeys* and in films like *Blade Runner* and *Mad Max.*[3] The popular culture and the media seems to play an important role in the formation of a new apocalyptic understanding among young people. Another boy among my informants addresses the same theme:

> We all have a fucking future ahead of us. Not only unemployment and poverty, but also more criminality. The pressure on nature will continue. The result will be the third world war. We could maybe avoid it by a revolution, but with the politicians we have at the moment and the flourishing of neo-Nazism no one knows what's going to happen. To conclude: Life's a bitch/shit happens/so be it!

Life is unstable, unpredictable, and inconstant. It is impossible to change anything, because in an unpredictable world, it's not possible either to make or carry out plans. The more complex the young see their world to be, the harder it becomes to predict outcomes of their actions.[4] From the Age of Enlightenment we have been taught that new knowledge would cause improvements and prosperity. This is not so among my informants, for whom new knowledge causes more anxiety than confidence and optimism. This problem is highlighted by another of my informants, a boy also aged eighteen:

> The future? Do we have any future? What use is it to think about the future? I live here and now and try to make the best out of it. To make plans in advance is not my style. I'm more spontaneous. I don't care about the future, we can't do much about it anyway. For me, the day today is most important, what happens tomorrow is important, but not today. Right now I feel a kind of hopelessness. I go to school every day, but what's the point of that?

Our common situation is difficult, uncertain, and out of control. This is also a common message in contemporary music and films. Such an understanding generates a kind of powerlessness that results in a regression or flight into a private sphere surrounded by a few intimate others. It is a kind of powerlessness because one cannot control anything but one's own life. This situation results in a focus on the present, here-and-now experience and on immediate gratification. The long line of time dissolves into a circle in which they themselves represent the center. The vision of the future influences motivation and strategies for action. One of the girls wrote this in her essay: "I want to get a good education, a good occupation, a husband and children. Old-fashioned? Maybe, but I like to dream of a safe and secure existence."

An intimate and secure life in the nuclear family is the main goal of this girl. The meaning of life is to live here and now. Nobody should waste time by thinking of things that are impossible to change anyway: "I look forward to falling in love with a man who loves me. I'm longing for children and a future full of love and enriching experiences. I want to travel a lot, have a good job, help people and be healthy."

Within these private and individual frames it's possible to establish a secure and happy life which also make it practicable to do something good for other people. She is concerned with those things in life that are possible to realize. Her optimism is tied to her intimate and private world.

I have tried to illustrate this situation described by my informants by using a diagram with two axes (see Figure 12.1). This diagram uses four squares: personal–optimism, personal–pessimism, global–optimism, and global–pessimism.

A short perspective with focus on attainable goals generates a kind of *personal optimism,* but at the same time, this short-sighted strategy reveals new and threatening problems that cause a distaste for the local situation. The regression or withdrawal from public (global) space is not without cost. Even though the global future is problematic, signs of hope still encourage further action.

Through a regression into a short-sighted, day-to-day perspective, my informants try to achieve a practical, meaningful, and less complicated life. Through this strategy, which also implies a negative view toward public life and institutions, they become agents of their own lives, able to design and create their own future. On this small "stage," they can play the leading role and be their own master. Within this small frame, planning and action do have meaning.[5]

To achieve their goals in life, they have to be skillful, competent, and lucky. In all this there is no one else to trust but themselves. Hard work, good marks, a good partner, good friends, and a bit of fortune will do the job. Everybody is an arbiter of her or his own fortune. The pessimistic views of the future can encourage activity but not so much solidarity.[6]

FIGURE 12.1

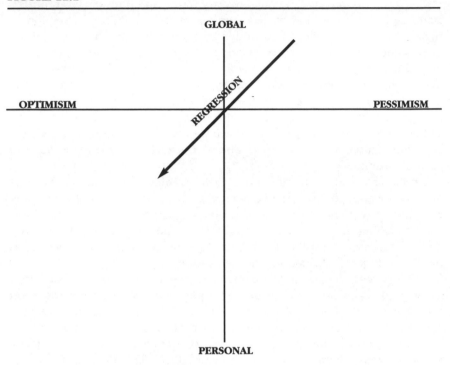

GLOBAL

OPTIMISIM   PESSIMISM

PERSONAL

After reading and rereading all the essays and interviews, I found it opportune to construct a new diagram visualizing the variety of causes of both remote (global) pessimism and near (personal) optimism. In the four squares I have listed the different themes mentioned by my informants in both their essays and interviews (see Figure 12.2).

To sum up: My informants' efforts to create a better future seem to have a very private character; the altruism tends to limit one's self to the group of intimate friends and family. The main focus is on education, family, body, occupation, and leisure. Further, my study shows ecological catastrophes, war, famine, natural disaster, and overpopulation to be the main fears in relation to the global future. Political action and commitment to the community seem to be lacking. Nevertheless, there might be a new way of thinking about political action, not by entering the traditional political institutions, but by using their power as consumers. They could have some influence here through strategic purchases and by boycotting companies they know.

In this respect, there is still a major shift in the youth-culture from the 1960s to the 1990s. Responsibility for the future is closely tied to the chance to change the situation. Without this opportunity, the young people do not feel responsible for our common future. An unpredictable future makes

FIGURE 12.2

	GLOBAL	
Make strategic purchase	Ecological catastrophe Atomic war Famine Natural disaster Over-population	
OPTIMISIM		**PESSIMISM**
Education —homework —good marks —future studies Family and friends —partner —children Body —health —appearance Occupation —interesting job —safe job —good income Spare time/leisure —exciting experiences —the possibility to travel	Fail at school —bad marks —lack of theoretical interest Fear of losing family/friends —divorce —loneliness Illness —death —health problems Unemployment —economical problems Boredom Violence, crime, gangs	
	PERSONAL	

planning for the time ahead difficult. Their capability, energy, and creativity are therefore directed at the private sphere. This situation does not auger well for the future. In Polak's major study of changing images of the future in Western society, he notes, "As long as a society's image of the future is positive and flourishing, the flower of culture is in full blossom. Once the image of the future begins to decay and lose its vitality, however, the culture cannot survive."[7]

This description throws a worrying light over the situation reflected in my study, and I therefore entirely agree with Hicks when he states that the crucial pedagogical dilemma is how to provide stories of hope that both liberate and empower the coming generations.[8]

"Body-building" as Survival Strategy

The development characterized by regression and privatization seems to result in a new focus on the body.[9] The body gets an important role in this situation. When the comprehensive structures in life in many ways seem to have broken down, and the future has lost its attraction, the body seems to be the last resort of hope.[10] When the old storytelling traditions and their stories of hope have become silenced and the communities of memories,[11] e.g., the family, the church, and so on, have been marginalized, the body is drawn into the project of building an identity and forming a self.

Some years ago I was working among young, unemployed boys in a dormitory town in the outskirts of Bergen, the second largest city in Norway. My friendship with these boys gave me a new understanding of this new role of the body. By building their bodies the boys also built their identity and a shelter for the future. Through body-building they became their own engineers. The mirror image in the fitness studio and the self image corresponded in an interactive process.[12] As important structures of life such as school, family, and occupation crumbled, the body beckoned.

There is, of course, also a close connection between body-culture, fashion, and lifestyle. In both cases the surface is what counts. The superficial achieves a depth because the identity is tied to the surface. In this respect, muscles, clothes, and dressing are far more than simply a means of bodily protection. They are means of symbolic display that gives external and material form to the self-identity.[13] The more posttraditional the setting in which the young people move, the more lifestyle concerns the very core of self-identity, its making, and remaking.[14]

THE FRAGILITY OF THE PRIVATIZED WORLD

Individualization and privatization give at the outset a lot of opportunities and freedom to create and construct one's own life, but at the same time they also bring problems for the new generation. They become separated from those larger communities, traditions and practices, stories, and narratives that earlier played an important role in forming a stable identity. From a Christian point of view, they are cut off from the great code of life, the code that gives them the key to "open up" and interpret the more existential questions. The signposts established by tradition are now blank. Young people have to make their own choice alone, without help from previous generations. But as the knowledge of the old generations fade out, the popular culture enters the stage ready to lead the young people in new directions. Movie and rock stars replace the old role models and become the new heroes, teachers, and tutors.

This emancipated, posttraditional, and privatized life is nevertheless a fragile life. When the future depends on what you yourself are able to do, the risk that something might fail is high (see Figure 12.2). Young people do therefore feel a pressure that I call a *local—or personal—pessimism*, a kind of postmodern melancholy, irony, or boredom. They have all experienced that life is fragile. A lot of dark shadows loom above their small, intimate, and privatized world. Failing at school, divorce, loneliness, illness, unemployment, boredom, violence, crime, and gangs are all threatening clouds on the horizon.

To protect their feelings from anxiety and boredom, young people also use such mental weapons as irony and cynicism. This kind of "defense weapon" is commonly used in the lyrics of their rock music. Rock music teaches young people how to deal with a world falling apart. Through irony they establish a protective zone between the complicated world and their own feelings. But this cure does not cure the illness. Instead it increases the problem. Irony prevents young people from altering their own situation. Irony just gives a short mental release.[15]

LONGING FOR BELONGING: THE NEW TECHNO AND HOUSE CULTURE

In this process of greater individualization I also find tracks of a deep longing for a new kind of belonging. This longing is present in one of the major youth movements in Europe in the 1990s, the House, Rave, and Techno Culture. The rapidly growing House, Rave, and Techno Culture is one of the strongest and most influential aspects of the European popular culture of the 1990s. By contrast, for adolescents in the 1960s *the road* was an extremely important metaphor reflecting the longing for freedom from repressive and binding traditions. The future at this time was full of promises and hopes. Young people believed that actual problems would find their solution in the future.[16] The notion of progress was still strong in the 1960s. Rock music reflected this understanding and became worldwide a powerful cultural force—the voice of an entire generation of young people.[17]

In the 1990s the unstable situation and gloomy prognoses from scientists have altered the understanding of both time and space, the road and travel. Young people in the 1990s are not so sure any longer that "progress," "the road," and "travel" will lead to a better place. They no longer possess the certainty of a radiant future and a final salvation, either religious or scientific. So why bother? Why strive to reach a place worse than what we already have?

Not the car and the road, but *the house* is the new metaphor for the 1990s. The *House Culture* signals a new way of thinking among young people in the West. Individualization, the experience of a world falling apart, and the loss of a utopian vision of the future have created a longing for community, for a place to rest, for a house, a home in which one could seek shelter and comfort. Bruce Springsteen sings that everyone needs "a place to rest, . . . a home" in his song, "Hungry Heart."[18]

The postmodern situation—a situation of intense change and transformation of old structures and traditions, loneliness, homelessness, displacement, boredom, and nomadism—seems to characterize the situation for a lot of young people. The nostalgic longing back to a safer place does not come as a surprise. Emancipation and progress seem to be replaced by longing for security and belonging. The individual seeks protection and belonging in a bigger entity, a house or a corporation. Berlin has in the last few years been the arena for the "biggest house party in the world." During one week in July, young people from all over Europe meet to dance, celebrate, and get a feeling of unity and fellowship.

In the summer of 1999 this very inclusive party gathered over 1.2 million young participants. The longing for unity and fellowship was expressed through an earlier slogan, "We Are One Family." The term *the family,* heavily attacked during the 1960s, is back in the 1990s, yet with an altered meaning: not as a nuclear family, but as one, big family collecting all kinds of people regardless of age, gender, religion, color, faith, and nationality. This giant party can be seen as an antimodernistic reaction. Instead of more freedom and individualization, we here see a wave of longing for unity, for a home, "a house." In a time when "all that is solid melts into air" (Marx), this longing is not difficult to understand. A lot of adolescents who come from broken homes are looking for an alternative place "to rest," as Springsteen expresses in his lyrics.

The roots of the House Culture are found not in Europe, but in the United States, in Detroit. During the 1980s, when the production of cars failed, young African-American boys and girls occupied the empty buildings and established a new kind of family.[19] This new family type replaced their broken homes and families.

The House Culture captures both a strong nostalgic longing back to a more premodernistic situation, and a progressive use of the new technology. Importantly, a new understanding of time emerges in this situation. Technology has lost its connection to thinking of time as a linear phenomenon. In the House Culture, time is more understood in terms of *points.* Disconnected points, a sequence of fleeting moments whose meaning is entirely grounded in the present point of time. Just points, no beginning and no end.[20]

Technology (e.g., techno-music) does not lead to progress but gives a "quick-fix buzz." The music, the dance, the drugs, and the intense feeling of fellowship help to participate in a new journey, not in time, but in space: an inner journey, a mind-expanding trip, or a shamanistic travel out of the body. In this situation the world around does not mean much more than problems. Maybe we here see the first traces of what we could call a kind of *techno-gnosticism*, a longing for a more harmonious spiritual world with fewer conflicts and problems?[21]

The House Culture marks a new era in the history of rock music. The political and the narrative aspect has evaporated, and the body and the senses are more than ever drawn into focus. The longing for freedom, so important in the beginning of the youth culture in the 1950s and 1960s, is now replaced by a longing for belonging and attachment.

LONGING FOR AN IDENTITY, LONGING FOR A BODY

It might be that the term *belonging* in many ways hits the very chord of what identity is. Identity is basically tied to a feeling of attachment, of belonging, a place where the surroundings respond, legitimate, and strengthen the self. We need someone to feed us, we need to get some *feed*-back. To have an identity is to be a part of an entity bigger than oneself. In a society in which community is replaced by communication, eating together is replaced by speaking together, and digitalized connection is more common than physical contact, the longing for a living body, a corporation, a community to move into becomes a pressing need—not so much to eat and consume as to be eaten and consumed by something stronger, bigger, and more solid than my own body.

The question is: How do important institutions in society meet this challenge, this longing for belonging on the threshold of a new millennium? Is there any *body*, or maybe as alternative, *house*, for the new generation to move into? One possibility is a transformed church.

Revisiting the church, which claims to be the *body* of Christ, the *house* of God, might give us an interesting perspective on the actual situation. Even though both a house and a body normally do have a visible appearance, it seems as if the church has become what Jacques Ellul calls a "disembodied wraith,"[22] a community without a body. A striking metaphor of this condition is the cheshire cat in Lewis Carroll's book, *Alice in Wonderland*. Alice meets the cat sitting on a branch, but slowly, beginning with the end of its tail, the cheshire cat begins to vanish until there is nothing left except a speaking mouth talking to Alice.

This small story might be a picture of the church in the modern world. The church has in many ways become a smile, a speaking mouth, a message without a body, without a community, an institution that finds it hard to offer, in the spirit of Matthew, young people protection, shelter, and fellowship. The House of God has become what Tom Waits (1999) calls a "House Where Nobody Lives."[23]

This is the story of the production buildings in Detroit after the depression, and it might also be the story of the church in many European cities.

From Latin we have the word *companion*, which literally means a person with whom you share your bread (*panis* is the Latin word for bread). The church, which started as a table society where the master himself shared the bread with his disciples with his companions, has become a disembodied, tableless society around words. The church has developed from *somebody* to *nobody*. It's not that easy for a new generation to find and join a corporation with *nobody*. Instead of an *eating-together community* we have got a *speaking-together community*, as in the rest of society.[24] Community is replaced by communication. The church has become more verbal and oral than corporeal.

But it's not only the body of the church that has melted into the air; other institutions seem to be suffering the same fate. The family also becomes more of a speaking than an eating community. The family as a small but important corporation gathering around the table is also vanishing. The small kitchen table society is losing terrain all over the Western world. Family members eat alone and "on the run." No wonder that eating-related disorders are on the rise among young people. This situation creates more freedom, but also more longing for real belonging. To develop a stable identity you need to belong somewhere, you need a "place to rest."

To establish and maintain a feeling of belonging, to be a member, to be a limb on some-body, one has to be remembered. To see is to remember. If someone is out of sight for a long time, he or she will also get out of mind. To see helps us to remind and *remember*. What is forgotten is invisible, it no longer exists in our mind. Remembering is an act of creating, it gives being, it's like a branch grafted onto a tree that becomes a part of a life-giving system. To be seen is to be invited into the house and to the community around the table as a member who is remembered.

My informants are afraid of being invisible, afraid of loneliness, of being forgotten. In a society in which young people are surrounded by faceless and disembodied voices on answering machines, the television or computer screen, and other electronic and digital transmitters, no wonder that a creepy feeling of invisibility makes itself felt. Patrick Batman expresses this fear in the horrible, but important book, *American Psycho:* "I mean, does anyone really *see* anyone? Does anyone really *see* anyone else? Did *you* ever *see* me? *See?*"[25]

New religious and political groups in this situation are able *to see* invisible young people. They offer a place to rest, a place of protection, experiences, belonging, and therefore also a new identity. Their odd and maybe devastating mission and goals are overshadowed by their promises of fellowship and friendship. To be eaten by a sect, a new religious movement, an extreme charismatic group, a criminal gang, a political corporation on the far left or right is better than to always eat and consume alone. To be a part of a *company* yields a more comprehensive and satisfactory life, at least at the outset. We also see some of the same mechanisms brought into play at big sport events. To be in a surging and roaring group of fans also gives an intense feeling of belonging. The problem is that an arena or a stadium can never be a permanent residence, or dwelling house.

THE FUTURE OF BELONGING

The future of new generations is at stake. How could we give young people a feeling of belonging and protection, a place where their own, fragile bodies could be a part of a bigger entity? Where could they find some-*body* to nurse and strengthen them and still give them freedom to move and develop? Some-*body* who could share the bread with them and walk two more miles together with them—not only a silent body, but a body with a mouth telling the new generations stories of hope that both liberate and empower them. Chris Rea describes the longing, not only for belonging but also for a narrative (or new spiritual mythology for the future) in his song, "Tell Me There's a Heaven."[26]

NOTES

(Some of the titles are the English translations from the Norwegian)

1. Paul Otto Brunstad, *Youth and Worldview: College Students' Faith and Expectations about the Future* (Trondheim: Tapir Forlag, 1998).

2. Karen Schousboe, *The Serpent in Paradise: Young People's Visions of the Future* (København: Undervisningsministeriet, 1990).

3. Joel W. Martin and Conrad E. Ostwalt Jr., *Religion, Myth and Ideology in Popular American Film* (Oxford: Westview Press, 1995).

4. David Hicks, "Retrieving the Dream: How Students Envision Their Preferable Futures," *Futures* 28, 8 (1996): 741–749.

5. Lars Erik Malmberg, "Finnish Adolescents' Future-Orientation: Effects of Educational Track, Gender and Self-Evaluation," *Nordisk Pedagogikk* 16, 4, (1996): 213–224.

6. David Hicks, "Retrieving the Dream . . . ."

7. Ibid., 742.

8. Ibid., 743.

9. Mike Featherstone, "The Body in Consumer Culture," In *The Body: Social Process and Cultural Theory,* eds. M. Featherstone, M. Hepworth, B.S. Turner (London: Sage, 1991): 170–196.

10. Alberto Melucci, *The Playing Self: Person and Meaning in the Planetary Society* (Cambridge: Cambridge University Press, 1996).

11. N. Robert Bellah, et al., *Habits of the Heart: Individualism and Commitment in American Life* (Harper & Row, New York, 1985), 152.

12. Thomas Johansson, "Gendered Spaces: The Gym Culture and the Construction of Gender," *Young* 4, 3 (1996): 32–47.

13. Anthony Giddens, *Modernity and Self-Identity: Self and Society in Late Modern Age* (Cambridge: Polity Press, 1991), 62

14. Ibid., 81.

15. Stanley Cohen and Laurie Taylor, *Escape Attempts: The Theory and Practice of Resistance to Everyday Life* (London and New York: Routledge, 1992).

16. Armin Nassehi, "No Time for Utopia: The Absence of Utopian Contents in Modern Concepts of Time," *Time & Society,* Sage 3, 1 (1994).

17. Ron Eyerman and Andrew Jamison, "Social Movements and Cultural Transformation: Popular Music in the 1960s," *Media, Culture & Society,* 17 (1995): 449–468.

18. Bruce Springsteen, *Hungry Heart,* From *Greatest Hits* (Sony Music Entertainment, 1995).

19. Friedhelm Böpple and Ralf Knüfer, *Generation XTC: Techno und Ekstase* (Berlin: Verlag Volk und Welt GmbH, 1996).

20.   Alberto Melucci, *The Playing Self: Person and Meaning in the Planetary Society* (Cambridge: Cambridge University Press, 1996), 12.

21.   Paul Otto Brunstad, "Mellom spiritualitet og virtualitet. Kristendtroen og den eletroniske motorveien," *Luthersk Kirketidende,* 14 (1996): 405–410.

22.   Os Guinness, *The Gravedigger File* (London: Hodder and Stoughton 1983).

23.   Tom Waits, *House Where Nobody Lives,* From *Mule Variations,* (Epitaph Europe, 1999).

24.   Pasi Falk, *The Consuming Body* (London: Sage Publications, 1994).

25.   Bret Easton Ellis, *American Psycho* (London : Picador, 1991), 238.

26.   Chris Rea,   *Tell Me There's a Heaven,* From *The Road to Hell.* (Magnet Music, 1989).

Chapter 13

Holistic Education and Visions of Rehumanized Futures

Jennifer Gidley

Much of the research presented in this book raises serious questions about the adequacy of contemporary mainstream educational theory and processes to equip youth to construct and face their futures positively. Key educational "futurists" have engaged in critical speculation about alternative forms of education that might better prepare youth for a rapidly changing and uncertain future, while also considering the needs of future generations. Several researchers recommend more holistic, integrated teaching methods using imagination, visualization, prosocial skills, and specific futures methodologies.[1] Intriguingly, many of these are crucial aspects of Steiner education.

STEINER EDUCATION: AN INNOVATIVE ALTERNATIVE APPROACH

Steiner education provides an integrated, holistic balance of intellectual/cognitive, artistic/imaginative, and practical/life skills education. The possibility that such holistic, imaginative styles of education might facilitate more confident, proactive, and hopeful outlooks toward the future provided the key focus for the research with Steiner-educated students discussed below.

Developed initially in Germany in 1922 by Rudolf Steiner (1861–1925), Steiner education has developed over the past seventy years as a large, nondenominational international schooling system of over 500 schools worldwide, underpinned by a holistic, spiritually based philosophy. This approach can be historically contextualized in the post-positivist movement of the late nineteenth century, which was a response to the positivist scientific view of the world that excluded notions of choice, freedom, moral responsibility, and individuality. Rudolf Steiner called for science to be reunited with art and metaphysics through "spiritual science."[2]

In the mode of a "Renaissance universal man," Steiner was a scientist, philosopher, and artist who contributed significantly to the fields of education, agriculture (biodynamics), architecture, medicine, and the arts. He gave more than 6,000 lectures and wrote more than sixty books, essays, and articles on history, religion, education, evolution, science, psychology, physiology, agriculture, and medicine. A futurist and grand theorist, he had a macrocosmic perspective on time in relation to what he called the evolution of human consciousness. With great foresight, he initiated the educational approach discussed here.

Underpinning Theories

Underlying this approach lies a holistic paradigm for viewing the world. The epistemological basis of the aesthetic, imaginative, and integral features of Steiner pedagogy is supported by art education theory. While this theory extends historically back to Plato (from a Western perspective), it has more recently been grounded in contemporary art education theory that draws on developments in the cognitive sciences springing primarily from Gestalt psychology.[3] This theoretical marriage of art education with Gestalt psychology has endorsed the value of the holistic, left-brain/right-brain patterning processes that enhance memory and learning through higher order meaning-making.

Speaking in 1922 of the qualities needed in education to prepare young people for the trials of the future, Steiner stressed the moral aspects of pedagogy:

> Pedagogy . . . is not merely a technical art. Pedagogics is essentially a special chapter in the moral sphere . . . only those who find education within the realm of morality, within the sphere of ethics, discover it in the right way.[4]

By contrast, Eckersley refers to the contemporary crises of youth discussed earlier in this book as reflecting "a profound and growing failure of western culture . . . to provide a sense of meaning, belonging, and purpose in our lives, as well as a framework of values."[5]

While the deconstruction of the metanarratives of modernity by postmodernism has left a "values vacuum" for our youth, Steiner education provides an approach that fosters a reinvention of human values to reincorporate the sacred. This approach is aligned to Thomas Berry's "postcritical naiveté," Morris Berman's "participatory consciousness," and David Tacey's call for a "postmodern spirituality,"[6] the impact of which will be evident in the student's visions.

In addition, Steiner education, underpinned by a holistic cosmology and spiritually based ontology, regards recognition of the interconnectedness of all things as a way of knowing. This aligns it also with many non-Western epistemologies that do not subscribe to the fragmented nature of learning underpinned by instrumental rationality. This recognition of the interconnectedness of all the discrete subjects is fundamental to the manner of planning of the Steiner curriculum.[7]

Conceptual Approach to the Cultivation of Imagination and Will

Steiner education uses an integrated approach to the development of the whole child. In particular, the cultivation of the students' imagination helps them envision prospective futures different from the present. In Steiner schools, the foremost tool for cultivating the imagination is stories, a preeminent medium of teaching. Also, Steiner schools widely use the creative arts to give meaning to every subject and promote intrinsic motivation and positive self-esteem. The value of this approach to cognitive development, in particular the development of an allusionary base for finding meaning in life, is supported by contemporary art educationists and psychologists.[8] Steiner himself linked the artistic education of the child with the development of initiative:

> If, through an artistic approach, which appeals to the whole human being, we gradually unfold in our teaching what has become purely intellectual in the world, our pupils will grow into complete and integrated personalities, capable of developing real initiative.[9]

ENVISIONING POSITIVE FUTURES: SOCIAL FUTURES AS PARAMOUNT

Because of my interest and involvement in both Steiner education and youth futures research, I decided to test speculations of educational futurists by researching the views and visions of young people educated in the system which, to my knowledge, was closest to the futures researchers' "ideal model." In this study, 128 senior secondary students from the three largest Steiner schools in Australia (Sydney, Melbourne, and Adelaide) participated. This chapter reports the Steiner students' visions of their futures (drawing on a combination of data sources) and presents a qualitative analysis of their "preferred" or desirable futures across various themes. As suggested in the wider research, Steiner students were just as inclined as other students and young people to have grave expectations about the future of the environment, social justice, and conflict. In spite of this, as reported elsewhere, it was shown that, unlike many mainstream-educated youth, they were not disempowered by those negative future expectations, but rather, they demonstrated a strong activist will to create more positive futures.[10]

In addition, this chapter shows that the Steiner-educated students have produced many richly imaginative positive visions of their preferred futures within the general thematic areas covered by the research. In addition to the themes provided to them (the environment, social issues, and war and peace), the students' qualitative responses and visions demonstrated that they see the quality and character of humanness itself as a major factor in the challenges they face and the futures they hope for. They imagine a better world in which human development, responsibility, and action are at the forefront.

Human Development as a Basis for Positive Future Images

When the students were asked to imagine living in the year 2020—when many of their hopes for the world have been realized—the positive changes they envisaged strongly centered on the importance of human development, with 75 percent of students citing some aspect of human development as important. As the human development factor appears to be fairly unique to this research, a more in-depth picture of the qualities the students described (activism, values changes, spirituality, and education for "future care") will be presented through direct quotations from the students' oral and/or written responses.

Activism. A rather impassioned plea for activism came from Katrina, an articulate, fully Steiner-educated tenth-year student with German parents:

> Obviously most people hope that the world will improve by the year 2020, but whether this is realistic or not is up to us. Everyone is able to do something in thousands of ways but people don't seem to see that. They think that the problems are too great for them to deal with by themselves and so there isn't even any point in trying. I believe that we can do something and that it is in our hands to change the future of the world. I am personally involved with the third-world organization called World Vision and I have seen the difference that single people can make. . . . So by educating children in schools about what they can and *should* do, more young people may take the initiative to act.

Katrina's comments not only sharply contrast the youth disempowerment referred to in many of the other studies, but indeed give us insights into, and point to possible resolutions for, this crisis of confidence among many of our youth.

Changes in values.   Two other girls demonstrated a similar depth of insight into the problems experienced by some of our youth today. Cathy expressed her views about the benefits of Steiner education:

> We need to start thinking on a global level, at the moment people are too tied up in materialistic values which only lead to unhappiness. People are just starting to realize this. I think Steiner schools will prevail over the state system in the future. State schools are breeding unhappy work orientated materialistic machines.

The other twelfth-year student, Jana, of Dutch parents, has attended the same Steiner school for over seven years. Her visions for positive changes that would bring about her ideal future world clearly showed her belief that a change in values can precipitate actual solutions to the global problems:

> There is more overall acceptance and tolerance for people of color, this has come about by realizing the importance of all cultures. . . . There is less pollution as people are concerned with the environment, together we have made an effort to be less selfish and more aware.

Many of the responses categorized in the values area referred to "changing attitudes." In a rather poignant statement of the seriousness of the issues involved and the urgency of the need for the attitude/values changes referred to here, Joshua, a twelfth-year student, revealed his anxiety about the very future viability of earth: "The future of the earth depends on the attitude of the community (both local and global). . . . The question is whether this point will be too late or not."

Some students clearly saw that the fearful prospects for the future of the earth that they, like other young people, are able to see can only be overcome by an urgent and vital change to less materialistic values. Their perception is a striking echo of much of the ecotheological and contemporary futures studies literature, and, of course of the spiritual scientific thinking of Rudolf Steiner himself.

Spirituality.   The general category termed *spirituality* is particularly distinguished by phrases such as "be more aware," "be conscious," "be awake." Several other subcategories have been included under this general term.

Consciousness development. The category of consciousness development represents the students' recognition that a mental or spiritual aspect underpins their actions. The mention of the need for an increase in "awareness" was a frequent response in this and other questions. That this is a central or driving factor as a basis for education and action was suggested by David, a fully Steiner-educated eleventh-year student: "I think it is very important to become aware and sufficiently educated in these topics, from there one can choose to tackle more active action."

Personal empowerment. This factor indicates the students' awareness of the value of each individuals contribution. It is well-exemplified by Sarah, quoted earlier, who seemed completely undaunted by the immensity of the global problems that have been identified by the students elsewhere:

> I can do everything in my own power to resolve my own conflicts peacefully and constructively and hopefully it will spread further. I can do good, be generous, do volunteer work for community health/charities and conscientiously make an effort to reduce my own and my family's pollution and waste. I'd like to also go to a third-world nation and do all I can there.

Community empowerment. On the other hand, a number of students also suggest that because the whole is greater than the sum of its parts, individual empowerment is tempered with community empowerment issues rather than individual egotism or power-seeking.

The need for a community effort was highlighted by James, who attended a religious primary school and Steiner secondary and is currently in his tenth year: "If everyone decided to do something about it then we could, but at the moment most people think it won't affect them. I think there are enough resources in the world to make everyone happy."

Interconnectedness. It is in the area of interconnectedness and respect for the sacredness of the earth (Gaia) that values begin most strongly to merge with the term spirituality. Sarah, who spoke earlier on the need to start with oneself, saw the environmental crisis as a springboard for spiritual development: "Because of the environmental crisis, the world's people realized that we have to work together to maintain our livelihood and we all have much more love and less greed."

Other students also referred to a link between environmental crisis or even catastrophe and a resultant regeneration or development of spirituality. These intuitions of the students are intriguingly consistent with the literature on spiritual emergencies in which a crisis often precedes individual spiritual initiation.[11] Joseph, a fully Steiner-educated eleventh-year student, came straight to the point, suggesting we need to "seek our meaning of existence to a greater level than now and search for true identity with the spirit." A similar scenario was envisioned by Kathryn, a twelfth-year student who has been Steiner-educated since her seventh year and wants to be a teacher or healer: "I tend to think that some huge catastrophe is going to occur either natural or man-instigated (world war), which will shake everyone up. After that there will be a kind of golden age. I don't think regeneration (of spirit and land) is possible without some kind of stirring/shocking event."

The extent to which this vision of environmental regeneration is holistically linked with some sort of spiritual integration within human beings was articulated by Yolanda, (quoted earlier), and who is in her twelfth year of Steiner education. Her vision of the positive changes needed for her ideal future world ensures that "humans use their abilities to their full potential balancing out the way we 'think' with our minds with the 'thoughts' we receive from our hearts."

Education for future care. This emerging issue is also in the human development arena. It seems that one of the things that thinking about the future has induced for these students is the realization that "the future" is something that needs to be addressed in schools. Alex, a twelfth-year student who had a Steiner secondary and state primary education, was quite emphatic in his view of future improvements in education, whereby "people are taught that as individuals they control the future."

Another fully Steiner-educated twelfth-year student, Damien, became a little cynical about the importance of listening to young people's views about the future: "The only thing that I can suggest is that people actually listen to what is being said by the young people of the day. After all, we are the ones who have to put up with all the crap that older generations dump on us by not thinking of the future."

SOCIAL EQUALITY, DIVERSITY, TOLERANCE, AND COMMUNITY

Almost two-thirds of the students (61 percent) regarded changes to the many social problems as vital to the creation of what they saw as socially equitable futures. The following issues are among the changes the students envisaged as necessary if their ideal futures were to be implemented:

- less/no homelessness, third-world countries, hunger/thirst, poverty
- no divisions according to race, class, gender, culture
- political freedom for all and land rights for indigenous peoples
- a reduction in health problems, social pressures

Jana saw the need for a deeper analysis of the issues in order to create the more equitable future she envisaged.

There is less homelessness as we are coming to understand the real reason why kids, for example, run away from home. We are coming to the root of problems and working on building stronger foundation as a way of prevention, rather than solving problems on a superficial level as they arise. . . . I believe that at the moment we are at a peak of self-centeredness and everyone is fighting their own battle of survival. As this is a peak there must also be a decline, where people realize that it is time to work together, towards a whole.

This concern for looking more deeply and broadly at issues was shared by Paul, who has attended Steiner schools all his life. His future vision requires "a 'system' that encourages people to think who they are and why they are here (stop thinking so narrow and short term)." An eleventh-year student, Shana, who has had a mixture of religious and Steiner education, decided to present her future visions in two scenarios that describe how she sees issues such as homelessness and racism resolving in the future:

> **Scenario 1**—No homelessness: Many people didn't even have homes. By opening many homes run by caring people, which offered free healthy food and comfortable beds, financed by money which otherwise would have been used on ridiculously unnecessary things like road work that isn't needed, nearly *all* homeless people, young and old, have places to live.
>
> **Scenario 2**—No racism: Classes were developed in every school that focused purely on racial difference and the problem of racism. Students were allowed to discuss opinions openly and were taught by intelligent knowledgeable teachers. Seeing as every child from a very young age grew up without purely prejudiced narrow-minded racist views, all great problems of racism faded away. Children with problems passed down from parents or developed due to a bad experience were counseled and given ways to deal with their feelings.

A PEACEFUL, COMMUNICATIVE WORLD

Somewhat less confidence was demonstrated when they considered creating visions of futures without war and conflict. Little more than one-third (37 percent) of the students were able to envision a peaceful future world. However, those who could saw this capacity beginning with themselves. The importance of listening to the other person's point of view in resolving conflicts was particularly stressed in one of the twelfth-year group dialogue sessions, where considerable discussion about the importance of relationships and dialogue in conflict resolution was encapsulated in the following comment by fully Steiner-educated Jake : "I think 'just relations' is the building block to everything—like communication and how you deal with people."

Shana, whose "socially just" scenarios were presented above, developed a more richly elaborated scenario depicting how peaceful futures might be fostered on a global scale. This seventeen-year-old girl's vision, of a peaceful world where global decisions are made collaboratively and in consultation, demonstrates a wisdom that many political leaders could learn from:

> **Scenario 3**—After much careful planning and deliberation, all world leaders and influential people met. A complete truce was called upon for this meeting even between warring countries. There were translators present and the leaders were made to listen to children and adults who had been decided upon before for having the best opinions and ideas, and an enormous agreement was made that all problems would be solved peacefully and without war. They realized how shocking and terrible and unnecessary it was for babies and innocent people to be killed brutally because of different religions or fights over land rights. Finally peace reigned and a few arrogant, blind, narrow-minded people didn't continue to destroy innocent lives.

RESACRALIZING OF NATURE AND HUMANITY

A unique and important finding was that none of the Steiner students saw technology as the savior in the future, as in Hutchinson's and other research, where the way out of global crises preferred futures for some students was into the "passive hope of techno-fix" solutions or "technocratic dreaming."[12] In addition, the Steiner students were somewhat cynical about technology; some consider technology needs to be "slowed down and people go back to basic living."

Images of Sacred Nature as Contemporary (Ancient) Wisdom

The fairly typical "clean, green, and safe" images of future environmental health and cleanliness are found to a degree in some of the other research investigating "preferred futures."[13] The Steiner students saw this as related to "overcoming corporate greed" and "putting the environment in front of money."

In addition, a small number of the Steiner students began to identify and describe, if somewhat tentatively, future images that echo a spiritual dimension only barely hinted at in the other research. Going beyond reductionist and materialist terminology, the following statements indicate a deeper reverence for the earth, which at least reflects a Gaia image if not a sacred image of the planet

- "People have realized their connection to the world around them."
- "We have to live for principles that are in harmony and respectful of the earth's existence."
- "We have learned to live more in harmony with the earth."

The esoteric underpinnings of Steiner education that incorporate an appreciation of epistemological interconnectedness began to emerge more strongly in the comments of Christina, a tenth-year student who has attended religious and Steiner schools. What she hoped for in the future is "a greater respect for the four elements earth, air, fire, and water and that they are seen as sacred."

Many of the students' visions of the environment in their preferred futures parallel the recommendations of the growing body of "green" literature on the vital importance of reversing destructive environmental trends in favor of sustainable development. Particularly interesting (in that they have not emerged from other research) were the students' visions, albeit a small number, that reflect images of "sacred nature." This somewhat romantic, idealist, even animistic view of the living environment is supported by an emerging body of literature that decries the environmental destruction that has resulted from three centuries of scientific reductionism and calls for a "re-enchantment of the world."[14] It should be noted also that some of this literature is remarkably consistent with the image of nature as inherently artistic, mysteriously alive, and imbued with spirit, a view held by many indigenous epistemologies, artists, and poets, as well as such philosophers as Goethe and Steiner.[15]

Utopian Dreams and Lessons

It might be cautioned that many of the visions presented above are utopian dreams divorced from reality or any hope of implementation. In fact, one fully Steiner-educated twelfth-year student, Melina, critiqued herself and balanced her own utopian vision in the following way:

> My imagined utopia, in which everything is perfect in everyone's eyes, would not have time to develop by the year 2020. Anyway I don't believe that it could ever be real because one can't live without some worries to balance one's life. However I believe that the situation in the world will improve and the problems that are now will be addressed.

An eleventh-year student, Julia, who has also attended Steiner schools all her life, further counter-balanced this view of utopian possibilities: "This earth will never become a place free of problems. That is not its destiny. This is a place where people come to learn and without problems we cannot do this. As the saying goes: 'Too much sunshine makes desert.'"

HUMAN DEVELOPMENT FOR SOCIAL FUTURES

In addition to the somewhat ubiquitous positive environmental images that the students created, more uniquely, they invested considerable imagery in "re-inventing" human values. Three-quarters of the Steiner students produced some kind of positive imagery of how human beings need to change in order for their "preferred future worlds" to be created. This capacity to richly envision aspects of human development as part of futures visioning has not been demonstrated in other research with young people, to my knowledge. Furthermore, it has been stated by Hicks (1996) that even when it comes to research of adult views and visions of the future, the emphasis has been on technological rather than on social futures. He quotes Johan Galtung on the general gap in the futures research on anything pertaining to "social futures":

> The future is seen in technical terms, not in terms of culture, human enrichment, social equality, social justice, or in terms of international affairs . . . . People may think of social future but regard it as unchangeable. But it seems more probable that they have only been trained to think technologically and have no other type of thoughts as a response to the stimulus "future". . . . [T]his will then become self-reinforcing since no one will be stimulated to think about social futures.[16]

The extent to which the Steiner students' visions also depicted socially just futures of equality and diversity, tolerance, and community further indicates that their capacity to envision "social futures" is quite strong. In addition, when envisioning futures without war, the students primarily related improvements in human relationships and communication, through dialogue and conflict resolution, rather than a "passive peace" image. Further suggesting a sophistication of social awareness rather than "protected innocence," even their "utopian dreams" were full of dialectic struggle, as is that of futurist Ashis Nandy, rather than a naive return to paradise.[17]

In summary, it is intriguing to compare the sense of responsibility that emerged in these students' visions of their futures with what Slaughter refers to as "responsibilities of young people for the twenty-first century." He lists such qualities as:

- looking beyond one's own personal needs
- participating in the global community
- acting as caring stewards of the environment and other species
- acknowledging the rights of future generations
- conserving and reinventing cultures
- subordinating technical concerns to human ones.[18]

In many respects, the Steiner students demonstrated what could be called "futures thinking," although they have not been formally introduced to futures studies education.

This research provides strong support for educational futurists' speculation that an education that is more integrated, imaginative, and proactive will better prepare young people for the future. The Steiner educational approach appears to foster in young people the ability to imagine positive social futures and the idealism and commitment to work for their creation.

NOTES

1. Ake Bjerstedt, "Future Consciousness and the School," in *Educational Information and Debate,* vol. 62., ed. A. Bjerstedt (Malmo, Sweden: School of Education, University of Lund, 1982); Hedley Beare and Rick Slaughter, *Education for the Twenty-First Century* (London: Routledge, 1993); Johan Galtung, "Schooling, Education and the Future," *Educational Information and Debate,* vol. 61 (Malmo, Sweden: Department of Education and Psychology Research, University of Lund, 1982); Francis Hutchinson, *Educating Beyond Violent Futures,* ed. R. Slaughter. (London: Routledge, 1996); Allen Tough, "What Future Generations Need from Us," *Futures* (December 1993): 1041–1050.

2. Rudolf Steiner, *A Modern Art of Education* (Lectures, 1923) (London: Rudolf Steiner Press, 1972).

3. J. Anderson, *Cognitive Psychology and its Implications* (New York: W. H. Freeman and Co., 1985); R. Arnheim, *Thoughts on Art Education* (Los Angeles, Calif.: Getty Center for Education in The Arts, 1989); Harry Broudy, *The Role of Imagery in Learning* (Los Angeles: The Getty Center for Education in the Arts, 1987); E. Eisner, *The Educational Imagination: On the Design and Evaluation of School Programs,* 2nd ed. (New York: Macmillan, 1985); Herbert Read, *Education Through Art* (Faber, 1943).

4. Rudolf Steiner, *The Younger Generation: Education and Spiritual Impulses in the 20th Century* (Lectures, 1922) (New York: Anthroposophic Press, 1967), 81

5. Richard Eckersley, "The West's Deepening Cultural Crisis," *The Futurist,* (1993): 10.

6. Thomas Berry, *The Dream of the Earth* (San Francisco: Sierra Club Books, 1988); Morris Berman, *The Reenchantment of the World* (Ithica, N.Y.: Cornell University Press, 1981); David Tacey, *Edge of the Sacred: Transformation in Australia* (Melbourne: Harper Collins, 1995).

7. Rudolf Steiner, *The Renewal of Education through the Science of the Spirit* (Lectures, 1920) (Sussex: Kolisko Archive, 1981).

8. Refer to note 3.

9. Rudolf Steiner, *The Renewal,* 86.

10. Jennifer Gidley, "Prospective Youth Visions Through Imaginative Education," *Futures* 30, 5 (1998): 395–408.

11. Stanislov Grof and Christina Grof, *Spiritual Emergency, When Personal Transformation Becomes a Crisis* (New York: Tarcher/Putnam, 1989).

12. Richard Eckersley, *Having Our Say about the Future: Young People's Dreams and Expectations for Australia in 2010 and the Role of Science and Technology* (Canberra: Australian Science and Technology Council, 1996); Francis Hutchinson, *Futures Consciousness and the School: Explorations of Broad and*

Narrow Literacies for the Twenty-First Century with Particular Reference to Australian Young People (University of New England: Armidale NSW, 1992).

13.   Ibid.

14.   Jerry Mander, *In the Absence of the Sacred* (San Francisco: Sierra Club Books, 1991); Theodore Roszak, Mary Gomes, and Allen Kanner, *Ecopsychology: Restoring the Earth; Healing the Mind* (San Francisco: Sierra Books, 1995); see also note 6.

15.   Rudolf Steiner, *Microcosm and Macrocosm* (London: Rudolf Steiner Press, 1968); Rudolf Steiner, *The Boundaries of Natural Science* (New York: Anthroposophic Press, 1983).

16.   David Hicks, "A Lesson for the Future," *Futures* 28, 1 (1996): 1–13.

17.   Ashis Nandy, *Traditions, Tyranny and Utopias: Essays in the Politics of Awareness* (Delhi: Oxford University Press, 1992).

18.   Richard Slaughter, *From Fatalism to Foresight—Educating for the Early 21st Century: Framework for Considering Young People's Needs and Responsibilities Over the Next 20 Years* (Melbourne: Australian Council for Educational Administration, 1994): 43.

Youth Essay 2

Voice of the Future from Pakistan

Bilal Aslam

Today's youth: tomorrow's world.

A statement which none can deny. So how is our future faring in today's world? What does it want? What does it feel? Once in a while everyone gives a thought or two to these questions. Some continue to ponder, others give a content smile imagining well-dressed, neat and tidy youngsters sitting in a lecture theater in one of the leading universities of the world, and of course there's the third kind, which outrightly dismisses any such thoughts saying: "Nah, they're just kids, what more could it be to them than jazzy sports bikes, loud music, and their girl/boy friends."

Then what does our future truly look like? To answer this question I would like to paint a picture before you and let you be the judge. Our picture has three faces. Each face represents a different individual from a different part of the world. Let me give you a brief background of our three characters.

Chris is the only son of a wealthy businessman living in a beautiful mansion in Beverly Hills, California, in the United States.

Nam is one of the eight children of a factory worker from Rawalpindi, Pakistan. Nam's father died a little while before Nam was born.

Liu is the only daughter of a middle-class government employee living in Tokyo, Japan.

At present all three of them are in their late teens.

On a cold November morning, Chris woke up at 8:00, slowly rolled back his doona, and wandered into his ensuite bathroom for a hot shower. After flicking through his many choices of expensive brand-name clothes for what to wear today, he went downstairs for some bacon, eggs, and coffee. After breakfast he picked up the keys to his new Porsche, which his dad got him for his eighteenth birthday and headed off to college. Chris was more then satisfied with his life. He was studying in one of the world's elite private colleges and his dad owned a business empire, which he was to take over. His main worry was which girl to take out this week.

On the other end of the globe, Nam was up at 6:00. It wasn't his mum who woke him but the unbearable cold, which hardly let him get any sleep throughout the night. He looked at the sky and shrugged in despair and horror. The sun was out and that meant he had missed the morning rush hour from which he earned quite a large part of his earnings for the day. Dressed in a shredded piece of cloth, which might have been considered a dress many years back when its owner donated it, he leapt to his feet and ran off to the city center in the hope of catching any traffic, which may be left. He approached the first traffic signal and saw a car stop at the red light. He rushed towards the car knowing that if he did not take back any money tonight, his family would sleep without dinner, their only meal in the day, and his mum wouldn't get her medicine. He tapped the cars window, making an innocent face and murmuring the words which he'd repeat throughout the day many a times: "Lord have mercy on you, please spare a penny, Lord have mercy."

Liu got up at 8:00 when her mum forced her out of bed, as her friend Amy would be here any minute and she was late for college. She got out of bed quickly, covering her arms so that her concerned mother couldn't see them. She got dressed, had a quick breakfast and the doorbell rung. It was Amy. The two girls were off to college on foot as they had been doing for the last couple of years. Midway to the college they suddenly slipped into a dark alley. After trotting hurriedly to avoid being seen they entered a door. A man welcomed them and after a brief conversation signaled them to sit. Liu unbuttoned her cuff button and rolled up her left sleeve, exposing her arm covered with black and blue marks. The man returned with a few syringes and handed one to Liu, who put the needle to her already numerously punctured arm and injected the blue liquid into her blood.

What is wrong with these three scenarios? What makes them different? Aren't all these three individuals human beings? Or is it that Chris chose to be born where he was? Nam made a mistake of being born in his family? Or maybe Liu was addicted from the day she was born? These are the true faces of reality, which are present today. And if this is the present, let us take a glimpse of the future.

Some twenty years down the line, on the seventieth floor of a New York skyscraper, in a huge office room, wearing an Armani suit, sits Chris, who is now the owner of a multinational business empire.

Back in Pakistan, under the naked sky, lay Nam on a bed hardly able to move. Now a father of five, Nam suffers from a plague, which spread due to the unhygienic water system. His wife died giving birth to their last child.

Nam anxiously awaited his older children's return with their day's earnings, which they earned the same way their father did his throughout his working life. He was hoping they'd have enough to get some milk for the little baby. His own medicines were simply unaffordable.

Liu's parents, now in their 80s slowly stepped out of their house. They kept walking for a little while and then stopped. Liu's mum, holding her dad's aging hand, fell on her knees and started crying, with her tears dripping on a tombstone on which Liu's name was engraved.

This is what the future would look like if the present is allowed to stay the way it is. In today's world, there aren't many Chrises present, but you would certainly find a large number of Nams and Lius, particularly in the third world countries like Pakistan, India and Sri Lanka, where a large percentage of the population lives below the poverty line, resources are extremely scarce, and the venom of drugs is spreading day by day.

I myself am a nineteen-year-old. What I see in front of me worries me. What kind of a world are we, the youth, going to take over from our elders? A world in which one teenager drives into a McDonald's in his shiny car, while another kid of the same age stands there with tears in his eyes begging the other for a penny, otherwise he'd sleep without having anything to eat? Why is there so much inequality? How did our elders let themselves be driven to this level of disparity? When God has made us the most intelligent of his creatures, why still every day do an increasing number of us give in to the demon of drugs? Why do we spend so much on wars and ways to destroy ourselves when we don't even have enough to eat? Why can education not be the right of everyone?

These are the questions present in the mind of today's youth. The answer to and the cure for all these problems is very simple if we consider just one key element. We are all born equal, everyone is born a human being, no one is a born thief, neither is anyone a born saint. We can be whoever we want to be. True, our surroundings and environment drive us to quite an extent to become what we are, be that criminals, or addicts, or whatever, but we must learn not to give in to these surroundings. That's why Lord has given us the insight to choose between right and wrong. Rather than giving in we must find ways to rectify the complexities around us. We have to change and we have to bring about a change. We have to change the way we think, the way we perceive, the way we prioritize, the way we attach so little value to human life. We need to change our attitudes and values.

As long as we maintain our approach of striving to be superior and bigger than the others, as long as we are bent upon destroying each other, as long as we don't consider humanity as one (rather than black or white), we cannot make a difference. Human life is the most precious gift of God, a gift which can not be sacrificed for the sake of our profits.

It's not just the elders on whose shoulders I place the burden of doing all this, but we the youth, together with our elders, have to make sure that everyone on this planet is considered equal. We have to make certain that those who sell death are stopped. Only by working together can we make this world a better place for us and our future generations. Together we can, together we must, and together we will.

Part III

Case Studies: Teaching Futures in Educational Settings

Chapter 14

From Rhetoric to Reality:
The Emergence of Futures
into the Educational Mainstream

Richard Slaughter

Young people do not need to be persuaded to consider the future. They already have powerful interests in the self-constitution of their own lives. A common complaint, however, is that they are seldom listened to or taken seriously. Despite much rhetoric to the contrary, their deepest needs, their highest ideals, do not figure prominently in most educational agendas. For some twenty years I have worked with a variety of schools, school systems, and tertiary institutions in several countries. What stands out very clearly is that forward-looking approaches appeal very strongly to the young, visionary educators, and those with progressive interests in education. I have seen many teachers, school principals, and schools take up and apply a wide range of futures tools with clear and documented success. But what has also stood out is that as soon as one passes beyond the middle level of any school system, futures approaches are of minor interest at best; they vanish like smoke on a windy day and are seen no more. Grassroots practitioners are denied the long-term support they need; initiatives die and are forgotten. If you return a few years later it is as if they never existed; business-as-usual rules.

Since the mid-1960s, innovative educators around the world have been exploring a different view. They have thoroughly understood the educational significance of the futures domain and have sought to incorporate it in theory, literature, and practice.

This chapter provides a brief review of the emergence of futures in education. It first considers the grounding of futures work in a cultural diagnosis, based on looking back to the past to understand the present. It then considers developments in practice. It asks: why did futures become an educational concern and what do young people actually learn? It suggests explanations for sources of resistance within educational systems. Finally, it outlines strategies to complete the process of making futures a fully main-stream concern.

LOOKING BACK TO LOOK FORWARD

The end of the twentieth century brought a flood of books and TV programs that attempted to come to grips with the recent past: what was the twentieth century and what, exactly, does it mean? These are not simple questions. Historians and social commentators will debate them for a long time to come. In order to say anything sensible about the future we must know "our place in time" or simply "where we are from."

Our present, our particular here-and-now, is in fact only one version of many that were once possible. Had key events in the past worked out differently we would be living in a very different world. So a careful look at the past reveals how our present world was constructed. And let us make no mistake that, like the calendar itself, our present reality is indeed a construction—albeit an exceptionally complex one. It did not arise by accident, but by the interweaving of a host of socially and historically contingent forces and factors. It is for such reasons that deep insight into the nature of our present must necessarily precede any attempt to explore possible futures. We do not begin from an objective starting point. Rather, we begin saturated with a host of "givens" which, because they are so familiar, tend to be seen as natural and even inevitable. But the fact is that if humanity is to have a worthwhile future, much that was taken for granted in the twentieth century will necessarily have to change in the twenty-first.

Some thirty years ago Lewis Mumford had this to say about a process he called "the removal of limits."

> To conquer nature is in effect to remove all natural barriers and human norms and to substitute artificial, fabricated equivalents for natural processes: to replace the immense variety of resources offered by nature by more uniform, constantly available products spewed forth by the machine.

He then added:

> From these general postulates a series of subsidiary ones are derived: there is only one efficient speed, faster; only one attractive destination, farther away; only one desirable size, bigger; only one rational quantitative goal, more. On these assumptions the object of human life, and therefore of the whole productive mechanism, is to remove limits, to hasten the pace of change, to smooth out seasonal rhythms and reduce regional contrasts—in fine, to promote mechanical novelty and destroy organic continuity.[1]

The conquest of nature, the removal of limits, and the pursuit of economic growth for its own sake are among the guiding commitments deeply inscribed within the global system at the dawn of the twenty-first century. These invisible but very powerful commitments frame the world in specific ways and color how that world is understood and how the great social formations, such as government, business, and education, operate. Though this growth-addicted civilization has been bumping up against global limits for some years, there remains an air of collective denial abroad: "economic growth is good for everyone; the problems are not that serious; we can find substitutes for scarce resources; new technologies will open out new options"; and so on.

The human species is nothing if not optimistic. But its powers of optimism are, perhaps, only matched by its powers of self-deception. The final element that makes this perceptual nightmare work, and work so effectively, is that in the Western industrial worldview, short-term thinking has become the norm. What this means is that while everyone is rushing around looking for short-term gains, attending to "the bottom line," gearing up for the next election, the downbeat, dystopian futures clearly implied by a culture in denial of limits are de-focused and put routinely out of sight. Hence, "the system" goes on in its destructive and literally myopic way, placing everyone's life and well-being at risk.

It comes as no surprise that young people already know this. They also know that there is much more to come and, moreover, that we are not at all well prepared for the revolutions ahead—what Jim Dator calls the "tsunamis of change."

Fortunately, the very forces of globalization, technical virtuosity, and environmental threat that characterize the early twenty-first century have also stimulated a range of responses. Among these has been the development of the field of futures studies itself and its progressive application within schools. In essence, futures studies explores the near-future context using a range of conceptual and methodological resources. What emerges from this process is, quite simply, a viable forward view or, rather, a number of them keyed to different needs and contexts.[2]

When people discover the rich understandings that the forward view offers, they find many, many uses for them. Individuals gain a new sense of purpose and direction; schools gain a new set of concepts and tools for exploring future options with the young; businesses enliven their necessary focus on strategy with the powerful insights that emerge from disciplined foresight. Governments, in those rare cases where they take the forward view seriously, can canvass entirely new policy options.

This, really, is the point. As futurists never tire of explaining, there is no one future. Rather there exist a very wide variety of possible, probable, and preferable ones. The whole point of exploring this array of future potential is to tease out the critical choices, strategies, and possible responses in the here-and-now and to apply these in a thousand different ways. In other words, the forward view fundamentally changes the way we operate in the here-and-now. That is essentially why the work of futures educators is vital to the well being of students, schools, and society. Questions about the future of education are of far lesser interest than those about futures in education. The former is an extrapolative exercise; the latter can transform practice in the present. The rest of this chapter looks at how futures education has evolved in response to these challenges.

DEVELOPMENT OF FUTURES EDUCATION PRACTICE

The earliest work in schools drew upon the wider field of futures research that originally developed in the context of the Cold War and its military scenarios. The techniques of planning, forecasting, war-gaming, and scenario analysis were seen to have value well beyond military applications. Government, business, and industry quickly assimilated into these and other techniques.

I have summarized elsewhere some of the rationales advanced for an explicitly futures-focused approach in education.[3] Briefly, they touch on:

- questions of rapid change;
- the fact that actions and decisions have consequences;
- that images of the future permeate the present;
- that the future is "a principle of present action";
- that education has its roots in the past but cannot move ahead only on that basis;
- that the past cannot be changed whereas the future can at least be shaped by human will and intention, and;
- when our implicit model of personhood sees people as agents (interpreters of culture and makers of meaning) there is a direct connection between futures and education.[4]

In the 1960s and 1970s such considerations provided *a priori* reasons why a futures focus in education seemed to be a good idea. The first school course was taught in the United States in 1966. Several pilot projects were funded by what was then called the Office of Education, and these led to the establishment of centers where futures were, and in some cases still are (e.g., the University of Houston at Clear Lake) studied and taught. The World Future Society entered the picture, and, by the early 1970s, its education section had a professional membership of several thousand. Conferences, publications, and seminars followed, spreading all over the United States and in other countries. By this time, a number of international networks and nongovernmental organizations (NGOs) had sprung up. Perhaps the most productive and durable of these is the World Futures Studies Federation.

In virtually every Western country, and increasingly in others as well, groups of innovators based in schools, colleges, and universities began to learn from each other and to perceive that they were part of a wider shift. It was a shift away from immersion in a taken-for-granted past and present toward a conscious evaluation of possible, probable, and preferable futures. Then, as practical experience accumulated, a range of highly desirable outcomes was observed. At least five key outcomes were frequently reported.

First, a working familiarity with the symbolic, and to a lesser extent, the methodological aspects of futures provides the basis for a futures discourse. This is missing from so many of the great institutions that structure social life: politics, economics, and, indeed, education itself.

Second, teaching and learning about futures enhances what may best be called "futures literacy." Thus, concerns that may have been unclear and poorly articulated are redefined to become the source of innovations, projects, and other creative responses. Those who develop these capabilities understand the risks, but they also understand that the key to resolving them lies in the nature of human and institutional responses.

Third, futures teaching specifically encourages constructive and empowering attitudes. As other chapters in this book make clear, young people are exposed to a great deal of negative and destructive material. Teachers of futures explore the significance of such material and lead students to understand its origins in industrialized cultures as well as the many routes and resources beyond it. Perhaps the most widely reported outcomes of futures courses are the constructive shifts in attitude that they engender.

Fourth, it follows that futures teaching helps people develop the skills of proactive citizenship and leadership. The latter is always leadership toward something, and futures-literate people are well-equipped to engage in dialogue and design concerning directions, processes, structures, and destinations.

Finally, such teaching and learning provide ways of grasping what is sometimes called "the big picture," that is, a clear overview of the processes of continuity and change, of challenge and response that structure and permeate our world.[5]

While the early gains of the futures education movement in the United States faltered under increasingly unfavorable political and economic conditions, a new generation of teachers and academics took up the work and improved upon it. Still in the United States, the foundation laid down by the pioneers continued through the work of people such as Kristen Druker, Ted Dixon, and David E. Smith. One of the strong continuities in this field is that established by Paul Torrence's work (initially with gifted children). From this emerged the Future Problem Solving Program (FPSP). According to a mid-1990s FPSP flyer, an estimated 200,000 students in all fifty states and numerous foreign countries were using the program's materials.[6]

No other country has yet been able to sustain this level of success or continuity in futures-related school curricula. In New Zealand and Australia a variety of tertiary courses had been offered, but when teachers returned to their schools they typically had very little continuing support. In Queensland, Australia, the Board of Senior Secondary School Studies (BSSSS) developed an innovative, four-semester, program in futures for years eleven and twelve. Early evaluations confirmed this to be a highly effective model for upper secondary work that deserves to be widely emulated.[7]

In Britain, Hicks' Global Futures Project continues to offer short courses and provide futures-related curricula for primary and secondary use.[8]

Futures programs at the Primary level have been developed in many areas but tend to be less well-documented. Many assume that you can't teach futures to young children. However, the junior school years provide ample opportunities for foundational work in futures. The work of Simon Nicholson and Ray Lorenzo, the Montclair futures school (New Jersey, United States) and researchers such as Hicks and Holden (United Kingdom) and Page (Australia) make it clear that a great deal can be achieved at this stage.[9] With the age and developmental stages of children taken fully into account, futures can be, and are, taught at the primary level and even earlier. Page's research is the first substantive work to explore the practical significance of futures in the early childhood context.[10] Cole Jackson's online futures project in Florida has successfully involved students from a range of schools in the United States and elsewhere and is described more fully in a later chapter of this volume.

The role of creative individuals and NGOs in the innovation process has been highly significant,[11] yet any attempt to provide a detailed picture would require a much longer work. One conclusion can be drawn, however: if teachers and schools stand any chance of integrating futures perspectives into their work, they will need much more durable structures of support than anything that has been provided.

Obstacles to Change

Futures education will thrive in the twenty-first century because, as suggested, it is driven by widely shared human responses to structural change. As one independent observer put it, "Futures concepts and curricula seem to me to be the most important rising paradigm in education. It addresses the ambivalence of postmodernism and focuses on proactive strategies that attend to the imperatives facing our world."[12] This singularly concise statement helps explain why futures education has such profound transformative potential. It is therefore surprising, at first sight, that the most serious impediments to the further development and integration of futures education into the mainstream are not external. Rather, they lie in the nature of the structure of school systems as they have evolved during the industrial period and prevailing modes of administration at the very highest levels.

Top administrators can cope with occasional extrapolative exercises regarding the future of education because they fit neatly within present bureaucratic thinking. But it is rare to see high-level interest in futures in education, which is a completely different matter. In order to explain this, I now turn to some of the powerful forces that constrain educational systems.

School systems are quintessentially "industrial era" organizations. They are rigid hierarchies, mandated and controlled by central and (at least in Australia) state governments, with top-down power structures. One of their key features, therefore, is inflexibility. Typically, there is a minister at the top; teachers and students are at the bottom—not unlike a nineteenth-century army. The "meat in the sandwich" is a layer of bureaucracy that must, at all times, obey prevailing political priorities. Teachers and students are reminiscent of marginalized, disempowered "foot soldiers." Indeed, prevailing "system imperatives" are not primarily about human beings, society, or, indeed, the future. They are largely abstract and may be summarized as power, control, economy, and efficiency.[13]

School systems are widely thought to serve some sort of human or social needs. In a limited, conventional sense, there is some truth in that view. The fact is, however, that they are not centrally concerned with human and social needs, or with where society may be headed at all. Rhetoric and public announcements repeatedly express such themes. But there are perhaps two key sets of forces, two worlds of reference, that set the major "rules" for such systems. Both, however, had become defective and incoherent by the end of the twentieth century. Politics is notorious for its short-term thinking and the ideological conceits of many of its practitioners. Economics lost sight of human needs and aspirations many years ago and remains a very long way from reforming itself. School systems have widely overlooked the fact that, as they presently stand, neither politics nor economics is capable of expressing, or responding to, widely understood human, social, and cultural needs. According to John Saul, behind both lies a powerful but regressive corporatist ideology.[14]

In summary, education systems tend to have the following characteristics:

1. They are inward-looking. Unlike comparable businesses, they have few systemic connections with the wider world, hence, they are largely insulated from processes of change in the global system.
2. They are past- and present-driven, hence, they have minimal capacity to create, or engage with, a forward view. This major structural defect requires urgent corrective action.
3. They are governed by fiat and powerfully resist any attempts to revise existing system imperatives, hence, they seek to marginalize educational leadership and attempts at systemwide innovation. This undermines their

social legitimacy (as agents of social well-being) and cuts them off from sources of human vitality that might otherwise be welcomed and used.

If education systems (from schools to universities) are to focus on the needs of a changing world, the needs of young people, and eventually future generations, then it is necessary to take action on a number of levels and in a number of different ways.

FUTURES EDUCATION IN THE TWENTY-FIRST CENTURY

A first step is to critique and replace the system imperatives currently operating. This will require sustained effort over a period of time. A second step is to insist on a number of perceptual and organizational innovations. Some of these are sketched out below. Third, paradigms of education (i.e., "what education is" and "what it is for") will need to be revised in the light of the conditions facing society and individuals in the twenty-first century. All entities within education systems, from primary schools to leading universities, will need to critically draw upon and use the tools of prospective analysis, understanding, and strategy-formulation that have been commonplace elsewhere (such as corporate environments) for a long time.

The drift to nonstate schooling is one of a number of social trends now actively creating a new "underclass." It does not take much foresight to realize that dysfunctional individuals will emerge from it to plague the rest of society. The rush to private schools is partly a result of government neglect of the state sector and partly a security reflex on the part of affluent parents. However, private schools are not immune from the defects mentioned. Many actively cultivate the image of tradition, of the past, but do no more than state schools to prepare young people for the opportunities and challenges of the real future they will live in. The long-term solution is not to opt out of public schooling but to revalue it and bring it up to a viable standard of operation. The pivotal contradiction of present school systems is that they ostensibly exist to prepare the young for active citizenship in the future. But, unlike most Fortune 500 companies, these systems have little grasp either of the big picture in the present or of what "the future" might actually mean.

For school systems to be able to comprehend and deal actively with the twenty-first-century context, the forward view must begin to permeate educational administration, thinking, and practice at every level.

In summary, the central strategies that will move education systems from a past to an explicitly future orientation are:

1. The active delegitimation of industrial-era notions of education based on redundant abstract principles.

2. The refocusing of education systems and universities away from the past and short-term present toward a substantive commitment to understanding the emerging near-term future.
3. The much wider utilization of the theory, literature, and practical capabilities that have been developed under the heading of "futures education," as outlined here.
4. The flourishing of a new type of ethically based and fearless generation of educational leaders who will overturn bureaucratic rationality, control, and so on, in pursuit of the public good in the long view.[15]

Futures Curricula in Practice

So what do futures teachers actually teach? During the early years, the focus is mainly on imagination, creativity, thinking skills, and the development of a futures vocabulary. Here is where the young are introduced to simple futures concepts (past, present, future; the extended present; alternatives and choices; images of the future, and so on) and to simple futures tools (time frames, futures wheels, cross-impact matrices, social inventions, and so on). Blindingly simple though it may appear, the key to inculcating the foundations of a futures perspective lies in providing the young with these very accessible conceptual and practical starting points.[16] At the secondary level, futures can be an interdisciplinary focus that permeates all subjects and/or a subject in its own right. For example, the BSSSS syllabus covered the following areas: the futures field; futures tools, techniques, and concepts; personal empowerment; social innovation; the state of the planet; pathways toward sustainability; and a unit on independent local study.[17]

Primary and secondary schools would face daunting obstacles if they operated in isolation. But both are powerfully supported by a knowledge base of futures studies, the discipline of foresight and futures enquiry in perhaps a dozen universities, and an impressive array of networks and NGOs increasingly accessible through the Internet.[18] Many syllabuses have been developed and tested, and authoritative accounts of futures teaching in schools and universities are available.[19] Too few teachers or lecturers have had the opportunity to pick up and apply these concepts and tools, which is a difficulty that needs to be quickly remedied. Those who have find the whole process personally and professionally rewarding.

ALL EDUCATION IS FUTURES EDUCATION

The challenge is to reinvent schools on a new philosophical and operational basis, rather than see them overwhelmed by economic rationalism, still less by the overhyped "communications revolution." The walls are certainly coming down around most built institutions, and schools cannot escape such powerful competitive forces as new media, entrepreneurial penetration and autonomous learning. The lure of "cyberspace" will make most industrial-era schools seem dull and unresponsive.

School systems are so change-resistant that they may be undermined by new circumstances. Alternatively they can choose to adapt and reinvent themselves. In the former case, public education will cease to exist as a viable entity, but the social consequences would be immense. Schools are vital locations for socialization and social cohesion. Without some shared locus of learning social fragmentation, the rise of exclusive subcultures and greater social conflict seem unavoidable.

It is difficult to see how humanity can respond to the coming transitions and "tsunamis of change" without maintaining socialization and social cohesion. Seen in this light, school systems must be regarded as assets, rather than costs. Above all, they should be protected from the irrationalities of economic rationalism and carve out for themselves a new futures-oriented *modus operandi* that more fully responds to deeper human and social needs. No one else will do it for them. The central task of foresight and futures studies is to help discern the foundations of the next civilization. The great opportunity for schools is to prepare the young to participate in this process of social innovation and deep design in every field of human endeavor.[20]

In so doing, they will necessarily take up the work of futures educators around the world and move beyond many of the assumptions and practices that flourished in earlier times. They will abandon the stale rhetoric that claims a vague and empty association between schools and "the future" for the reality of a substantive involvement with the forward view at every level.

NOTES

1. Lewis Mumford, *The Pentagon of Power* (New York: Harcourt, Brace, Jovanovitch, 1970).

2. Richard Slaughter, *Futures for the Third Millennium—Enabling the Forward View* (Sydney: Prospect, 1999).

3. Richard Slaughter, "An International Overview of Futures Education," *UNESCO Future Scan* 1, 1 (1992): 63–64.

4. Malcolm Skilbeck, "The School and Cultural Development," in *Curriculum Design,* ed. David Golby (London: Open University, 1975), 27–35.

5. Richard Slaughter, "The Knowledge Base of Futures Studies—What Do Students Learn?" *UNESCO Seminar Papers* (Vancouver, June 1992): 6–7.

6. Kirsten Druker, et al. "Futures Studies at an Urban High School," *World Future Society Bulletin* 15, 2 (1981): 15–21; Ted Dixon, "Futures Studies for Juniors," course syllabus (Milford High School, Ohio, 1982); Richard Smith, "Laying the Foundation: Basic Theories for a Futuristics Course," *World Future Society Bulletin,*

15, 2 (1981): 22–24. Also Paul Torrence, "Creativity and Futurism in Education: Retooling," *Education* 100, 4 (1980): 298–311.

7.   Board of Senior Secondary School Studies, Pre-Pilot Senior Syllabus in Futures (Brisbane, 1999).

8.   David Hicks, *Global Futures Curriculum Document* (Bath Spa University College, United Kingdom, 1997/8).

9.   Simon Nicholson and Ray Lorenzo "Future Perfect," *Undercurrents* 36 (1979): 12–14; Montclair Public School Brochure (Montclair, New Jersey, 1980); David Hicks and Cathie Holden, *Visions of the Future: Why We Need to Teach for Tomorrow* (London: Trentham Books, 1995).

10.   Jane Page, *Reframing the Early Childhood Curriculum—Educational Imperatives for the Future* (London: Routledge/Falmer, 2000).

11.   Richard Slaughter, "An International Overview . . . :70–72.

12.   Paul Inglis, Queensland Institute of Technology, (1998).

13.   John Saul, private communication, *The Unconscious Civilization* (London: Penguin, 1997).

14.   Ibid., 162.

15.   Patrick Duignan, "A Quest for Authentic Leadership," *BMAS Annual Conference Papers* (Oxford: Balliol College, 1995).

16.   Richard Slaughter, *Futures Tools and Techniques, and Futures Concepts and Powerful Ideas* (Melbourne: Futures Study Center, 1999). Also see Thomas Lombardo, *The Odyssey of the Future* (Rio Salado College, USA, 1999).

17.   Board of Senior Secondary School Studies, Pre-Pilot Senior . . . .

18.   Richard Slaughter, ed., The Knowledge Base of Futures Studies, vols. 1–3, (Melbourne: Futures Study Center, 1996). Also, with Sohail Inayatullah, *The Knowledge Base of Futures Studies* vols. 1–4, CD-ROM (Brisbane: Foresight International, 2000).

19.   Howard Didsbury, *Prep 21 Course Guide* (Washington: World Future Society, 1986); David Hicks and Richard Slaughter, eds., *Futures Education—World Education Yearbook 1998* (London: Kogan Page, 1998).

20.   This is a vast topic and there are many rich sources. Three contrasting treatments are: Paul Hawken, et al., *Natural Capitalism—The Next Industrial Revolution* (London: Earthscan, 1999); David Tacey, *Reenchantment—The New Australian Spirituality* (Sydney: Harper/Collins, 2000); and Ken Wilber, *Integral Psychology* (Boulder, Colo.: Shambhala, 2000).

Chapter 15

Re-Imagining Your Neighborhood: A Model of Futures Education

Carmen Stewart

REVITALIZING SOCIAL PLANNING

In recent years there has been substantial research on young people's images, hopes, and fears for the future and how these perceptions encourage or discourage their participation in society. Futures researchers such as Elise Boulding, Polak, and Zeigler, have contributed to our understanding of the crucial role that our images of the future play in determining our present actions. "Polak was one of the first thinkers to call attention to the atrophy of our capacity to visualize a wholly different future."[1] In translating Polak's reading of history, Elise Boulding describes the important role images play in motivating social change: "In eras when pessimism combines with a sense of cosmic helplessness, the quality of human intentionality declines and, with it, the quality of the not-yet. . . . Societies in that condition live bounded by the present, with no social dynamic for change available to them."[2]

A dynamic link exists between our capacity to imagine and believe in a sustainable future and our present ability to respond to issues of social and ecological survival. Developing our capacity to imagine significant aspects of a healthy future is a crucial and timely motivation for change.

Numerous reports prepared by researchers, including Richard Eckersley, Frank Hutchinson, and David Hicks, raise concerns about trends of youth pessimism. The findings from this research indicate that young people are aware of and affected by the growing complexity and challenges of our world.[3] Their greatest concerns include environmental degradation, violence, employment prospects, war, and relationships. Not surprisingly, their concerns reflect the major social and environmental concerns of communities globally. The apathy we must confront is not due not to a lack of information about the problems, but to a lack of information about the possibilities for a healthy and sustainable future.[4]

Trends of youth pessimism are not inevitable. Numerous educators have been developing tools and methods to help young people imagine a life-giving future that encourages social confidence and action. Jennifer Gidley's 1997 study focused on a holistic, imaginative, and artistic approach to educating about the future. In investigating the views of Steiner-educated students, she found that:

> . . . educational input can potentially facilitate a positive, prospective outlook, thereby empowering students for their future lives. . . . It is argued that the qualities that strengthen this need to be taken seriously. This research demonstrates that it is vital that the current emphasis on "head knowledge" in mainstream education be balanced in the future by: the cultivation of the imagination through story telling and the arts; a reinvention of human values to include activism, spirituality and future care. [5]

Similar findings have been cited in studies by Boulding, Hicks, Slaughter, and Hutchinson.[6] Young people can experience social confidence, vision, and an energetic enthusiasm to participate when presented with a holistic context for exploring the future. Such learning and empowerment is necessary for the emotional well-being of young people. It is also central to motivating a positive and critical exploration of the future in ways that can revitalize social purpose and planning.

RE-IMAGINING YOUR NEIGHBORHOOD

This chapter will introduce "Re-Imagining Your Neighborhood" (RYN), a futures education project developed by Imagine the Future Inc. The project was first piloted in 1997 in Melbourne's western suburbs. Since then over 150 young people have participated in this project to imagine and articulate what a socially and environmentally sustainable future for their neighborhood could be like. The project's broader objective is to develop young people's hope and resilience by helping them explore the possibilities for future health.

The methodology of RYN is situated within the emergent, empowerment-focused futures education approach. Ideas and methods have been drawn from the work of several of the futurists mentioned as well as the UNESCO Growing Up in Cities project.[7] In addition, the project's focus on issues of youth participation and use of public space reflect my background as a youth worker.

This school-based project operates for sixteen weeks. So far, students aged nine to twelve from both state and Catholic education systems have participated. These students have focused on a variety of curriculum areas including English, Environmental Studies, Australian Studies and Media. The content of RYN has been designed to adapt to the curriculum requirements of existing subject areas and year levels. There is validity in establishing a separate futures studies curriculum, as discussed by Richard Slaughter in the previous chapter. In designing the project, however, we felt it was more important to present the future as relevant to all areas of inquiry.

We begin the project by asking students to talk about their concerns for their world and neighborhood. We then facilitate an education program that explores positive strategies to deal with these issues. Students are encouraged to imagine significant details of what a healthy neighborhood could look and feel like and to identify what we need to do to create it. Their active participation in determining their environment is encouraged through dialogue with local government, conducting interviews, community art, tree plantings, and designing public spaces.

I would like to introduce the methods used in RYN by referring to some of our 1997 findings from a survey conducted with students regarding their expectations for the future. This comparative survey was carried out in weeks one and fourteen of the project to gauge how participation in RYN changed their perceptions (see Table 15.1).

The findings of this comparative survey indicate that RYN has effectively in helped students develop a greater sense of hope and possibility. The following is a summary of some of the key methods used in RYN that have facilitated this positive change in perspective.

Connection to the Local Environment

Students participating in RYN are encouraged to discuss both global and local issues. However, the focus of our future visioning and problem-solving is kept local. It is our aim to create not only a positive vision of the future, but also an understanding of how such a future could function and be created. Tangible achievements in visioning and problem-solving can be made at a local level where there is a high degree of relevance to life experience and understanding. Fiske et al. describes this relevance to one's personal life as image salience. The greater the salience, the greater the opportunity for action.[8]

At the beginning of the project, a lot of the students expressed a desire to see their neighborhood improved but displayed little sense of connection to it. As Karen Malone from the UNESCO Growing Up in Cities project said to me, "How do you expect young people to develop a sense of connection with the future, when they don't have a sense of connection with the present?" Belonging to a cohesive community culture and having accessible and stimulating public spaces are very important to young people. Talking about their own experiences of growing up, learning about

TABLE 15.1

Responses to survey 1 (held in week 1) are recorded under S1 and responses to survey 2 (held in week 14) are recorded under S2. F1 corresponds to responses by females in survey 1, and F2 are responses received in survey 2. M1 corresponds to responses by males in survey 1, and M2 are responses received in survey 2.

1. Thinking about Australia in twenty-three years time, that's the year 2020, do you think that our overall quality of life will be better than it is now, about the same, or worse than it is now?

	S1	S2	F1	F2	M1	M2
Better than now	37%	68%	23%	58%	55%	77%
About the same	21%	28%	31%	42%	9%	15%
Worse than now	42%	4%	46%	—	36%	7%
Don't know	—	—	—	—	—	—

2. Do you expect things to get better, remain the same, or get worse in Australia between now and 2010 in the following areas?

	Better		Same		Worse		Unsure	
	S1	S2	S1	S2	S1	S2	S1	S2
Our natural environment	26%	60%	4%	20%	70%	20%	—	—
Crime and violence	13%	20%	9%	36%	74%	28%	4%	16%
Our Physical health	39%	60%	26%	28%	35%	12%	—	—
Our Mental health	30%	52%	44%	40%	22%	8%	4%	—
Racism	44%	72%	30%	12%	26%	8%	—	8%
Gap between rich and poor	13%	24%	26%	44%	44%	24%	17%	8%
Family life	35%	40%	52%	52%	13%	4%	—	4%
Substance abuse	26%	20%	22%	40%	39%	12%	13%	28%
Justice and equality	39%	56%	35%	40%	22%	4%	4%	—
Employment prospects	22%	48%	17%	28%	35%	20%	26%	4%
Australia's economy	54%	44%	25%	16%	13%	36%	8%	4%

their region's history, expressing their concerns, and learning about initiatives for change gave students a greater sense of connection to the present through the context of their neighborhood.

We spent several lessons going for walks around the local creek, housing, entertainment, industry, and shopping strips. On these walks we discussed aspects of the natural and built environments and asked students to imagine a variety of scenarios for the future landscape of their neighborhood. Students took us to the places they liked to hang out and explained their significance their lives. They also showed us the places they avoided for fear of being hassled or threatened. This provided us with very important insights into how young people see, value, and experience their physical environment. What was clear from these exercises is the intimate knowledge that young people have of their locality. These walks have proven to be a very powerful medium for helping students ground their understanding and imaginings.

Developing a Confidence that Other People Care

The students valued the opportunity to name, discuss, and debate their concerns in class. It validated their concerns and provided a space to reflect on how these issues affected them personally. Many commented that it was positive to learn that peers shared their individual concerns—it broke a sense of isolation. A lot of the students' initial feelings of hopelessness stemmed from a belief that other people, particularly adults, don't care about our world and that change therefore is impossible. The educational content was designed to provide examples of individual and community efforts to achieve change. This included guest speaker presentations on the local environment, sustainability initiatives, community safety, multiculturalism, and the history of their bio-region. The content provided students with information that they don't normally access in mainstream education—information aimed at inspiring social confidence and an understanding of practical ways of acting. As Martha Rogers and Allen Tough explain in "Facing the Future is not for Wimps": "In order to feel empowered, people need to hear or read success stories where individuals have made a difference, and they need to experience hope and cautious optimism from those who 'know the facts' but are able to sustain hope and commitment."[9]

Providing Young People with an Experience of Participation

Having the confidence and opportunity to take action is an empowering reinforcement of a person's ability to effect change. The local neighborhood is an important forum for the authentic and active participation of young people in policy-making and community life. The UN Convention on the Rights of the Child (CRC) includes a series of articles on young people's rights of participation. This was built upon in "The Habitat Agenda," which reports that:

The needs of children and youth, particularly with regard to their living environment, have to be taken fully into account. Special attention needs to be paid to the participatory processes dealing with the shaping of cities, towns and neighborhoods; this is in order to secure the living conditions of children and youth and to make use of their insight, creativity and thoughts on the environment.[10]

The participating students initially displayed little confidence in the effectiveness of making formal recommendations to local government. They wanted to help determine their neighborhood but didn't feel their opinions would be respected. Young people are very aware of the token gestures of adults seeking their passive involvement. To establish a relationship with local government, students were provided with an affirming and authentic opportunity to participate in policy-making and the design of public space. Youth futures research has identified an emphasis on young people's rights to participate in decision-making as an important precursor to active citizenship.

For the students, the process of submitting recommendations to local government was a form of social action; they felt that this act contributed to the future of their community. Their recommendations reflected realistic and well-considered ideas for change. The changes they wanted were relatively selfless desires: restore their creek to health, strategies to develop community pride, accessible services, the cleaning and beautifying of their built environment, and a commitment to alternative technologies. They had realistic ideas of how to implement these steps understood the social and personal responsibility involved in creating this change. Their recommendations reflected an intimate knowledge of their neighborhood and a genuine concern for its long-term social and environmental health.

Development of the Imagination

In week one of the project, students were asked to draw or write about the sort of future that they would "like" to live in. Approximately 35 percent of the students drew pictures of life on other planets, bombs exploding, gray skies, and a planet on the brink of environmental destruction. The students who documented in writing focused on what they hoped would no longer exist, such as violence, destruction, pollution, and so on. It was difficult to move beyond the strength of their negative imaginings even when asked to document what they would "like" the future to be like. The only positive responses were concepts of peace and colors of green land and blue skies. None of the students had the capacity to truly imagine in any detail the sort of future that they would like to live in.

To create relevance to the lives of the students, it was important to move beyond concepts of future peace and a clean environment to an understanding of how such a future could look, function, and be created. Concepts alone do not hold the strength needed to create an empowering belief in the possibility of a healthy future, nor do they indicate with clarity the actions needed to create it. As Elise Boulding discusses, we need to develop strong and relevant visions of the future if we are to encourage social confidence and action.

> A critical feature of . . . social therapeutic imaging is that the imager must be able to picture significant details of . . . a healthy society. . . . The significant aspect of imaging is that human beings construct social reality in their minds prior to the sociophysical task of constructing the external reality.[11]

One of the difficulties I encountered as a facilitator was finding visual and written resources to aid the imaginative process. I found many examples of initiatives emerging out of Europe and a few Australian-based projects, such as the design of the Halifax Ecocity.[12] They were valuable for their examples of possibilities, particularly for urban design, but lacked a relevance to the student's present experience of life in their neighborhood. One of the images I used as an example of a sustainable future was from David Hicks.[13] Students were asked to discuss the benefits of living in such a community. While they preferred Hick's example to the future they expected, their responses focused on the lack of choices and suggested that such a model of local sustainability would be lacking in interaction and stimulation. One student wrote that "this future seems very balmy and peaceful, but I'm not sure that I'd like to live in it. The environment is healthy but I think I'd get real bored seeing everyone in my community all the time and everything being the same." There is a need to further develop visual and written resources that capture aspects of both sustainability and life in a dynamic and stimulating social environment.

Students' varying abilities to imagine healthy futures developed along with their understanding of the possibilities for sustainability. As mentioned, the relevance of the visioning process to the local environment and lived experience of participants was also a crucial and grounding factor. To further strengthen this visioning process, community art and urban design were incorporated as major project components. These activities effectively helped students articulate and imagine the sort of future that they would like to live in.

Visual Arts

At the beginning of the project, students are asked to create a major art piece depicting a healthy and sustainable future for their neighborhood. With the assistance of an artist, they participated in an intensive process designing images that incorporate significant details of social and environmental health. A mix of art media, including murals, mosaics, and painted tiles have been used. The students' designs have included images of nature corridors, native flora and fauna, appropriate technologies, cultural diversity, entertainment, art, sport, public transport, community pride, street life, and a stimulating built environment. All of the artwork has been permanently installed in prominent public places in their neighborhood.

Community art has proven to be a very effective medium for developing young people's abilities to imagine and understand concepts of healthy futures. It has also proven effective in developing student's self-esteem. The quality and descriptiveness of their work has attracted significant recognition from local government, peers, family, and media.

Urban Design

At the invitation of local government, students participated in a process of researching and drawing site plans for a major pedestrian thoroughfare in their neighborhood. The objective was to provide students with an opportunity to physically transform their environment and to develop their understanding of healthy urban design.

The students began by conducting 170 surveys with local residents and workers regarding their ideas to improve the site for use as a public space. They then participated in workshops with an urban designer and learned about principles of healthy design and creating contexts for social interaction and stimulation. Their ideas were developed into a series of site plans that were submitted to local government for inclusion in the final design. Their work displayed a heightened awareness of the social, environmental, and aesthetic considerations of urban design. It also provided an opportunity to participate in applied visioning.

Developing Links with Local Government

As suggested, a partnership was established with local government to include students in urban design and community planning processes. As well as benefiting the consultation initiatives of local government, this relationship validated the sense of worth and potential of young people to contribute and participate. By initiating links with local government, we are hoping to develop a model of education that optimizes opportunities for the authentic participation of young people in determining the future of their neighborhoods.

A MODEL FOR EMPOWERMENT

In designing "Re-Imagining Your Neighborhood," we are hoping to develop a model of education and consultation that can empower young people to help create healthy futures. The methodology of this project is relevant to both the education sector and local government. If education aims to prepare students with a positive outlook for their future roles and responsibilities, then it must integrate processes that can cultivate social confidence and vision.[14] It is also important to acknowledge the important contributions young people can make in the present to determining the future of their localities. By cultivating imagination, hope, and an experience of participation, young people can develop the motivation and will necessary to actively participate in creating sustainable and stimulating communities.

NOTES

1. Elise Boulding and Kenneth Boulding, *The Future: Images and Processes* (Thousand Oaks, CA: Sage, 1995): 95.

2. Ibid., 96.

3. Richard Eckersley, "Young Australian's Views of the Future: Dreams and Expectations," *Youth Studies Australia* 15, 3 (1996): 11–17; David Hicks and Cathie Holden, *Visions of the Future: Why We Need to Teach for Tomorrow* (Stoke-on-Trent: Trentham Books, 1995); Francis Hutchinson, *Educating Beyond Violent Futures* (London: Routledge, 1996).

4. Joanna Macy, *Despair and Personal Power in the Nuclear Age* (Philadelphia: New Society Publishers, 1983), 10–30.

5. Jennifer Gidley, "Transcending Violence Through the Artistic Imagination," in *Futures Studies: Methods, Emerging Issues and Civilizational Visions*, eds. Sohail Inayatullah and Paul Wildman (Brisbane: Prosperity Press, 1998).

6. Elise Boulding and Kenneth Boulding, *The Future: Images and Processes* (Thousand Oaks, CA: Sage, 1995); David Hicks, "Retrieving the Dream: How Students Envision their Preferable Futures," *Futures* 28, 8 (1996): 741–749; Francis Hutchinson, "Valuing Young People's Voices on the Future as if They Really Mattered," paper prepared for Youth and the Future Conference, Victoria (July 1997); Richard Slaughter, "Why Schools Should Be Scanning the Future and Using Futures Tools," *For The Practising Administrator* 4 (Melbourne: Futures Studies Centre, 1996).

7. The Australian site of the 1997 UNESCO Growing Up in Cities Project was conducted in Melbourne, Australia, under the direction of Dr. Karen Malone from Deakin University Geelong.

8. Susan Fiske et al., "Citizens' Images of Nuclear War: Content and Consequences," *Journal of Social Issues* 39 (1983): 41–65.

9. Martha Rogers and Allen Tough, "Facing the Future Is Not for Wimps," *Futures* 28, 5 (1996): 495.

10. United Nations, *The Habitat Agenda* (1996).

11. Elise Boulding and Kenneth Boulding, *The Future: Images and Processes* (Thousand Oaks, CA: Sage, 1995), 98.

12. Halifax Ecocity is an ecological development proposal for an ex-industrial site in the heart of Adelaide, South Australia. This project was launched in 1992 and is a joint venture of Urban Ecology Australia and Ecopolis Pty. Ltd.

13. David Hicks, *Educating for the Future: A Practical Classroom Guide* (London: World Wide Fund for Nature, 1994), 70.

14. David Hicks and Cathie Holden, *Visions of the Future,* 18.

Chapter 16

Learning with an Active Voice: Children and Youth Creating Preferred Futures

Cole Jackson, Sandra Burchsted,
and Seth Itzkan

Do not confine your children to your own learning, for they were born in
another time.

—Traditional proverb

"SCHOOL'S OUT"

Schools, like other social institutions, are struggling to cope with the scope and rate of change that has occurred in the latter part of the twentieth century. Educational institutions and educators are reacting to the changes instead of approaching the future creatively and generating fresh visions of alternative futures for teaching and learning. Therefore, it is doubly ironic that we still often hear the remark that a time traveler from the nineteenth century would recognize one place in contemporary societies: the school campus.

Thus, to paraphrase Lewis Perelman, "school" as we have known it in the last several generations, is out.[1] Most educators recognize that the old ways no longer meet the needs of students, that "school is out," but they lack a clear vision of what "schools" and "schooling" needs to be in order to engage children in learning that is relevant to their lives and adequately prepares them for a future that promises to be so different from the past. As Ron Brandt points out, "If we are to design schools for the twenty-first century, we must have some idea what life will be like in the years ahead. How can we educate students without having some idea what we are educating them for?"[2]

If the antiquated social constructs we know as "schools" are out, what is in? Are personal growth and wisdom being sacrificed on the altar of the

push for "world-class" standards in academic achievement usually measured by standardized assessments? Should we be in the business of producing better technologists, investment bankers, policy wonks,
hyperthryroidic professional athletes, and popular-culture entertainers, or
of developing better people or "all of the above"? If the answer is "all," then
why, when the personal development of youth is proposed for curricula at
almost any level of education today, do so many educators begin to
backpedal away as fast as they can from dealing with hearts and spirits? Is
not the whole child/person a complex amalgam of cognition and affect? By
default, we educators leave to whim the very ethical and value foundations
that feed not just the head, but the heart. We have left to the uncertain
winds of serendipity the crucial question Allen Tough continually asks us:
why should we care about the next forty years, not just the next few
months or few years?[3] Indeed, why should children and youth care about
futures generations? This is a paradox in itself, because *they are the future
generations!*

The genesis of the Orange County Public Schools Images of the Future
Project and the Creating Preferred Futures initiative, the two case studies in
youth futures discussed in this chapter, was triggered by a recognition that
our students were experiencing much anxiety about their future and that,
to a large extent, education has been slow to respond to the new learning
needs of our children, who will be spending the greatest parts of their lives
in radically different social, technological, economic, and cultural conditions.

We began to realize that schools successfully relate the past to the present, but the link to the future was more nebulous and vocationally utili-
tarian, particularly in terms of students realizing the future implications and
consequences of their actions in the present. Perhaps more than ever
before, today's students need to understand that they are not helpless,
hopeless pawns in the face of an uncertain future—that in fact, they have
a tremendous range of positive choices that affect them both as individuals
and as knowledgeable, confident participants in a democratic society. They
can proactively help take their own futures through a forward-looking educational process.

Survey after survey in many Western countries have shown that the
young are fearful about the future, especially about issues like the production of nuclear weapons, environmental decline, and economic instability.

In the United States, three-quarters of the adults surveyed by the Harris poll and
two-thirds of all high-school seniors surveyed by *Scholastic* magazine say they
believe that the United States will be a worse place ten years from now than it
is today. . . . If these people do not acquire some constructive vision of purpose
for themselves, they are likely to be very destructive, counter-progressive forces

in society throughout their lives. We already see that. One recent estimate is that one-sixth of all sixteen- to twenty-four-year-olds in America—mostly males—are currently "disaffected and disconnected." They are not associated with any formal role in society, nor are they in any formal relationship with another person. These are the folks who are joining the gangs in center cities and swelling the ranks of rural militias. They see no roles for themselves in an informated society, and they are angry about their empty future.[4]

The discontent of American children and youth is also reflected in a dramatic increase in psychiatric illnesses. A recent study in the *Journal of the American Medical Association* found that Ritalin prescriptions for patients aged two to four had tripled between 1991 and 1995 and prescriptions for antidepressants in the same age group had doubled.[5] The number of American teens and preteens taking antidepressants has been estimated at more than half a million.[6] To provide some scale of this phenomenon, the use of selective serotonin re-uptake inhibitors—the class of antidepressants that includes Prozac—has increased 103 percent in patients under eighteen during the past five years, while rising only 21 percent in adults.[7] While suicide rates among adults have steadied or even declined over the past few decades, in the 1998–99 school year, an estimated 2,700 young people ages ten to nineteen took their own lives.[8] "Where it used to be your grandfather, now it's your son," said Tom Simon, a suicide researcher at the United States Center for Disease Control and Prevention. He added that more Americans under age nineteen now die each year from suicide than from cancer, heart disease, AIDS, pneumonia, lung disease, and birth defects combined. Moreover, for every teenager in the United States who commits suicide, 100 more will try.[9]

Perhaps more than ever before, young people need to understand that they really do have a tremendous range of positive choices about their futures. Students need the information base and they need to see the interconnectedness of different aspects of the world around them, from technology to the arts, and the relevance of what they're asked to do in school in order to achieve success in the twenty-first century workplace and in life and society in general.

RATIONALE FOR INTEGRATING FUTURES THINKING INTO CURRICULUM AND INSTRUCTION

Futures studies offers twenty-first century learners an empowering set of perspectives and methods to cope with and achieve success in this age of uncertainty. Commonly, when children are asked about the future they express feelings of fear, anxiety, and impotence. Many feel that the future will be much worse than the past and that they are powerless to change it. However, when these same children learn the tools and perspectives of futures studies the future becomes more tangible; they gain a greater sense of responsibility and connection to it and they feel a sense of empowerment about their roles in creating the future.[10] Our experience has been that when futures thinking is seamlessly infused into curriculum and instruction in a seamless fashion, children and youth acquire and demonstrate an understanding of complex systems, the nature and process of change, our interdependency as it relates to the global "commons," and process skills that enable them to analyze and synthesize disparate pieces of information.

Indeed, futures education works best when blended into the regular classroom experience, as opposed to an "add-on," and it involves the community and has practical applications for children and youth in their daily lives.

The rationale for incorporating a more systematic treatment of the future into the learning and instruction of all children and youth is multifold. Futures-oriented learning empowers students to identify and create images of their preferred futures. Additionally, it helps them connect present choices and actions to future consequences, thereby sensitizing them to the needs of future generations. On the cusp of this millennium, the time in which our children and youth will be living the greatest portion of their lives, will be very different from the past. Therefore, new ways of thinking, learning, "being," and doing will be required for them to successfully traverse the complexities of tomorrow. In the words of Donna Carter, former president of the Association for Supervision and Curriculum Development:

> The global aspect of any futures education initiative is indispensable. In the face of extensive economic, technological, and political changes, we must learn more about the economics, education, environmental conditions, cultures, and technologies of our global neighbors and how our decisions affect each other. The multidimensional quality of each issue demands that we consider the perspective of those indigenous to the cultures of all stakeholders, understanding that a specific point of view is often shaped by the viewing point. We must accept the interrelationship of our futures and share the responsibility to prepare students to critically assess information gathered across time and cultures as they craft new world policies for times to come.[11]

THE IMAGES OF THE FUTURE PROJECT: AN OVERVIEW

The Images of the Future Project, the only existing futures program in the United States for kindergartners through twelfth-graders (K–12), operates in the Orange County Public Schools in Orlando, Florida, and is coordinated by Cole Jackson. Internationally, futures as a distinct field of study has yet to find a substantial foothold in K–12 school education.

The Orange County district is the fifteenth largest public school system in the United States, with over 150 schools and more than 35,000 students. Since 1990, thousands of students in elementary, middle, and high schools have received services as a result of the project. A futures center, a clearinghouse for futures studies and resources that support the activities, was originally established at Edgewater High School and today is centered at Corner Lake School.

In the decade since the project was established with seed money from the Florida State Department of Education, futures curriculum units have been developed, teachers have been trained in futures methodologies, and partnerships have been formed between schools and local organizations and businesses to provide students with real-life applications. Many of the students in the Orange County district are required by their individual educational plans to effectively demonstrate at least one futures tool before they graduate from high school. This provision alone was an enormous victory for the original cadre of "futuristas" in the school system because it signaled official acceptance of futures studies and thinking as a viable enhancement to the overall educational experience of children and youth. Additionally, for the past eight years, a "futures fair," featuring student-made futures projects, has been a popular event in the district each spring.

The desired learning outcome for students participating in the project is to demonstrate the following: enhanced cooperative and collaborative learning; improved problem-solving, decision-making, and conflict-resolution abilities; better understanding of technology and how to apply various technologies appropriately and in a sustainable framework; improved process skills such as gathering, analyzing, and synthesizing information; increased ability to globalize their perspectives about learning; enhanced ability to imagine and create informed and plausible alternative futures; and increased capacity to approach the future with confidence and personal empowerment. In essence, at the same time they learn essential life-long skills and applications, children and youth learn they can shape, not only react to, their futures.

Some of the futures-related projects Orange County students have produced are included:

- Career exploration for the twenty-first century
- Futuristic transportation systems
- Environmentally sound waste management
- Alternative water systems in Florida (lakes, aquifers, rivers, wetlands, the Everglades, Gulf of Mexico, and Atlantic Ocean)
- Implications for society, social security, and healthcare in the United States due to the aging of the Baby Boomer generation
- Futures of virtual reality

- Rainforest futures
- Space travel and exploration futures
- Alternative futures of world peace and conflict resolution

One of the most satisfying results of futures imaging in Orange County has been surveys indicating change in student attitudes toward the future. A survey of nearly 90 percent of participating students indicated they had more in their ability to change or influence the future rather than be merely passively subject to it. A comparable percentage of the students said they had expanded their visions of their community, nation, and the world. More than 75 percent had altered their visions of the future in positive ways and over 90 percent had begun to feel more hopeful about the possibilities of positive change, up from 65 percent in the preparticipation self-assessment.

THE CREATING PREFERRED FUTURES PROJECT: AN OVERVIEW

Creating Preferred Futures (http://www.planet-tech.com/preferred_ future) is an interdisciplinary, Web-based concept, designed and facilitated by the authors, that links students around the globe in an interactive futures education experience. This unique program combines the elements of traditional futures education, such as trend analysis, expert interviews, and scenario writing, with the methodologies of multiclassroom Internet-based instruction and collaboration.

The premise of Creating Preferred Futures (CPF) is familiar: that the future that children and youth will inhabit promises to be radically different from the present. Young people need to learn to recognize patterns of change, identify trends, draw implications, and create alternative futures scenarios so they will be better equipped to anticipate and plan for future challenges. Creating Preferred Futures is designed to provide students with processes and tools that will allow them to face the future with confidence. In addition, CPF has an international community of professional futurists online to join students in discussion and evaluation of their projects. Some of the prominent names in the field who have participated as mentors include James Dator, Sohail Inayatullah, Graham May, and Richard Slaughter. And it is the only online futures program of its kind in the world specifically geared to K–12.

Once on board with the project, participating teachers receive access to all the teaching materials in order to familiarize themselves with the learning modules. Subsequently, their students may begin at any time. Because the project is global and involves students from different countries around the world and various time zones and school schedules, project entry/exit is flexible. CPF therefore serves as a cybernetic hub for a networked futures curriculum.

To illuminate the assumptions that children and youth bring to futures thinking, test those assumptions, and develop alternative futures, students from around the world engage in research (using a variety of media to explore and synthesize information from multiple sources); communicate and think critically (discussing self-selected topics with peers, teachers, and experts in the field of futures research); creatively imagine (participating in an exercise designed to facilitate insight into what future generations need from them); and create scenarios of their preferred futures.

The project exposes students to a variety of futures research tools and techniques, including environmental scanning, futures wheels, cross-impact matrix, visioning, guided cognitive imagery, environmental scanning journals, reversing the negative, interviewing futurists, and scenario construction. It further engages students in constructive discussions concerning their present actions and the potential consequences of those actions on future generations.

To date, ignificant innovations and products developed to anchor CPF in the discipline and spirit of futures education include: (1) connecting students and teachers in the United States and globally in collaborative and individual learning projects that can be both content-specific and cross-disciplinary, and (2) establishing interactive forums for discussion and sharing ideas about futures-oriented curriculum and instruction to reinforce and enrich the diversity of the content and futures toolkit.

In the first phase of the project, students create a personal definition of futures studies. They post them to the student forum for everyone to read and comment on. Below is a select sampling of the students' definitions.

As we travel through our life and future, we are blind as to what may come. Future studies will give us an idea about this unwritten future. Future studies will help us to cope with situations pertaining to the future. Futures studies is the tool to our future without it, we are lost.

Futures is not just about creating a sustainable future for generations to come, but also to understand how everything is relevant to the way we interpret what goes on around us. It is also about how we can take an active part in learning how to take control over our individual future.

Futures studies helps us gain knowledge of how to deal with the future without panicking and figure out what may happen and the effects of what may happen.

Students have completed projects on topics such as the future of global peace, space colonization, population decline in Russia, youth violence, and future housing.

CHALLENGES TO SUCCESSFUL IMPLEMENTATION
OF FUTURES STUDIES IN K–12 EDUCATION

Challenge One: Linking the West and North with the East and South

An ongoing challenge for CPF as a Web-based project is the dearth of communications technologies in the South and East. Even within the advanced technological nations and wealthier societies, there are excessive disparities in educational services provided for youth and children. As Jonathan Kozol has pointed out, it has long been a source of shame in the United States that children in many rural areas and learners in the lower socioeconomic communities of our large urban centers receive far less in both quantity and quality of educational opportunity and services delivered.[12]

Our plea for future generations of educators, as well as national and international policy-makers, is to contrast in our minds the child in Kenya or Irian Jaya or Bangladesh or Cameroon or Kashmir with the child in Beverly Hills, as Bilal Aslam has done in his essay in this volume. Are there any trends or other reasons we should expect education to be that much better or different in Dacca in 2025 than it is now? Our experience on several continents tends to support the notion that the huge gap in human potential realized between resource-rich and technologically advanced nations and poorer regions of the world continues to grow at an exponential rate. According to UNESCO, this abyss is exemplified by the 900 million illiterate people around the world and the 130 million school-aged children who are out of school, compounded by conventional educational systems (where they exist at all) that fall short of embracing the cornucopia of new ideas that enrich learning processes. While the United States and Singapore report nearly universal wiring of schools for the Internet, in Mozambique, even a used computer, let alone a high-speed, graphics-capable modem to go with it (given the hardware is even compatible in the first place), costs around U.S. $4,000! And think for a moment: if your electricity can't be depended upon, how will you run the hardware even if you have it!

Distant learning and e-mail and Internet links between learners of different cultures and perspectives offer exciting new tools for closing the knowledge gap in the "global village," but only if less technologically developed regions have more universal access to these powerful modalities. Wealthy nations could help close the gap by evolving to understand that our less economically and technologically blessed planetary co-inhabitants have much to offer our present and future generations and, therefore, it is in everyone's best interest to embrace this massive task of helping those who are having such difficulty finding a sustaining place in the nanosecond new millennium.

Challenge Two: Perception of Futures Education by Educators

Futures studies is considerably more mundane than Star Wars and infinitely more rational and systematic than reading tea leaves in the bottom of a teacup. Futures studies has been widely applied in government, business, and industry in order to cope with the unparalleled dynamics of rapid change in every sector of society. The concepts and technologies developed through decades of futures studies and research need to be put to use in educational contexts. When applied appropriately, they can provide students who will be living and working in the twenty-first century with the knowledge, understanding, leadership skills, and technical expertise they will require to competently cope with, and not be completely confused by, the uncertainties of further change in their personal and working environments. Inherently sensitive to the transformations taking place around them, the students therefore can learn to take part in exploring, defining, and choosing desirable futures that support a more active and alert notion of democratic citizenship.

Still, futures studies as an organized approach in content areas has been a tough sell, and it will continue to be as long as the educational establishment misperceives futures-orientation as intrinsic to all that it does—despite the reality that the overwhelming amount of what children and youth consume in schools is past- and present-oriented. The inability of teachers to imbue their lessons with a methodologically sound futures orientation should not be interpreted as blaming the victim. However, the inherent conceit at the higher levels of K–12 curriculum administration that the "future" is what they are all about, combined with the steamroller effects of an increasingly crowded curriculum and heightened accountability for results measured by high-stakes standardized assessments, portend an ongoing threat to innovations in classrooms.

Challenge Three: Lack of Futures-Oriented Methodologies in Curriculum and Instruction

Some universities and colleges have instituted a number of thriving futures-oriented programs (some of the most notable have been established at the University of Hawaii, the University of Houston-Clear Lake and the Metropolitan University in Leeds, United Kingdom). Unfortunately, the application of futures thinking in elementary and secondary schools has been a void of wishful thinking and misapplication. A review of the literature turns up little more than isolated efforts at futures-related components in primary and secondary education. Moreover, because most of the curricula are designed for tertiary undergraduate and postgraduate consumption, they are complex and didactic for even secondary-level students.

Because futures education is so new to teachers, any attempt to infuse futures thinking and project-based approaches should be supported by an appropriate staff development program so that teachers can more confidently and competently introduce students to cognitive and affective futures themes and topics. One of the reasons futures studies has yet to take root in the public school curriculum is the relative dearth of developed, ready-to-use curriculum units. Teachers today often do not have time to develop their own curriculum units and welcome "turnkey" approaches to integrating futures-related content and methodologies into existing courses of study.

Challenge 4: Fragmentation of the Education Process

A school should not be a preparation for life. A school should be life.
—Elbert Hubbard

Another obstacle to the use of such interdisciplinary themes in education as futures studies is fragmentation in the educational process. Particularly at the compartmentalized secondary level, links between subject areas tend to be weak. From a systems perspective, this weakness arises not so much from the inadequacies of instructional methodologies deployed by teachers as from the lack of "connections" among the disciplines. Therefore, as educator and systems expert Jay Forrester observed:

> Students are stuffed with facts but [they are left] without a frame of reference for making those facts relevant to the complexity of life. Schools teach a curriculum from which a student is expected to synthesize a perspective and framework for understanding the social and physical environment. But that framework is never explicitly taught. A student is expected to create a unity from the fragments of the educational experience.[14]

Unfortunately (and Forrester also makes this point), the contemporary response to students' underachievement usually is a demand for still *more* standardized content and assessments in an already overcrowded curriculum, rather than movement toward a common foundation that pulls all fields of study into a unity that becomes mutually reinforcing.

FUTURES EDUCATION: A SPRINGBOARD TO HOPE

German philosopher Goethe once wrote that as mere mortals, we may not be able to solve the ineffable problems of the universe, but we can teach our children how to put their fingers on the pulses of the problems so that they may keep them within the limits of the comprehensible.

In his survey of Australian youth attitudes toward the future, Richard Eckersley captured the essence of the dilemma in education and community vis-à-vis futures thinking:

Any consideration of education must take into account the whole person - his or her outlook on life, expectations of the future, and values and attitudes. These qualities will shape a person's approach to all aspects of life, including education, work, citizenship and personal relationships. If young people believe in themselves (not just as individuals but also in their ability to contribute to society), and have faith in the future, anything is possible. If they lack these qualities, as the evidence suggests many do, no amount of conventional policy adjustment will deliver the results we seek.[14]

The first task of education is to liberate. Noted educator Hannah Arendt said it very well:

Education has two tasks. One is to introduce students to the values of their society. Students should know their country's constitution, they should know their country's values, they should know its history. But the second task is to prepare students to go into the future that they will have to create. So we have to open them up; we have to teach them that the values of the past, although we stand by them, are not values that we can extrapolate into the future. Education should ground students in the past but allow them to soar into a future that is different from past or present.[15]

This is especially true in view of the growing intercultural, international nature of the future young people will inhabit in decades to come. The planet grows more multiracial, multiethnic, multicultural, and multilingual even as we speak. Individuals are flowing across national boundaries in the same way that material and financial capital now flow relatively unimpeded across borders. We suggest that integrating futures studies methodologies into elementary, middle, and high-school curricula, as we have described in this chapter, can be a useful framework for teaching twenty-first century thinking and process skills. In addition to the natural fit of constructivism in futures education, other promising practices that find fertile ground in a futures-oriented learning landscape are multiple intelligences, multiculturalism, peace education and conflict resolution, community-referenced instruction, and authentic assessment of student performance. Perhaps even more important, a consideration of applied futures in learning can be a springboard for providing hope for a better future by empowering our children and youth to imagine, construct, and act on more positive, preferred alternatives for the new millennium.

NOTES

1. Lewis J. Perelman, *School's Out: A Radical New Formula for the Revitalization of America's Educational System* (New York: William Morrow & Co., 1992).

2. Ron Brandt, "Public Education in the 21st Century," *International Electronic Journal for Leadership in Learning* 1, 1 (1997): 2.

3. Allen Tough, *Crucial Questions about the Future* (Lanham, Mary.: University Press of America, 1991).

4. David Pearce Snyder, "The Revolution in the Workplace: What's Happening to Our Jobs?" *The Futurist* (March/April 1996).

5. Stephen Fried, "Sex, Meds, and Teens," *Rolling Stone* (May 11, 2000): 53.

6. Ibid., 53.

7. Ibid., 53.

8. Jessica Portner, "Complex Set of Ills Spurs Rising Teen Suicide Rate," *Education Week* (April 12, 2000): 22.

9. Ibid., 22.

10. Oliver W. Markley and Sandy Burchsted, "Experiencing the Needs of Future Generations with Adults and Children," *Futures* 29, 8 (1997): 715–722.

11. Donna J. Carter, in *Global Education: From Thought to Action,* ed. Kenneth Tye (Alexandria, Virg.: Association for Supervision and Curriculum Development, 1990): v.

12. Jonathan Kozol, *Savage Inequalities* (New York: Crown Publishers, 1991).

13. Jay W. Forrester, *A Systems Basis for High School Education* (Cambridge, Mass.: Sloan School of Management, Massachusetts Institute of Technology, 1989).

14. Richard Eckersley, "Dreams and Expectations: Young People's Expected and Preferred Futures and Their Significance for Education," *Futures* 31 (1999): 74.

15. Hannah Arendt, as cited by Stephen Keen in *Educational Leadership* (September 1989): 75.

Chapter 17

I Don't Care about the Future (If I Can't Influence It)

Sabina Head

DISCOVERING FUTURES STUDIES

I went to a futures workshop as part of a teaching inservice in the area of studies of society and the environment (SOSE) in 1996 and decided to attempt some futures work for a final unit in a graduate diploma in media. It seemed that futures addressed the need for the human race to develop some collective and long-term planning skills for itself and the well-being of the planet as a whole, since we had become powerful enough to alter our surroundings drastically. Our awareness of the possible effects of these changes we imposed seemed to be limited, however, along with our similarly limited capacity for self-awareness. Education appeared to be a worthwhile field for the development of a personal commitment to a futures perspective, and it has proved to be very rewarding. Students seem to be receptive to futures ideas and can develop confident, positive attitudes toward the future in an encouraging environment. Their contribution in futures work has been beneficial and at times inspiring. I have done futures work with lower secondary SOSE students, as well as Drama students in the lower and upper secondary areas, with some encouraging results.

Support for futures studies in the field of education in Queensland has been in the form of a futures perspective written into all syllabuses in the eight key learning areas, from preschool to year ten, legitimizing and encouraging development in the area. Much of SOSE work is already futures-oriented in terms of examining current issues in a geographical context and learning from past as well as current issues in a historical context. A more explicit focus on the future and ways of dealing with it was added to the course after the initial survey.

Gathering Students' Opinions on Futures Work

This paper is based on two surveys carried out in the first half of 1997, before and after the students had undertaken some futures work in the area of Studies of Society and the Environment. It was modeled on the work of Hicks and Holden (1995) in the United Kingdom.[1] The students were about thirteen-years-old and were in their first year at a girls high school. In both surveys, the questions were open-ended to allow as much freedom as possible for the students to respond naturally, without direction from the teacher.

The first survey of 88 students established a baseline of attitudes to the future for themselves, their local area, and the world, in terms of their predictions, hopes, fears, and their own influence on the future (results shown in Table 17.1).

Specific futures work included some futures tools and techniques:

- Futures timelines were introduced with one horizontal line in the past, separating at the "now" point into at least three branches (possible, probable, and preferable futures).
- The 200-year present was given as the structure of a personal timeline for the students, helping them to see the mutual influences and links with parents and with grandparents 100 years back, and with their own children and grandchildren 100 years from the present.
- The students completed a worksheet on the short- and long-term possible consequences of decision-making (hypothetical and real).
- A "Local Area" unit integrated futures topics so that students completed a land-use survey on the local area around the school, investigating two historic colonial houses and a Chinese temple, a busy main road, a creek, and a residential area. They then wrote a report explaining their plan for redeveloping the area by 2020, including a future map.
- The "Stone Ages" unit consisted of a worksheet based on group discussion of the effects of hypothetical change, and the pace of change, as well as personal reactions to change itself. The girls were asked to consider alternative futures if Aboriginals had become farmers and herders rather than remaining hunters and gatherers, and what would happen if a new Ice Age came to southern Australia within several different time frames. They were asked to discuss and record their reactions to big changes in their own lives, local area, and world conditions, with or without prior knowledge.

The second survey, completed by 107 students who had taken part in the futures work, asked for reactions and recommendations for teaching futures within and outside the SOSE course. They were asked for personal reactions to the work and advice on the inclusion of futures work in the SOSE course, as well as other suggestions for SOSE. They were also asked

TABLE 17.1   *Initial Survey Before Futures Work*

There were eighty-eight responses. Multiple answers were acceptable. Thus the percentage may total over 100 percent. Very low percentages were deleted due to lack of space.

PREDICTIONS

Personal (I will...)		Local Area (There will be ...)		Global (There will be ...)	
Be Employed	49%	More buildings	80%	Advances in technology	33%
Have a family	34%	Population growth	19%	More pollution	23%
Be married	32%	New types of transport	18%	More conflict	19%
Be educated	16%	Environment degradation	13%	More population	15%
Own a home	11%	More industry/commerce	11%	More computers	9%
Have traveled	10%	More roads	7%	A new transport system	7%
		More cars	7%	More transport	6%
				Forests destroyed	6%
				World peace	6%

HOPES

Personal (I will...)		Local Area (There will be ...)		Global (There will be ...)	
Be employed	53%	More parks, trees, bushes	30%	World peace	56%
Have a family	24%	Clean environs	17%	A cleaner world	36%
Be married	22%	More shops	13%	Improved world health	19%
Own a house	17%	More amenities	7%	No starvation/poverty	15%
Have traveled	11%			A drop in crime	10%
Have money	10%			Technology advances	8%
Be happy	10%			Stable/lower population	5%
Have a car	6%			Forests preserved	5%
Be healthy	5%			Full employment	5%
Healthy relatives	5%				

FEARS

Personal (I will face ...)		Local Area (There will be ...)		Global (There will be ...)	
Death of self/relatives	64%	Increase in population	33%	War	57%
Unemployment	19%	Decrease natural environment	15%	Pollution	28%
Illness	9%	Increase in crime/violence	15%	Overpopulation	11%
Failure in study/work	8%	Increase in roads/traffic	11%	An increase in crime	10%
Lack of finances	6%	More built-up areas	10%	The end of the world	9%
Family breakup	5%	A wasteland/a mess	9%	Deforestation	7%
		Houses turned to apartments	9%	Resource depletion	6%
		Increased commerce/industry	9%	Disease outbreak	5%
				Starvation	5%

PERSONAL INFLUENCE ON THE FUTURE—WHAT I CAN DO?

Personal (I can ...)		Local Area (I can ...)		Global (I can ...)	
Have studied	45%	Take environmental action	51%	Blank/little/nothing	32%
Have employment	14%	Take political action	23%	Take environmental action	20%
Have strategies/attitude	25%	Blank/nothing/don't know	9%	Take personal action/charity	18%
Have specific actions/				Take political action	17%
variety	19%				
Work hard	9%				

how to best prepare for the future, and the best attitude toward it. Thus a practical experiential component combine with a consultative planning process to produce the data. Results are reported in the body of this chapter.

Does futures work change the way students think and feel about the future?   After completing the activities, students reported changes in their thinking about the future, noting a broadening of their awareness and a more tolerant attitude. One said, "Instead of thinking about my personal future only, I now think of the world's future (e.g., transport, computers, the environment, and so on)." Another added, "I have a more open eye to different cultures." Some seemed to be more grounded, as these two were: "It made my mind more open when we did the section on decisions having consequences" and, "I now have what I think to be a more realistic view of the future—about the good things and the bad."

The simple act of looking at possible futures seems to demystify the students and make them more accessible. This encourages a realistic approach. The students exhibited a variety of emotional responses to their increased understanding of the future. It was interesting to note that exactly the same percentage of students (39 percent) felt better after increasing their understanding of the future as those who felt worse. Fourteen percent felt both better and worse after the work. One girl was "amazed to find out that what we do affects the environment dramatically," which points to the value of students' direct personal experience and observation. Planning exercises helped this student feel better:"Having to think of changes, I drew a future map which helped a lot. You could then see the differences."

Students recommended futures work in schools.   An overwhelming 87 percent thought that futures work should be taught in SOSE, and 75 percent thought that everybody should learn futures in school "because it might make people more aware of the present," and "it will help them take their place in society. "This student said: "Yes, to tell people to look forward to the future and not feel it will be completely different, because people will always be people."

Some said that it would help students understand current situations and know how to prevent or assist in these situations, and that students needed to know what would happen "if we keep treating the world badly." One girl suggested: "They should learn it by doing some research about the past and see how much has changed in certain years and try to compare it for the future."

They were happy that the course was delivered in a mix of field trips, books, and videos, and rated discussion and debate as equally important ways of learning. After the data was gathered, students' computer access substantially increased in the course and would have perhaps rated a mention.

Students' made recommendations about their needs in SOSE.
The most pressing need, students saw, was for a knowledge of international current affairs, followed by international history ("to see which communities worked best"), followed by Australian history ("so we have more of an idea about where Queensland/Australia is in the scheme of things"). The environment needed special attention, and people need to acquire the skills to care for it, on a local and global level. One student felt the need to see "the consequences we face with pollution in the long term, rather than short." Suggestions included the need for knowledge of "good possibilities and bad possibilities of the future so we are aware of them" and "future management skills." One girl said: "Students should know how to write letters of complaint, and so on, so that they might be able to stop any changes going on in their area that aren't in the community's best interest, or changes that could damage the environment."

If students feel they can contribute to the issue by taking action, they feel influential and empowered in their relationship with the local and global communities.

Students' suggestions for preparing for the future. According to 28 percent of the students, "care for the environment" is the most important thing to do to prepare for and create the future. They offered some very thoughtful responses on this topic, focusing on building awareness and understanding of people, history ("why things happened and how"), consequences ("what will happen if you do something to our world [ozone layer, forests, and so on]"), methods ("how to help today to help the future"), and cooperation. The need for a practical and positive approach was described by one girl as "not only to state problems but give answers as well." She also said, "I think students should be heard."

The response from this student is encouraging: "We should have a very open imagination. I love thinking about the future, planning very high-tech things. We can think up the unbelievable, wish for something exquisite and try to make it something believable for the future."

All the students had studied advertising in a media course, leading to the following suggestion: "Advertising and world-wide companies could be set up to help the environment and get more people involved.' At the school level, this student advised changing the curriculum to accommodate the futures aspect: "Learn how to change school work questions into real-life situations. Change some of the content to suit the topic (what should everyone learn to do to help them prepare for and create the future?), or one day a week have time set aside for different things."

One girl suggested "learning creative thinking," and another wanted to use "physical activities, where we would actually go out and do something about (caring for) the earth and the environment." In practice, the suggestions may be difficult to implement and maintain, but they reflect the seriousness with which the students regard problems of the environment and society and a willingness (if only in theory) to engage with such problems.

Students recommend the best attitude toward the future.   This question was most valuable after the students had been engaged in futures work, when they were speaking from a more knowledgeable and confident standpoint. Half the students surveyed stated that the best attitude toward the future was a positive one, and 14 percent mentioned an open/accepting/ready attitude. One student had in mind "a positive, friendly, and good-hearted attitude, because we must hold on to one of our most important and sole quality that machines don't have, and that is *feeling*!"

Another elaboration was "knowing that what you think and do will make a difference—getting students involved in every discussion so they think their opinion is worthwhile."

Students have articulated a need for positive as well as negative information. This girl suggested: "Focus on the good things, not the negative ones. Teachers could tell students only a few negative aspects of the future but many positive predictions. Then people will not worry so much and can face problems when the time comes."

Advertising campaigns were also suggested as a way to create positive attitudes.

A positive attitude toward the environment was also seen as important:

Live in harmony with nature. It should be taught to kids from a very young age, all through school. Bigger fines for litter, pollution, cutting down trees, poaching, etc. . . . Positive thinking/action taken toward the matter of pollution/ozone layer. . . . protesting and TV ads, school projects, class discussions and class videos.

This mature and flexible student recommended: "an open mind. No one knows for sure what will happen and we have to go into it with an open mind and a changeable attitude. Teachers need to nurture and encourage this attitude. You can't change the future if you're not willing to see it. It is those with an open mind who can better the future."

In summary, the essence of futures work with these students hinges on creating and nurturing an enduring relationship between the students and their surroundings (global and local) so that their future is known and felt on as many levels as possible, to be inextricably linked with that of their world. From their responses, this relationship would currently appear to be tenuous and starved of sufficient linkage to have much validity for them. Thus they see their future as separate from their physical and societal surroundings. They see themselves as discrete individuals who, rather than interacting as aware, contributing, and influential members of a global and local community, are merely pawns to be carried along toward whatever future someone else is responsible for.

Thus there is a need to make conscious and constant connections between the students and the global picture, and to a lesser extent the local picture, by using strategies that directly involve the students so that they can engage with the issues. This would help build the students' perception that they have a place in the scheme of society as valued members of it.

Students' Recommendations

In the course of the process, the students expressed a number of ways that their conrtribution to the future could be achieved:

- They see a need to be better informed about current affairs and their placement on global, national, and local maps. The wealth of information available is not necessarily consciously accessed by the students and may overwhelm to the point of apathy without guidance and some simplification for the age level. Their relationship with the world is based on knowledge of the world.
- They see a need for positive as well as negative information. Apparently, negative events and issues can be examined in terms of both basic attitudes. (Positive for whom? Negative for whom?) Students can be made aware that there is often a choice of attitude.
- They need to know that their opinions are valued. Surveys of student responses help them clarify their own thoughts, and personal reflection after a topic has been concluded reinforces the connection between student and issue. However, they also need feedback from surveys to reinforce the sense of self-worth and a feeling of community with the other students.
- To help build regard for themselves as participating and influential members of the community, they need to know action taken is based on their opinions and suggestions. Their sense of self-worth is partly based on an active relationship with the community.
- They would like to know more about methods of taking action open to them, whether they be pastoral, environmental, or political. This will help create a feeling of empowerment in their relationship with the community.
- They see a need to engage with environmental issues at local and global levels. Many students feel this is a priority in its own right.

Future Directions: the Challenge of Shifting Viewpoints

Futures work in schools need not necessarily generate extra course content; rather, a shift in viewpoint and unit planning could integrate futures thinking into the whole context of the work undertaken across the curriculum, while students still practice essential skills and processes within that context. In compiling this work I have learned that the students themselves, far from being uncaring adolescents, hunger for a sense of community and purpose to which they can attach themselves so that they can make worthwhile contributions according to their individual skills and interests.

The challenge for the future is to prepare the circumstances in which the students can explore and build this sense of community so that they are supported in their preferred attitudes toward the future—positive, open, accepting, and ready for anything.

NOTE

1.   David Hicks and Cathie Holden, *Visions of the Future: Why We Need to Teach for Tomorrow* (Stoke-on Trent: Trentham Books, 1995).

Chapter 18

Rural Visions of the Future: Futures in a Social Science Class

Shane Hart

My interest in exploring future studies stemmed from my own experience as an Australian exchange student in Denmark when I was sixteen. In the early 1980s at the height of the Cold War, the village I lived in was halfway from Moscow to New York. My life was incredible, I was learning so many new things, yet deep down I felt an overwhelming sadness for the future of the planet. Obsessed with the nuclear predicament, I, like many people concerned about the future of the planet, felt paralyzed to act. Despite this, my year ten teacher at Jels Folkeskole, Flemming Carlsen, managed to turn around my fears through what I now understand to be activities associated with the field of futures studies.

This case study focuses on the visions of the future of twenty-five students in a small rural Queensland state high school. This case study was born out of a need to make teaching more relevant and empowering for adolescents and to overcome students' negative attitudes toward the future. Similarly, this approach builds on the work of many environmental educators who have linked the future to objectives of environmental education.[1] Indeed, Hicks and Holden have argued that "the future per se is the missing dimension in environmental education."[2]

My experience in schools has shown that, while teachers may produce outstanding units of study on global environmental issues, the outcomes often leave students with a passive adoption of a dystopian future. This has been reflected with my own classes with comments such as, "So what? Our world is completely stuffed." The central thesis of this case study is that asking students to visualize probable, possible, and preferable futures creates the context for hope and action. If students can begin to act for their individual and collective visions of a preferable future, then both students and teachers will have moved from a narrow concept of environmental education that teaches about environmental problems to a broader one that educates for the future.

CONTEXT OF THE CASE STUDY

Two years ago, the school and community were shocked by the suicides of two male students at the school. This prompted extensive training in suicide prevention and intervention and was a major motivation for me to explore futures education to move students away from fatalistic attitudes to the future. This study took place in a social science class during a six-week unit titled "Towards the Year 2030" (three seventy-minute lessons each week). The unit that preceded the study focused on the third world, which helped develop many of the critical thinking skills and concepts needed for this unit, particularly "thinking globally." The class was highly representative of a typical rural Australian high school year ten class, although it is the most multicultural class I taught at the school, with students from Thai, Croatian, Maltese, Dutch, German, Italian, and English migrant families. The stories within this article were recounted verbally and/or in writing during a qualitative study for a masters of environmental education thesis.

At the start of the unit, students were issued a journal and were requested to write about their feelings, concerns, and hopes for the future. These journals were collected daily or weekly, which gave me the chance to chart their feelings, alter planned activities, and develop strategies to hold their interest, provoke their thoughts, and challenge their initial perspectives. A delicate balance was required to separate the roles of teacher and researcher. I was most conscious of maintaining distance so that the data collection methods didn't become a form of social control. Triangulation (the use of three data collection methods) and face validity (in which the students confirmed the data collection and the discussion of my findings) assisted in ensuring that the research reflected the student's thoughts, visions, and fears, rather than mine.

Beginning: The Future Is Not an Empty Place

The unit's starting point was exploring what the future meant to the students. My rationale for this was that before students can visualize a preferable future, I wanted them to explore their own, their peers', and other people's perceptions of the future. I asked students to write three questions about the future. The varied responses predominantly included references to their perceived future lives. I then asked them to write about how they see the future. Many of the responses revealed that young people are very actively engaged in the future. For example, Heather wrote, "The future for me is a path that I will take. Although I don't know what is ahead. I am the only one that can take the corners. But the ups and downs are just fate."

Rory chose to draw an image of the future—a tree—in his journal, under which he wrote, "I see the future as a tree. The root system represents our past, the trunk is the present, and the future is the branches and leaves."

In contrast, a small number of students wrote that humans have no control over their futures: "Whatever happens in the future happens and there is nothing you can do about it" (Jill) and "Nothing can change the past or the future" (Nick).

Challenging Visions of the Future: The Challenge Is Ours

I believed it was important to introduce some "futures tools," resources designed to jolt the passivity of students such as Jill and Nick and to motivate all students in this case study to see how their attitudes toward the future help shape it in positive or negative ways. In this way students were also able to see a range of probable, possible, and preferable visions of the future.

The final lesson of the first week drew on two future scenarios entitled Green Times 2040/Hard Times 2040,[3] which are some of the best "future tools" I have used with students. They chart a day in the life of Mary Wilkins in two different futures. Hard Times explores a future world in which people cannot stay outside for long, in which her grandchildren play "refugees and border patrol," where schooling is TV lessons year 'round, and where deserts have spread and farmlands dried up. In the conclusion, Mary Wilkins tries to develop a response to her granddaughter's question, "Why did people let things get so bad"?

In sharp contrast is Green Times, in which Mary Wilkins watches with joy as her grandchildren dress up for the Independence day parades (independence from fossil fuels). This scenario explores the previous fifty years of the Age of Ecology (the name for a sustainable society). This futures resource is of an American origin, yet it has proven very successful with Australian students.

Students were deeply moved by both scenarios and were extremely quiet as we read Hard Times. During the debriefing, I noticed how quickly students moved from positions of concern to positions of denial. I quickly took the opportunity to get students to write about their feelings. Walking around, two students—Tanya and Katrina—asked, "What can we do about this?" Therein lies the great power of future scenarios: they provide an opportunity to move beyond what Rogers[4] called "awakening the mind" stage to the "awakening the heart" stage. Again, some student's responses, such as Charmaine's were impressive: "I think Hard Times is very possible and it's scary to imagine that one day I could be that grandmother and I'm telling my grandchildren that their lives are very bleak."

In contrast that above statement, a number of boys, including Nick, felt that while it might be a possible future, it would certainly not be in 2040: "Hard times will not be possible by 2040, maybe in five or six hundred years' time."

During our reading of Green Times, students again were intensely engaged. Once we finished the readings, students were asked to reflect on the two futures. The responses again were varied: "I like Green Times better, the things they did to improve the world worked. We could do that if everyone cared." (Tanya) and "The second is much better because it gives us hope, and the other one means we have no hope." (Rory)

Both comments emphasized the advantages of using futures tools and other people's visions. Yet some students strongly rejected Green Times as a realistic future world. Virginia wrote, "Green times is a lot better and how people want our world to be like. I think that "hard times" is a more realistic world for the year 2040. People aren't going to change. If anything they are going to have much more wars and conflict which will harm the world."

While Virginia's statement reflects a passive adoption of a "harder" future, the activity has jolted her thinking about the future. I still felt that she and many other students needed to explore a wider range of possible futures before we could envision our own preferable future. It is interesting to note that the same experience gave other students a sense of hope that the future can be a positive place.

Using David Hicks' activity, Choosing the Future,[5] students were required to reflect on four different futures: more of the same; technological fix; edge of disaster; and sustainable development. One of the great aspects of this future tool is that the cartoon drawings depict each future as both an urban and rural setting. The rural settings proved popular with this group of students. Charmaine summed up the futures in her journal: "In more of the same, the people are depressed, in technological fix they used electricity for everything. In edge of disaster, everyone was in famine. The one I liked best was sustainable development because it was healthy and stable."

Karri also noted this when she wrote, "I guess it's all depressing for the first three scenarios and the last one (sustainable development) is like a dream, that's not going to come true too quickly."

During the debriefing, we explored how these possible futures came about. Many students appreciated the choice of four future scenarios; however, many doubted that humans are capable of making the changes required to bring forth a sustainable future. It was interesting to note that the class was beginning to be polarized into two groups: those who were internalizing the issues and those who were rejecting them.

Developing a "Voice"

The final activity of the week was a simplified adaptation of the deep ecology workshop (A Council Of All Beings),[6] in which students are required to choose and speak to a council from the perspective of a non-human species. Its purpose was to get students to explore a different activity, take risks, and reflect on the human–nature relationship.

The entire lesson was done outdoors and started with a cooperative hoola-hoop game, which established cooperation and trust and focused the group. Students then reflected on the beauty of a photograph of our planet taken from the moon in 1969. We then discussed the changes to the planet since 1969. This worked well because the year 2030 is also about thirty years away. A list of extinct animals that have passed from our lives and memories was read out, and students were asked to clap their hands. The echo sounded like a guillotine. I read some examples of humans expressing themselves from an animal's perspective, then students went to a space by themselves and prepared their own presentations.

The gamble of trying something different had worked well, and many students spoke about how they enjoyed the lesson. The activity catered to many different learning styles and provided an opportunity to awaken the heart and speak out, although some students wrote in their journal that the activity was "weird." Students were also asked to predict the future human–nature relationship in 2030. Some of the responses included, "I think that most people do care now and more people will care in the future, hunters will be outnumbered and outpowered by those who care about the future" (Karri) and "In the year 2030, humans will improve their attitude and try to help but in some cases it's too late" (Sean).

Building on The Council of All Beings activity, I asked students to write about their hopes and fears for the future. This was also an attempt to prepare them for the envisioning activity. It was obvious that girls found this task easier than the boys. It was interesting to note that many of the hopes for the future were global, such as world peace, nuclear disarmament, solution to the greenhouse effect, better leadership and less violence. More girls than boys expressed global hopes. Many of the boys hoped for successful careers, a happy family, and an expensive car. While some girls hoped for careers and family, none wrote about material possessions.

From Voice to Vision

Many of these activities were designed to challenge student's perceptions of their roles in the future as well as attempt to motivate them to develop a voice and a vision for a preferable future.

I believed that students were now prepared to begin to explore their own visions of the future. I adapted Elise Boulding's *Envisioning the Future Workshop*,[7] and while some students did manage to visualize a preferable future and wrote about their visions, overall the activity did not achieve its purpose. Many students gave up on the challenge. I became despondent about the outcome and disappointed that students who had put so much effort into previous activities had "opted out" during the visioning activity. While I felt it was a complete disaster, it turned out to be a good basis of exploring visions. After some further discussion of the value of mentally picturing something before we do it and a further step of breaking into smaller groups, some visioning did ensue.

The outcomes of the smaller groups were very different. Building upon Boulding's work, but simplifying the language and stages, most students did visualize a future; many were negative rather than positive futures, however. One of the most disturbing visions was from Heather, who drew (rather than described) an urban environment with the words atom, bomb, and explosion written over a rather obscure image of fire and chaos. She drew five people, all of whom are crying.

From Individual to Collective Visions

Regarthering as a large group, the class was asked to develop an individual and then a collective vision of a preferable 2030. The process involved exploring everyone's individual vision and then deciding on those that had everyone's support. The developed visions were for a future with:

- Less pollution
- Less violence and wars
- A ban on nuclear energy and weapons
- Striving for clean air
- Greater protection for endangered species and wilderness areas
- Greater equality between men and women
- Greater equality between all humans (first and third world)
- More emphasis on health

Once the class agreed on these, students brainstormed actions that we could take now as a class and in the future. After making a large list, students decided that they really wanted to "speak out" about their concerns for the future, but they felt that they needed to research specific topics, such as logging and uranium mining, and would then produce letters to national and international politicians expressing their concerns. Some did not want to take action but agreed to participate. It was interesting to note that those who were most committed and dominated the process were those who engaged positively in the envisioning activities.

The students' letters to politicians were impressive. All students received a response from politicians acknowledging their concerns and answering their question. This gave students some sense of speaking out, although they were possibly left deflated with the response.

DISCUSSION OF RESEARCH FINDINGS

Success!

One of the most important issues raised in the focus groups was the need for effective education. As in the research of Hutchinson, and of Hicks and Holden,[8] students in this case study took the opportunity to speak angrily at the irrelevance of their education in general: "I didn't really know about things until we did this. I knew there were problems and stuff but until we did this, I didn't think there was much we could do. It's important that people realize and are taught how to help." (Rory)

When asked about the success or failure of teaching with a futures focus, Tanya responded: "This unit was great. It was about what we think rather than what you think."

Similarly, Rory contemplated futures studies in other subjects: "Science should do futures studies, you can't do it in math because that stuff never changes, but in science there is all this stuff like nuclear power plants. But science people think opposite to what green type people think. . . . They say virtually the opposite to what you say."

This research confirmed the success of futures tools. These "tools" provide opportunities to link theories to practical learning experiences and to move beyond knowledge to commitment and action. Many of the students found the future tools jolted their passivity. This confirms the Johnson thesis concerning big-picture questions.[9] When confronted with the reality of choice provided through these "futures tools," students forced to have some engagement with the big-picture issues.

Pepper[10] argues for a critical education that seeks to draw out what students already know and believe. This strongly influenced the design and teaching approach of this study. In addition, the future tools provided the opportunity for students to bring forth what they knew. For example, in the first focus group interview, Tanya raised this issue: "The future is not about one person, it's about us all."

This data clearly shows that students are trying to work through their thoughts about the future and how their lives, attitudes, and practices affect the future. This is clearly identified by this response:

> Author: Tanya, you wrote in your journal that you already knew your actions affected the future. Can you explain how?
> Tanya: Because growing up on the farm and clearing land—you know it's affecting the future but it's a way of life and you have to do it.

Such comments reflect that many dilemmas, opportunities, and issues were confronted throughout the study. While the knowledge may always have been there, some students were now speaking about their concerns in terms of the future. It is also very clear that Tanya has internalized these dilemmas and issues as evidenced in her outstanding letter to Senator Robert Hill concerning poor agricultural practices of the past and their future consequences. Similarly, Craig's responses reveal considerable futures foresight:

> Author: Craig, you seem to be clearer than anyone else in the class about what you want to do with your life. In the year 2030 you are most likely to own a

cane farm. Yet the one concern you write about is that a nuclear war will pre-
vent that. Is there anything you can do over the next thirty-two years to prevent
that?
Craig: I suppose I could support other people!
Author: What sort of people?
Craig: People who protest against things like that, you know, Greenpeace.

This represents a huge attitudinal change from people in Craig's situation. In previous environmental units in this community, students were left
feeling disempowered, and they identified green ideologies as belonging
to other people. Craig's personal sense of responsibility to the future led to
this commitment and conviction. Craig added that "caring about the environment is something you have to do if you live on the land" and that "this
community doesn't fear organizations like Greenpeace, but fear that some
green organizations may be able to prevent their livelihood by restrictions
to farming. . . . Greenpeace is there to stop the stupidity of nuclear
weapons."

Failures?

A major puzzle of this research was that some students did not develop
any futures foresight. Jill and Trent represented the two extreme positions
of this group. Trent was largely negative and fatalistic. At the end, his attitude was even more pessimistic than it was at the start of the study. While
it could be argued that he clearly represents what Shields[11] argued when
she writes such people are "stuck in a victim's role," it is very clear that this
approach has failed such students. None of the activities gave him any
sense of hope or awareness that our visions actively shape the future.

Jill represents a different resistance that is based less on ideology than
on a lack of understanding about the world. Jill wrote about her life as if
global environmental issues would not affect her.

It is easy to conclude that despite all the quality future tools used, neither Trent nor Jill was able to develop a sense of human activity shaping
their world. When challenged about this, they simply found the work
"weird and pointless." Despite these examples, I will continue to utilize
futures studies because the need for students to develop futures foresight
is crucial to our survival. The success of this futures approach is evident in
Rory's conclusion: "I don't know about the rest of the class, but I know that
I'm more aware and concerned about the future of the environment that I
am going to live in."

FUTURE VISIONS AND CHANGE

This case study has documented how some students were able to
change their visions of the future with the approaches developed. Not all

students progressed through all the stages, yet many moved through Jensen's model:

- Knowledge
- Commitment
- Visions of the future
- Experience taking action to move from fatalistic attitudes to the future to ownership of preferable visions.[12]

Jensen's model starkly contrasts some approaches to teaching about the environment that rarely progress beyond the knowledge stage. Many of the future tools are cleverly designed to move learners from knowledge to commitment, or from "awakening the mind" to "awakening the heart." This research has revealed that positive images of the future (Green Times, Sustainable Development) help some students create their own images of the future and subsequently focus on what they want in a preferable future, rather than simply fearing the future. It was fascinating to find students stating such things as: "Schools are falling behind the times, I reckon they don't prepare us for the future, maybe a 1950s future but not the 1990s we don't learn enough about the environment and what we can do." (Rory)

Rory's insight is a distinctive call for the need for massive change in our schools, and, indeed a justification for more futures education. All it takes is our own vision of a better educational approach and the commitment to try new experiences and to build from success.

BUILDING ON THE ENERGY OF YOUNG PEOPLE

This case study revealed how some students engaged positively in a range of futures studies activities. These activities have sought to challenge students on four levels. First, students challenged their perceptions about the future. The second challenge was for students to explore a range of future images and decide which they preferred. The third challenge required students to envision a preferable future, and the fourth challenge required students to act for that future.

Herein lies the value of futures studies: it enables educators to build from the energy and optimism of young people. The process-oriented approach to futures studies described in this study drew out what students really thought, and enabled and empowered some of them to move from their fears to their hopes for the future. Youth are part of the solution; they must have an education that empowers them to feel this. Even most of the students who were distinctly negative at the beginning of the study were able to see the need for change. Many students, changed their attitudes to ecology and the future as they began to see the connection between their attitudes and their actions.

Postscript. Like the students of Jels Folkeskole year ten class in 1982, many students in this study were able to use their visions of the future to actively act and embrace a preferable future. The students in this study chose to build a time capsule which included their individual and collective visions of the future. In the year 2030, we shall all return to the community and hopefully celebrate our collective vision of the future.

I hope in the year 2030 I will own my own farm and completed all my goals that I have mentioned in this journal, most of all I hope that no major wars starts and my family is safe and secure. I also hope that when we return to open the time capsule we remember all we learnt in social science with Mr. Hart. (Craig)

NOTES

1. Elise Boulding, "Image and Action in Peace Building," in *Preparing For The Future: Notes & Queries For Concerned Educators,* ed. David Hicks (London: Adamantine Press Limited, 1994), 63; Richard Slaughter, "Critical Future Study—A Dimension Of Curriculum," *Curriculum Studies* 6, 2: 64–68; Richard Slaughter, *From Fatalism To Foresight: Education for the Early 21st Century* (Hawthorn, Victoria: Australian Council For Educational Administration, 1994), 52.

2. David Hicks and Catherine Holden, *Visions of The Future* (Staffordshire: Trentham Books, 1995), 186.

3. G.T Jnr Miller, "2040 A.D., Hard Times On Planet Earth" and "2040 A.D., Green Times On Planet Earth," *Living in The Environment*, 8th ed. (California: International Thompson Publishing, 1994), 290.

4. Martha Rogers, "Student Responses to Learning About Futures," *World Yearbook of Education 1998: Futures Education,* ed. David Hicks and Richard Slaughter (London: Kogan Page, 1998), 206.

5. David Hicks, *Education for the Future: A Practical Classroom Guide* (Staffordshire: Trentham Books, 1994): 55–71.

6. John Seed, Joanna Macy, Pat Flemming, and Arne Naess, *Thinking Like A Mountain: Towards A Council Of All Beings,* (Philadelphia: New Society Press, 1988), 100–109.

7. Elise Boulding, "Image and Action in Peace Building. . . ."

8. Francis Hutchinson, *Educating Beyond Violent Futures* (London: Routledge, 1996): 70–86.

9. David Hicks and Catherine Holden, *Visions Of The Future*: 79–112.

10. Charles Johnson "Asking the Right Questions," keynote address, Future of Education Conference, Albuquerque Academy (October 1996).

11. D. Pepper, "Red and Green: Educational Perspectives," *Green Teacher* 4 (1987): 11–14.

12. K. Shields, *In The Tiger's Mouth: An Empowerment Guide For Social Action* (Newtown, Sydney: Millennium Books, 1991), 23.

13. David Hicks and Catherine Holden, *Visions Of The Future*: 45.

14. B. Jensen, *Research in Environmental and Health Education* (Copenhagen: Research Center of Environmental and Health Education and the Royal Danish School of Educational Studies, 1995): 155.

Chapter 19

Youth, Scenarios, and Metaphors of the Future

Sohail Inayatullah

While other chapters in this book present nation-based case studies, mainly from Australia, this chapter develops insights based on studies around the world. Most of the case studies presented here involved the teaching of futures studies to young people and explored how they imagine their preferred futures and the type of alternative futures they see emerging. These case studies should be seen as indicative instead of conclusive.

CASE STUDY 1: UNDERGRADUATE STUDENTS AT THE CENTER FOR EUROPEAN STUDIES

The first case study is based on a sample of ten students attending a month-long intensive course on civilization and the future. The course was held June 1999 at the Center for European Studies, University of Trier, Germany. After a four-week introduction to critical and multicultural futures studies, the following scenarios emerged.

Community/Organic Futures

The first and most popular scenario was the community/organic. In this scenario, young people move away from the chemical corporate way of life and search for community-oriented alternatives. Local currency networks, organic farming, shared housing, and other values and programs favored by the counterculture are preferred. Dioxin contamination in Belgium (with similar scares in the future even more likely) could lead to quite dramatic changes away from artificial, pesticide-laden, and genetic foods in the long run. These young people imagine a community household system in which goods and services were shared. However, one participant imagined Europe not within the urban/community dichotomy but saw all of Europe as community-oriented. This meant a clear move away from the view, "I shop, therefore I am" to "I relate, therefore I am."

Family Future

This focus on relationships was also central for other participants. Indeed, the return to a strong family life determined how they saw the future of Europe. Taking care of children—and ensuring that the state provided funds for this—taking care of the elderly, and, in general, making familial relationships far more important than exchange relations was a foundational value. In contrast to the community scenario, this future was far more focused on the nuclear family—the family future. Indeed, some participants considered efforts to maintain this institution crucial, especially with the rise of genetic engineering and the possibility of test-tube factories in the not-so-distant future. While more formal visioning workshops with technocratic experts examine scientific variables,[1] these students asked, "Will I have children? How many? How will I spend my time with them?"

Plastic Europe

Other participants believed that new technologies would dominate and that we should rejoice rather than of resist them. We should celebrate artificial intelligence, plastic surgery, and gene enhancement, creating plastic Europe. Anonymity in fact gives freedom from other; it allows the individual to express his- or herself, while community and family suppress the individual. The new technologies promise great wealth. Some argued that single life was far more important than family life. It gave choice; it was not steeped in outdated institutions such as marriage. Europe was flexible and it should remain so when it came to formal relations.

Fears of Disaster

However, behind these preferred futures was the reality of disaster. One participant argued that oil reserves would certainly run out, and Europe would quickly decline, while Africa, with its plentitude of sun, and eventually solar energy, would rise. Mass unemployment in the context of Castle Europe—keep the barbarians out—was the likely future. AIDS, Ebola, and many other disasters loomed ahead. Nuclear technology could also lead to serious problems, and new forms of energy were needed. Unless alternative forms of energy were developed, the future was bleak.

Techno-futures

A last perspective was of technology positively transforming the future. The new technologies create the possibility for a network of national identity. They allow creativity to grow, and, along with more spiritual views of what it means to be human, let humans transcend their narrow limitations. Europe could offer a multilingual focus, a vision of a multicultural society. It was this gift Europe wanted to give her children, to ensure that they could speak German, Swahili, French, English, and Mandarin, for example.

In summarizing this case study, the focus on family was the main difference between the preferred futures offered by this group of young people and others I have studied—getting married or searching for alternative partnership models, was central to these young people.

CASE STUDY 2: HIGH SCHOOL STUDENTS, TRIER, GERMANY

Instead of a visioning exercise, this case study used the more traditional methodology of a questionnaire to explore how German high school saw the future using.[2]

To the question, "Are you hopeful or worried about the future?," 56 percent were hopeful and 45 percent were worried or very worried. In itself, this is meaningless. What is interesting is that those who were worried stated the official reasons of unemployment, pollution, natural catastrophes, and population. Those that were hopeful generally felt they would have good jobs and a good family life, and it made no sense to worry.

To the question, "Do you think the world would be a better place or a worse place in twenty-five years?," generally 45 percent felt it would be worse, 45 percent believed there would be no change, and a small response of 11 percent felt there would be change for the better. The reasons for "worse" were as above; responding "no change," students felt that humans would counteract these negative trends, largely through technology. Thus, positive human agency would counteract negative trends.

Most interesting to me, however, were the scenarios these young people preferred. The four scenarios offered for consideration were continued growth, green, collapse, and transformation.

Both the continued growth scenario (as defined by progress, integration, and globalization) the collapse scenario (overdevelopment, wars, and genetic technology) were preferred by 17 percent of the class. The green/sustainability scenario (progress is controlled, meditation and inner consciousness become very important, as do issues of environment, gender cooperation, and solidarity with the third world) was ascribed to by 28 percent. The last scenario preferred by 38 percent, was transformation. It was written as the Internet, aging, multiculturalism, and postmodernism change what it means to be human. A world governance system emerges and we begin to move into space. Spiritual technologies develop exponentially. However, comments focused far more on the inevitability of technology than on spiritual consciousness.

Intriguingly, 50 percent felt they could have some impact on the future, and the other 50 percent felt they would have little or no impact.

A study by Pere Fontan of young people in Catalonia confirms young people's concerns about the environment and human rights violations throughout the world.[3] This should be read as idealism, as a solidarity with nature and others. Of course, the number one issue in the Catalan study was employment. Generally, however, Spanish youth have a strong concern for others. Enric Bas[4] found that issues such as ecology, human rights, racial inclusiveness, and volunteerism receive the highest degrees of sympathy from young people in Spain. Furthermore, in terms of youth activities, social volunteerism, ecological movements, and human rights movements rank the highest.

This finding highlights part of the problem for youth. The reality is that postindustrialism is taking away the possibility of full employment—the famous 90 percent unemployed with 10 percent working formula—and yet political leaders still promise jobs.[5] This is the lie that leads to an age cohort crisis. The message is that there are jobs if you become an economic rationalist, but if you follow your ideals, there is no work. Young people do understand that technologies lead to automation, which leads to the elimination of work.

These issues are echoed by Richard Eckersley in his research on youth futures. Eckersley writes that young people "expect to see new technologies further used to entrench and concentrate power and privilege." For example, they were almost twice as likely to believe that governments would use new technologies to watch and regulate people than they were to believe that these technologies would empower people and strengthen democracy. They want to use new technologies to create closer-knit communities of people living a sustainable life.[6] This is in essence a mixture of the green/sustainable and transformational futures preferred at the Trier high school and the community/organic future of Trier university students.

However, these results are consistent with findings from other nations. In a similar visioning workshop in Taiwan, the following emerged as preferred futures.

CASE STUDY THREE: TAIWANESE STUDENTS AT TAMKANG UNIVERSITY, TAMSUI, TAIWAN

This study was conducted with undergraduate university students in Tamsui, Taiwan in May 1999. One group imagined a globalized Taiwan with each citizen being super-rich and owning a personal airplane (the globalist artificial society). The main thrust of this scenario was travel and individual rights. This was the payoff after fifty years of sacrifice (not by young people but by their parents).

Another group imagined a softer, slower, organic future where farming was crucial (the communicative-inclusive). Technology linked them globally but there was no email imperative. Quality of life issues were as crucial as wealth issues. The China/Taiwan issue would be resolved by both entering a supranational federation where nation did not matter any more. The vision was that territorial identity would recede and identity would be increasingly global, created by the development of the knowledge economy.

This latter scenario was quite surprising to older participants (one saying that it was a dangerous vision for the nation) but not puzzling, given that this younger new-age cohort does not have the memory of fleeing China or of the poverty of fifty years ago. As with their Western counterparts, these students demonstrate a development/science and technology fatigue and a desire for a far different life—a green, spiritual future. This future is quite similar to the community/organic future expressed by young persons from the University of Trier.

CASE STUDY FOUR: ISLAMABAD, PAKISTAN

In Pakistan in the early 1990s, a visioning workshop was held with a mixed age group. Some participants were young, but many were in their forties and fifties. The main point that emerged from this workshop was that metaphors of the future are not universal but particular.

The workshop presented four general metaphors to describe the future. The first was the ocean, representing unbounded choice, agency. The second was the roller coaster, representing the ups and downs of life. The third was the raft, flowing down the rapids, using quick reflexes to avoid dangerous rocks. The fourth was the dice, representing chance. For Pakistani participants, the missing metaphor was that of facing Mecca in unison. Unbounded choice—the postmodern metaphor—seemed not only foundationally problematic, but strange, incomprehensible.

This case study is important because it contests some of the conventional metaphors used in the West to understand the future.

CASE STUDY FIVE: UNIVERSITY OF QUEENSLAND, HISTORY OF THE FUTURE STUDENTS

For three years (1997–1999), an annual course, titled History of the Future, was taught at the University of Queensland, Brisbane, Australia. Generally, 200 students (in two separate groups) participate in this course. Each year, I engage the students in a two-hour discussion on trends, images, and metaphors of the future. The first hour is generally a lecture on macro-history—the grand patterns of change from Islamic, Indian, Sinic, Pacific, Western, Gaian, and feminist perspectives. The second part of the class explores their visions and metaphors of the future. Metaphors help youth understand how they see the future as well as how the future can be used to liberate, to move them out of the present.

Among the preferred metaphors presented are the following:

- The future is like a tree. It has roots in history, the branches represent inter-connection, organic growth.
- The future is like a spider web—deep connections but also a feeling of being trapped.
- The future is like being in a room without any doors—trapped with no choices.
- The future is like a spaceship—rapid speed going into the unknown.
- The future is like a can of beer—delicious while it lasts. That is, we are enjoying today but taking away the future from future generations, who won't have any beer.
- The future is like a game of hopscotch. Fun but with many hurdles, obsta-cles, to jump over.
- The future is like a fork. Which direction should we go—graduate school or work, for example?
- The future is like a motorcycle—riding toward the horizon.
- The future is like an onion—reality has many layers; we need to peel each one to be in truth with ourselves.
- The future is like the *Titanic*. Western civilization appears invincible but it is about to hit an iceberg (limits to growth).
- The future is like a closed door—no choices, no possibilities.
- The future is like a roundabout. There are ways in and ways out, and if one is not careful, one can keep on going around, endlessly.
- The future is like a mouse wheel—action with no purpose, effort with no direction, meaningless struggle.
- The future is like an ant hill—hundreds of us all working hard to create a col-lective future.
- The future is like a machine. We have little agency.
- The future is like the movie *Star Trek*—to boldly go where no man has gone before, adventure, progress, high-tech, but also learning about alien civiliza-tions.

These metaphors speak to transformation, connection, adventure, but also to meaninglessness, to action without purpose. Their richness testifies to the imagery that youth are endowed with.

FROM DICHOTOMOUS FUTURES TO EMPOWERED FUTURES

The findings from the case studies presented here in general confirm my claim in Chapter 2 that most youth visions of the future fall into two foun-dational (and dichotomized) scenarios. The first is the globalized artificial future, and the second is the communicative-inclusive future.

The globalized scenario is high-technology and economy-driven and could be further conceptualized into the following:

- Genetic prevention, enhancement, and recreation—new species, germ line engineering, and the end of "natural" procreation

- Soft and strong nanotechnology—end of scarcity of work
- Space exploration—promise of et contact or, at least, species continuation in case an asteroid hits earth
- Artificial intelligence and ultimately the rights of robots
- Life extension and aging—gerontocracy and the end of youth culture
- Internet and the global brain

In contrast to this is the communicative-inclusive society, which is values-driven and could be conceptualized in the following ways:

- Challenge is not solved through technology but through creating a shared global ethics
- Dialogue of and between civilizations in the context of multiple ways of knowing is the way forward
- *Prama*—balanced but dynamic economy—technological innovation leads to shared cooperative "capitalism"
- Maxi-mini global wage system—incentive linked to distributive justice
- A soft global governance system with 1,000 local bioregions
- Layered identity, moving from ego/religion/nation to rights of all
- Microvita (holistic) science—life as intelligent

However, there are also examples of youth not having a dichotomous position toward the future. For example, in a Queensland study,

One student . . . foresaw that he would invent new DNA technology to bring back extinct animals and endangered rainforests. Others imagined themselves developing renewable energy transport, and living in homes with compulsory worm farms for composting organic waste. Still others could see Sydney Harbor regenerating as a dolphin habitat, and communication around the world being as simple as talking into your "lip phone."[7]

To summarize, research on how youth see the future should not merely be about collecting and analyzing their responses to how they see the future but working with them to uncover and unpack their preferred futures—the futures they want to create.

Ultimately, youth futures is about empowering young people to enter the future, and to create it in their own imaginations.

NOTES

1. See, for example, Sohail Inayatullah, "Futures Visions of Southeast Asia: Some Early Warning Signals," *Futures* 27, 6 (July/August 1995): 681–688.

2. The sample size consisted of a mere 18 students and thus the research should be seen as indicative.

3. Pere Fontan, "Youth and Future Values," *Papers de Prospectiva* 6 (1997): 37.

4.   Enric Bas, "Youth and Future Values: An Overview of the Spanish Surveys," in *The Youth for a Less Selfish Future,* eds. Erzsebet Novaky and Tamasa Kristof (Budapest: Budapest University of Economic Sciences and Public Administration, 2000): 77–78.

5.   Jeremy Rifkin, *The End of Work* (New York: Putnam, 1995).

6.   Richard Eckersley, "Portraits of Youth. Understanding Young People's Relationship with the Future," *Futures,* 29 (1997): 247.

7.   Reg Anderson, "Forward to an Exciting Time," *The Courier-Mail* (November 28, 2000): 8.

Youth Essay 3

Shared Futures from the Philippines

Michael Guanco

Why should I think of the future when I am here at the present, still struggling to live decently and perhaps struggling to live up to my own personal expectations of myself? Don't you find it quite absurd that we're actually being led to an illusion of a future? Can we not do something about our present situation so that it will set a tone for a brighter tomorrow? Who the hell will care for the future when my stomach is empty or all of my trusted friends have turned their backs on me? These are the things that I often encounter when I ponder what kind of future I would like to see. This is most especially true when I am really depressed and I feel that there are so many burdens on myself. Thus, I have a hard time convincing myself that, indeed, I have a stake in the future. Difficulty in believing that, indeed, I can create or move toward whatever future I prefer.

I remember the time when one of my professors told me casually, when I started confiding about my subtle problems, "Mike, you have to dream, it's free, and nobody will take it away from you." Then it dawned on me that this dreaming is not an illusion but the kind wherein we are allowed to dream a future into reality. When I started envisioning my goals, my life became "light," as if a positive energy has emerged from within. And whenever these workable dreams fail, there are still options. The beauty of dreaming is that ideas are simple but as vast as the space, and the choices are ours.

To be with my preferred future, I must also know what is going on at present. Otherwise, my visions are blind. Man fails whenever he or she fails to recognize the sea of humanity that we are all floating in. Humans are not capable of living without the other, but they often assume that they can. Our preferred futures are not possible if people will not diminish their selfishness. We need to share and cooperate with each other.

But today, few people realize that sharing and cooperation are necessary for survival. The concepts of profit and globalization simply point to the demands of our egos to accumulate wealth and keep it for ourselves. The United Nations Development Program Human Development Report 99 stated that globalization has further worsened the incidence of poverty. That is a reality that is existing before our eyes, yet nobody recognizes it. While there are some economic benefits that globalization has ushered into the economy, it does not guarantee justice and the eradication poverty. A classic example is the oil industry in the Philippines. The aim of deregulation is to reduce prices due to competition. But there is no fair competition, and the opposite is now true. Also, infrastructures are now found almost everywhere and are generally regarded as the main indicator of development. In an interview, the traffic commander of Iloilo City was asked: "How is the situation of the traffic in the city?" He said, rather convincingly, that the traffic was getting worse but, nonetheless, for him it was a clear indication that the city is progressing.

Can we use traffic as an indicator of progressive economy? With traffic comes air and noise pollution. Maybe if Iloilo River dies, they will also say that this is a sign of progress since all the pollutants came from the factories and shopping malls surrounding the area.

Although it is clear that the government and societal structures do play vital roles in the mess that is today, let us not forget to see how we ourselves are involved in creating the said mess. The people that run the government are human themselves. As humans, we have a higher inner self covered by animal instincts. We are rational, and coupling this with our instincts makes us worse than animals. Instead of trying to use our rationality to benefit the totality of the planet Earth, we used it to exploit everything else. Aren't we spoiling the water we drink by disposing of toxic waste in the streams and the other bodies of water? How about the forests? Don't we just love to enjoy the fruits of our nonlabor?

Are these the sole products of human ingenuity—massive industrialization that results in massive exploitation of earth's resources? Even human resources are exploited. But these will have no future unless we do something about it. Unless we realize that we are co-existing with all other species on earth, the scenario that I have painted here for the present generation is a glum one.

My alternative vision of the future is sharing. A shared future, a shared vision, it is my desired future to see a world where everybody shares. Communal heaven! But it's neither utopia nor the second coming that I want. My reason for a shared future is one of practicality.

Perhaps we can have a shared economy where money is no longer at the heart of economics. The new economics will be founded on the survival of all. A shared security, wherein everyone feels secure wherever he/she is. A military to protect and promote peace. They won't have heavy armaments, rather they will have strength of character and the courage to live in peace—a shared culture, where everyone respects other cultures without bias—a shared intelligence, where everybody is concerned with the preservation of wild life; a shared wealth, communal wealth that will allow us to no longer see hungry stomachs; a shared faith, where regardless of religious affiliation respect reigns supreme and lastly, a shared personhood where the sense of personhood extends to all others.

That's my vision of the future and my desired future. It is not far from reality. It's workable, but it will take time. Still, it's worth it. The best quotation to describe this is from the words of the Second Plenary Council of Philippines (the council of the local Catholic bishops): "Nobody is so poor that he/she has nothing to give, and nobody is so rich that he has nothing to receive"—the basic principle of sharing. Help and be helped. Know where you stand and look up to the future with bright and wide eyes.

Concluding Reflections

Sohail Inayatullah and Jennifer Gidley

To summarize and synthesize what has been stated elsewhere in the book, "youth" (as an "issue") have begun to affect the agendas of world governments, big corporations, and NGOs because they have begun to be perceived over the last ten to fifteen years as having economic and political importance. This "importance" centers around key areas:

1. **The economic importance** (to the corporate world) stems from the concept of "youth as market share." Big business and its marketing managers recognize that the two billion (approximately) youth worldwide are potentially a sizeable chunk of their profits and resultant share prices. As Elissa Moses argues in her book *The 100 Billion Allowance: Accessing the Global Teen Market*. They are true-blue consumerists, aspiring to own as much as possible, as quickly as possible (spending currently $U.S. 100 billion per year in cities—and her figures do not include the twenty to twenty-five age group that is part of youth). However, paradoxically, as discussed in Chapter 1, this "buying power" of youth can be, and is being, manipulated by youth themselves for altruistic purposes, (for example, the antisweatshop movement), creating an Achilles heel for big business.

2. **The political importance** that youth have recently claimed ("youth as victim") centers in the West around rising mental health issues and youth suicide rates, dilemmas prompting a proliferation of funding "sweeteners" to demonstrate a "caring side of government," in spite of failure to address the issues at their systemic and foundational roots. In the non-West, this "youth as victim" scenario centers more centered on broader health issues, such as nutrition, HIV–AIDS, teenage pregnancy rates, and, more recently, exponential rises in heroin addiction.

3. **The demographic importance** is obvious as their numbers increase, especially in the third world, and they become what the World Health Organization has called the global teenager. Their hopes and visions, their pathologies and fears, are no isolated from the grand questions of our time: how to create a global ethics; how to transform the ocean of poverty and misery; and how to innovate so that the islands of prosperity do not lead to a further divided—ethnic, digital, genetic— world? If young people do not see a positive future for themselves, if they do not believe or do not develop the capacity to create a better world, then not only they, but the entire world is threatened. This relates directly to a fourth theme that has been the focus of this book.

4. **The sociocultural importance** of youth as creative agents of change needs to be urgently recognized by educators, politicians, and economists. The hopes, dreams, and visions of the young people discussed in the essays of this book can sow seeds from which new policies could grow—idealistic policies that include respect for the earth and for each other, just and equitable policies that would put people and planet before profit. Paradigms, as research suggests, are born from outside the corridors of power. It is youth who have provided, and will continue to provide, the energy for new paradigms of transformation.

The youth who speak through these pages have a destiny that comes with being born into these crucial times. Many of them, angry about the damage to the earth they have inherited from previous generations, are strongly committed to trying to change things for the better. Gidley is reminded of her own your when her seventeen-year-old son says, idealistically, "Mum, we will be the generation who will 'turn things around'." Yet, a growing commitment of the elders of our global cultures is crucial to ensure that we don't get in their way.

POLICY SUGGESTIONS

We now conclude with a clear message to the policy-maker. Based on the theoretical and empirical research from this book and the ideas of the youth themselves, we advise the following:

1. Youth must actively participate in creating desired futures. This means not merely providing content on the knowledge base of the future but ensuring that they participate in envisioning the futures they desire.

2. Policy must be proactive, not merely responding to the latest crisis (youth suicide), but scanning for change and developing policy that can deal with youth's changing needs.

3. Policy must be systemic and holistic because focusing only on the visible level of the problem ignores the deeper systemic issues (how technology leads to joblessness, for example) and worldview issues (the breakdown of meaning and community in modern and post-modern society). The policy must also address the deepest metaphorical level of personal narrative—the story youth tell themselves and others.

4. Policymakers also need to recognize that there is a cultural sea-change (paradigm shift) occurring, namely, popular disenchantment with the dominant materialist worldview that grounds Western culture. Youth are part of this desire to see ethical and spiritual values become central to policy and action in all spheres of life.

5. Merely stating over and over that youth are the future ignores the reality of demographics in Western societies, which show aging to be a more important issue.

6. Moreover, there is not one future but a range of alternative futures. Public policy—educational policy, employment policy, cultural policy—needs to explore the full range of alternative futures. This means opening up the future, not closing it.

7. Generally, the scenarios that are most important are the globalized-artificial society, the communicative-inclusive society, and the feared societal collapse. Youth can be integral participants in a dialogue on the visions preferred by communities and regions.

8. If youth are to be involved in genuine consultation, the form of the visioning of the future should not be in nineteenth-century technologies, that is, town hall consultations. Rather face-to-face, collaborative workshops are more likely to engage youth (not excluding online forums and video processes).

9. Finally, youth desire futures based on truths. Can we create a world incorporates integrity and authenticity? If not, of what use are the futures we are creating?

Bibliography

Ananda Rama, Avadhutika. *Neo-Humanist Education*. Mainz, Germany: Ananda Marga Publications, 2000.

Beare, Hedley, and Richard Slaughter. *Education for the Twenty-First Century*. London: Routledge, 1993.

Bjerstedt, Ake. *Future Consciousness and the School*. Malmo, Sweden: School of Education, University of Lund, 1982.

———. "Preparation for the Future as an Educational Goal," *Educational and Psychological Transactions* 68 (1979).

Boulding, Elise. *Building a Global Civic Culture: Education for an Interdependent World*. Syracuse, N.Y.: Syracuse University Press, 1990.

———. "Image and Action in Peace Building," *Journal of Social Issues* 44, 2 (1988).

Brown, Mary, ed. *Our World, Our Rights: Teaching about Rights and Responsibilities in the Primary School*. Washington, D.C.: Amnesty International, 1996.

Burns, S., and G. Lamont. *Values and Visions: A Handbook for Spiritual Development and Global Awareness*. London: Hodder and Stoughton, 1996.

Bussey, Marcus. "Critical Spirituality: Neo-Humanism as Method," *Journal of Futures Studies* 5, 2 (2000).

———. "Sustainable Education: Imperatives for a Viable Future," *Encyclopedia of Life Support Systems*. Oxford: EOLSS Publishers, 2001.

Calleja, J., and A. Perucca, eds. *Peace Education: Contexts and Values*. UNESCO in association with the International Peace Research Association, Leece, 1999.

Dator, James, ed. "Futures Studies in Higher Education," *American Behavioral Scientist* 42, 3 (1998).

Davis, Mark. *Gangland: Cultural Elites and the New Generationalism*. St. Leonards, NSW: Allen and Unwin, 1999.

Didsbury, Howard, ed. *Prep 21 Course Guide*. Washington, D.C.: World Future Society, 1986.

Eckersley, Richard. *Casualties of Change: The Predicament of Youth in Australia. An Analysis of the Social And Psychological Pressures Faced by Young People in Australia.* Melbourne: Australia's Commission for the Future, 1988.

———. "The West's Deepening Cultural Crisis," *The Futurist* (1993).

"Education for Transformation," *New Renaissance* 8, 3 (1998).

Eisler, Riane. *Sacred Pleasure.* San Francisco: HarperCollins, 1996.

———. *Tomorrow's Children: A Blueprint for Partnership Education in the 21st Century* Boulder, Colo.: Westview Press, 2000.

Elkind, David. *The Hurried Child.* Reading, Mass.: Addison Wesley, 1981.

Fitch, Robert, and Cordell Svengalis. *Futures Unlimited: Teaching about Worlds to Come.* Washington, D.C.: NCSS, 1979.

Fontan, Pere. "Youth and Future Values," *Papers de Prospectiva* 6 (1997).

Galtung, Johan. "On the Last 2,500 Years in Western History, and Some Remarks on the Coming 500." In *The New Cambridge Modern History, Companion Volume,* ed. Peter Burke. Cambridge: Cambridge University Press, 1979.

———. *Schooling, Education, and the Future.* Malmo, Sweden: Department of Education and Psychology Research, University of Lund, 1982.

Galtung, Johan, and Sohail Inayatullah, eds. *Macrohistory and Macrohistorians: Perspectives on Individual, Social, and Civilizational Change.* Westport, Conn.: Praeger, 1997.

Gidley, Jennifer. *Imagination and Will in Youth Visions of their Futures: Prospectivity and Empowerment in Steiner-Educated Adolescents. Education, Work, and Training.* Lismore: Southern Cross University, 1997.

———. "Prospective Youth Visions through Imaginative Education" *Futures* 30, 5 (1998).

Gidley, Jennifer, and Paul Wildman. "What Are We Missing? A Review of the Educational and Vocational Interests of Marginalized Rural Youth," *Education in Rural Australia Journal* 6, 2 (1996).

Glines, Don. *Educational Futures.* Millville, Minn: Anvil Press, 1980.

Hicks, David. *Educating for the Future: A Practical Classroom Guide.* UK: Godalming, World Wide Fund for Nature, 1994.

———. "Envisioning the Future: The Challenge for Environmental Educators" *Environmental Education Research* 1, 3 (1995).

Hicks, David, and Catherine Holden. *Visions of the Future: Why We Need to Teach for Tomorrow.* London: Trentham Books, 1995.

Hicks, David, and Richard Slaughter, eds. *World Yearbook of Education 1998: Futures Education.* London: Kogan Page, 1998.

Hillman, James. *The Soul's Code: In Search of Character and Calling.* Sydney, Australia: Random House, 1996.

Holden, Catherine, and N. Clough. *Children as Citizens: Education for Participation.* London: Jessica Kingsley Publishers, 1998.

"Holistic Education," *New Renaissance* 6, 3 (1996).

Hutchinson, Francis. "Valuing Young People's Voices on the Future as if They Really Mattered, *Journal of Futures Studies* 3, 2 (1999).

————. *Educating Beyond Violent Futures*. London: Routledge, 1996.

————. *Futures Consciousness and the School: Explorations of Broad and Narrow Literacies for the Twenty-First Century with Particular Reference to Australian Young People*. Armidale, NSW: University of New England, 1992.

————. "Making Peace with People and Planet: Some Important Lessons from the Gandhian Tradition in Educating for the Twenty-First Century," *Peace, Environment, and Education* 3, 3 (1992).

Illich, Ivan. *Deschooling Society*, Middlesex: Penguin Books, 1976.

Inayatullah, Sohail. *Alternative Futures: Methodology, Society, Macrohistory and the Long-Term Future*. Taipei, 2000.

————. "Possibilities for the Future, " *Development* 43, 4 (2000).

————. "Causal Layered Analysis: Poststructuralism as Method," *Futures* 30, 8 (1998).

Inayatullah, Sohail, and Jennifer Gidley. *The University in Transformation: Global Perspectives on the Futures of the University*. Westport, Conn.: Bergin & Garvey, 2000.

Inayatullah, Sohail, and Paul Wildman. *Futures Studies: Methods, Emerging Issues and Civilizational Visions*. A multimedia CD-ROM. Brisbane, Australia: Prosperity Press, 1998.

Jain, Manish. *Unfolding Learning Societies: Challenges and Opportunities*. Vimukt Shiksha Special Issue, Udaipur: Shikshantar, 2000

James, A., and A. Prout, eds. *Constructing and Reconstructing Childhood*. London: Palmer Press, 1997.

Jennings, Lane, and Sally Cornish, eds. *Education and the Future*. Washington, D.C.: World Future Society, 1980.

Johnson, Lynell. "Children's Visions of the Future." *The Futurist*, (1987).

Jungk, Robert and Norbert Mullert. *Futures Workshops*. London: Institute for Social Inventions, 1989.

Kauffman, Draper. *Teaching the Future*. Palm Springs, Calif.: ETC Pubs, 1976.

Kierstead, Fred (et al). *Educational Futures: Sourcebook 1*. Washington, D.C.: World Future Society, 1979.

Klein, Naomi. *No Logo: Taking Aim at the Brand Bullies*. London: Flamingo, 2000.

Lasn, Kalle. *Culture Jam: the Uncooling of America*. New York: HarperCollins, 2000.

Macy, Joanna. *Despair and Personal Power in the Nuclear Age*. Philadelphia: New Society Publishers, 1983.

Male, Mike. *Framing Youth: Ten Myths about the Next Generation*. Monroe, Maine: Common Coverage Press, 1999.

Marien, Michael, and Warren Ziegler. *The Potential of Educational Futures*. New York: Charles A. Jones, 1972.

Masini, Eleonora. *Why Futures Studies?* London: Grey Seal, 1994

————. and Yogesh Atal, eds. *The Futures of Asian Cultures*. Bangkok: UNESCO, 1993.

McGregor, Peter. "Visions of the Future." In *Studying the Future: The Introductory Reader*, Richard Slaughter, ed. Melbourne, Australia: Commission for the Future, Bicentennial Futures Education Project, 1989.

Milojevic, Ivana. "Globalization, Gender and World Futures." In *Encyclopedia of Life Support Systems*. Oxford: EOLSS Publishers, 2001.

Milojevic, Ivana, and Sohail Inayatullah. "Feminist Critiques and Visions of the Future," *Futures Research Quarterly* 14, 1 (1998).

Moses, Elissa. *The $100 Billion Allowance: Accessing the Global Teen Market*. New York: John Wiley and Sons, 2000.

Nandy, Ashis. *Tradition, Tyranny, and Utopias*. Delhi: Oxford University Press, 1987.

Novaky, Erzsebet, and Tamas Kristof, eds. *The Youth for a Less Selfish Future*. Budapest, Hungary: Budapest University of Economic Sciences and Public Administration, 2000.

Page, Jane. *Reframing the Early Childhood Curriculum: Educational Imperatives for the Future*. London: Routledge, 2000.

Redd, Kathryn, and Michael Harkins, eds. *Education: A Time for Decisions*. Washington, D.C.: World Future Society, 1980.

Rifkin, Jeremy. *The End of Work*. New York: Putnam, 1995.

Rogers, Martha, and Allen Tough. "What Happens When Students Face the Future." *Futures Research Quarterly* (Winter 1992).

Rubin, Anita. *Growing up in Social Transition: In Search of a Late-Modern Identity*.University of Turku, 2000.

———. *Unfolding Tomorrow: Adolescents' Images of the Future as the Strategies for Coping with Transition*. Losarvi, Finland: 1996.

Rushkoff, Douglas. *Children of Chaos*. New York: HarperCollins, 1996.

Russell, Glenn, and Bernard Holkner. "Virtual School," *Futures* 32, 9/10 (2000).

Sallay, Maria, ed. *A New Vocational Training Model for Hungary*. Budapest, Hungry: General Press, 1996.

Sardar, Zia, ed. *Rescuing All of Our Futures*. Twickenham: Adamantine, 1999.

Sardar, Zia and Jerome Ravetz, eds. *Cyberfutures*. London: Pluto Press, 1996.

Sardello, Robert. *Love and the World of Soul: Creating a Future for Earth*. New York: HarperCollins, 1995.

Sarkar, Prabhat Rainjan. *Discourses on Neohumanist Education*. Calcutta, India: A.M. Publications, 1998.

Saul, John Ralston. *The Unconscious Civilization*. Ringwood, Australia: Penguin Books, 1997.

Schiller, Frederick. *The Aesthetic Education of Man: In a Series of Letters (1795)*. New York: Ungar, 1977.

Scott, David, and Susan Awbrey. Transforming Scholarship, *Change* (July-August 1993).

Shane, Harold. *The Educational Significance of the Future*. Bloomingham, N.J.: Phi Cappa Delta, 1973.

Slaughter, Richard. *From Fatalism to Foresight—Educating for the Early Twenty-First Century: A Framework for Considering Young People's Needs and Responsibilities over the Next Twenty Years*. Melbourne, Australia: Australian Council for Educational Administration, 1994.

———. *Futures Concepts and Powerful Ideas*. Melbourne, Australia: Futures Study Center, 1996.

———. *Futures Tools and Techniques*. Melbourne, Australia: Futures Study Center, 2000.

———, ed. *The Knowledge Base of Futures, Studies*, Vols. 1–3, Melbourne, Australia: Futures Study Center, 1996.

———, ed. *Studying the Future: An Introductory Reader*. Melbourne, Australia: Commission for the Future, Bicentennial Futures Education Project, 1989.

Slaughter, Richard, and Sohail Inayatullah, eds. *The Knowledge Base of Futures, Studies*, vols. 1–4 CD-ROM. Brisbane: Foresight International, 2000.

Steiner, Rudolf. *The Evolution of Consciousness (Lectures, 1923)*. London: Rudolf Steiner Press, 1926.

———. *Human Values on Education (Lectures, 1924)*. London: Rudolf Steiner Press, 1971.

———. *The Younger Generation: Education and Spiritual Impulses in the Twentieth Century (Lectures, 1922)*. New York: Anthroposophic Press, 1967.

———. *Toward Imagination: Culture and the Individual*. New York: Anthroposophic Press, 1990.

Tarnas, Richard. *The Passions of the Western Mind*. London: Random House, 1991.

Toffler, Alvin, ed. *Learning for Tomorrow*. New York: Vintage, 1974.

Tough, Allen. *Critical Questions About the Future*. Boston: University Press of America, 1991.

———. "What Future Generations Need from Us," *Futures* (December 1993).

Wilber, Kenneth. *Sex, Ecology, Spirituality: The Spirit of Evolution*. Boston: Shambhala, 1995.

Wildman, Paul, and Jennifer Gidley, eds. "Holistic Education: Preparing for the Twenty-First Century," *New Renaissance* 6, 3 (1996).

Wildman, Paul, Jennifer Gidley, and Ros Irwin. "Visions as Power: Promises and Perils of Envisioning Desired Futures with Marginalized Youth," *Journal of Applied Social Behavior* 3, 2 (1997).

Wildman, Paul, and Sohail Inayatullah. "Ways of Knowing, Culture, Communication, and the Pedagogies of the Future," *Futures* 28, 8 (1996).

Ziegler, Warren. "Envisioning the Future," *Futures* (1991).

Index

ABOUT THE EDITORS
AND CONTRIBUTORS

JENNIFER GIDLEY is an educational psychologist and futures researcher. She has researched and published widely in the youth and education futures fields, most recently co-editing the book *The University in Transformation: Global Perspectives on the Futures of the University* (Bergin & Garvey, 2000).

SOHAIL INAYATULLAH is visiting professor, Department of Futures Studies, Tamkang University, Taiwan and professor, International Management Centers Association. He is co-editor of the *Journal of Futures Studies*. Among his books is *Macrohistory and Macrohistorians* (Praeger, 1997).

BILAL ASLAM is 19 years old and has just finished his advanced levels in Rawalpindi, Pakistan. Besides studies his interests are computers and outdoor sports.

PAUL OTTO BRUNSTAD is associate professor at the Norwegian Teacher Academy, School of Religion and Education, Norway. He is also a member of a research group at the Center for the Study of European Civilization at the University of Bergen.

MARCUS BUSSEY is a teacher and musician who has written numerous articles and reviews on futures, futures education, holistic education, neo-humanist education, artistic practice, culture, history, Montessori education, and cognitive theory. He is currently senior teacher at Harmony Montessori School, Buderim, Queensland, Australia.

SANDRA BURCHSTED is a former elementary teacher and founder of Prospectiva, a futures-thinking consulting firm in Friendswood, Texas.

RICHARD ECKERSLEY's research currently covers two main areas: measuring progress and quality of life; and sociocultural aspects of young people's well-being. In 1995, he initiated, planned, and participated in a major study of young Australians' expected and preferred futures for their nation.

RIANE EISLER is a cultural historian and systems scientist best known for her international bestseller, *The Chalice and The Blade*. Her most recent book is *Tomorrow's Children: A Blueprint for Partnership Education in the Twenty-First Century*. She has taught at the University of California, Los Angeles, and is president of the Center for Partnership Studies in Tucson, Arizona.

MICHAEL GUANCO has a Bachelor of Arts in Community Development Economics from the University of St. La Salle. He works in development banking and is also involved with the World Futures Studies Federation secretariat.

SHANE HART's teaching interests include indigenous cultures, sustainability, and the future. He writes poetry and his book *With The Eyes of The Wandjina* will be published in 2002.

SABINA HEAD has been teaching for 12 years. Before that, she was involved in various aspects of theater and is interested in using drama as a teaching aid and implementing futures studies across the school curriculum.

EVA HIDEG is associate professor, Futures Studies Center, Budapest University of Economic Sciences and Public Administration. Beside teaching futures research, she is researching postmodern paradigms of scientific theory, the futures research application of models of chaos and evolution, and future orientation.

CATHIE HOLDEN is a senior lecturer in education at the University of Exeter, United Kingdom. She taught in primary schools for many years and now lectures in primary humanities and education for citizenship. Her research focuses on the perspectives of children, parents, and teachers and the practical implementation of education for citizenship.

RAINA HUNTER is 20 years old and returning to university after a year of full-time work. She will be completing a Bachelor of Arts degree in politics and psychology at Adelaide University.

FRANCIS HUTCHINSON is senior lecturer, Faculty of Social Inquiry, University of Western Sydney, Australia. He has an extensive background in curriculum consultancy (kindergarten to year 12) in areas such as antiviolence education, human rights education, and futures education. Among his publications are *Educating Beyond Violent Futures*.

SETH ITZKAN is a futurist, web site designer, social architect, and founder of Planet-TECH Associates. As an educational technology consultant, he has been designing and hosting programs in online collaboration and youth empowerment for over a decade.

COLE JACKSON served for over two decades in the public schools as a teacher and administrator. He is founder of Learning Ventures International in Orlando, Florida, focusing on educational innovation, design, support, and staff development. He is also codesigner and cofacilitator of Creating Preferred Futures, a distance-learning project for secondary-level students and teachers, and consults and writes on futures education.

ERZSEBET NOVAKY is professor and head, Futures Studies Center, Budapest University of Economic Sciences and Public Administration and vice president of the Futures Research Committee, Hungarian Academy of Sciences. Beside teaching futures research, she is researching behavior of complex large systems, chaos and forecasting, and future orientation.

ALFRED L. OEHLERS teaches courses on the Asia-Pacific economies at Massey University (Albany), Auckland, New Zealand. His research focuses on the processes of social, economic, and political change in Southeast Asia, and most particularly, Singapore.

ANITA RUBIN is a sociologist and futurist working at the Finland Futures Research Center. She has studied the images of the future held by young Finns, especially how those images reflect social transition. She is involved in futures education projects into virtual education.

RICHARD SLAUGHTER is Foundation Professor of Foresight at Swinburne University of Technology in Melbourne. He is a consulting futurist, president of the World Futures Studies Federation (WFSF), and a professional member of the World Future Society. In 1997 he was elected to the executive council of the WFSF. His most recent books are *Futures for the Third Millennium—Enabling the Forward View* and *Gone Today, Here Tomorrow—Millennium Previews*.

CARMEN STEWART worked with Imagine the Future Inc. (Melbourne) for several years as the designer/facilitator of Re-Imagining Your Neighborhood. She recently developed the Making Places project, a futures education and consultation initiative facilitated by local government and services.

DAVID WRIGHT is a doctoral candidate with the School of Communication, Queensland University of Technology, Brisbane, Australia. His doctoral investigation involves a poststructural analysis of Japan's twenty-first century discourses of the nation's postbubble futures. His main research interests include communication futures, images of the future in arts and aesthetics, and the futures of work.

UNIVERSITY OF WALES, NEWPORT
LIBRARY
AND
INFORMATION
SERVICES
CAERLEON

UNIVERSITY OF WALES, NEWPORT
LIBRARY
AND
INFORMATION
SERVICES
CAERLEON